always!
Mark
11-3-12

Messages for Educational Leadership

9-27-12

Colleague
I hope you enjoy
this tribute to
Dr. Constance Clayton!
Sincerely,
Diana T. Slaughter-Defoe
(dianasd@gse.upenn.edu)

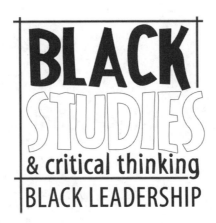

BLACK STUDIES
& critical thinking
BLACK LEADERSHIP

Judy Alston, *Series Editor*

Rochelle Brock and Richard Greggory Johnson III
Executive Editors

Vol. 34

The Black Studies and Critical Thinking series
is part of the Peter Lang Education list.
Every volume is peer reviewed and meets
the highest quality standards for content and production.

PETER LANG
New York • Washington, D.C./Baltimore • Bern
Frankfurt • Berlin • Brussels • Vienna • Oxford

Messages for Educational Leadership

The Constance E. Clayton Lectures
1998–2007

DIANA T. SLAUGHTER-DEFOE, VOLUME EDITOR

PETER LANG
New York • Washington, D.C./Baltimore • Bern
Frankfurt • Berlin • Brussels • Vienna • Oxford

Library of Congress Cataloging-in-Publication Data

Messages for educational leadership: the Constance E. Clayton lectures
1998–2007 / edited by Diana T. Slaughter-Defoe.
p. cm. — (Black studies and critical thinking; v. 34)
Includes bibliographical references.
1. Education—Social aspects—United States. 2. Educational leadership—
United States. 3. Clayton, Constance E. I. Slaughter-Defoe, Diana T.
LC191.4.M47   306.430973—dc23   2012001054
ISBN 978-1-4331-1631-5 (hardcover)
ISBN 978-1-4331-1630-8 (paperback)
ISSN 1947-5985

Bibliographic information published by **Die Deutsche Nationalbibliothek**.
Die Deutsche Nationalbibliothek lists this publication in the "Deutsche
Nationalbibliografie"; detailed bibliographic data is available
on the Internet at http://dnb.d-nb.de/.

The paper in this book meets the guidelines for permanence and durability
of the Committee on Production Guidelines for Book Longevity
of the Council of Library Resources.

© 2012 Peter Lang Publishing, Inc., New York
29 Broadway, 18th floor, New York, NY 10006
www.peterlang.com

Printed in the United States of America

Table of Contents

Foreword

Bernard C. Watson

Educator

The children come first. That statement defines the educational philosophy and practice of my good friend and colleague, Dr. Constance Clayton. A native Philadelphian, Connie graduated from Girls High School, earned degrees from Temple University and, with a Fellowship from the Rockefeller Foundation, earned her doctorate from the University of Pennsylvania.

Rising through the ranks of the Philadelphia Public Schools, Connie developed and helped write the Afro-American History and Culture curriculum and, with her colleague, Milt Goldberg, developed and expanded the Early Childhood Program throughout the school system and in the process made it the model for other school systems throughout the country.

Growing up, the most significant influence in Connie's life was her mother, Willabell Harris Clayton, an accomplished singer, pianist, and choir director who inspired a love of the arts. Connie studied and played cello and to this day is involved in supporting and enjoying the arts. Connie was expected to do well academically and to adhere to the highest level of ethics. I know from personal experience how proud Mrs. Clayton was of her daughter.

During a period in our history when opportunities for African Americans were limited, Connie became the first African American and the first female superintendent of the Philadelphia Public Schools, a position she occupied for eleven years. To this day, that is an unusual tenure for a big city urban superintendent. Despite the challenges of the position, she was able to introduce a standardized curriculum in science and mathematics in all schools; required art and music instruction in all elementary schools; introduced Algebra in middle schools, and, in collaboration with Dr. John Chen and his 21st Century Mathematics Center at Temple University, provided math courses and innovative instructional methods for public school teachers who needed additional education to become effective teachers. Elementary school libraries and instructional materials centers were staffed with certified librarians. Although her tenure as superintendent was characterized by change, Connie was able to work effectively with the seven unions represented in the public schools. Five strikes had occurred in seven years. There were none during the eleven years of her tenure.

Following her retirement, Dr. Clayton became a professor in the Pediatrics Department at Hahnemann University Medical School, Administrator of the School of Public Health and, after the tragic death of the dean in an airplane crash, became Interim Dean of the School of Public Health. The University of Pennsylvania established the Endowed Dr. Constance Clayton Chair in Urban Education, and Connie taught in the Harvard University Graduate School of Education.

Still active in education and the arts, Connie serves on the Board of Trustees of the Philadelphia Museum of Art, and is a former trustee of the University of Pennsylvania. In my opinion, she is a role model for those who aspire to become teachers and administrators. They should remember: The children come first.

1. Introduction and Overview: The Constance E. Clayton Lecture Series

DIANA T. SLAUGHTER-DEFOE
University of Pennsylvania

Background to the Clayton Lectures

I am a developmental and clinical psychologist by academic background. However, urban education, by definition, is an interdisciplinary field, characterized by an attempt to bring as many perspectives as possible to the study of research pertaining to urban educational policy, and to the practice of education with children and youth whose lives unfold in densely populated areas—whether city or suburb. Thus, psychiatry and public health; sociology; developmental, experimental, and social psychology; history and foreign language studies, as well as education, are disciplines and fields represented among the Clayton lecturers and respondents in urban education in this volume.

I think the concept of urban education as it addresses African Americans and other "underrepresented minorities" really emerged and evolved over the past two generations, following the publication of the late Allison Davis' 1948 lecture at Harvard University, *Social Class Influences Upon Learning*. A social anthropologist by disciplinary background, Davis received an academic appointment in the Department of Education at the University of Chicago, and thus began to apply concepts from his disciplinary field to the problems of education—problems that he addressed in his time by emphasizing how schools needed to appreciate the cultural differences linked to the socioeconomic backgrounds of children from impoverished backgrounds, irrespective of their ethnic or racial origins. Professor Davis was the doctoral dissertation mentor of my dissertation advisor at the University of Chicago, Professor Robert D. Hess. In research published in the early 1950s, Davis and Eells (1953), with Hess as one of their graduate assistants, attempted to develop "culture-fair" tests for school pupils.

In 1998, I established, with the gracious support of former Dean Susan Fuhrman, the Clayton Lecture Series in the Graduate School of Education at the University of Pennsylvania, to further honor Constance E. Clayton, the African American woman and educational leader for whom my chair was endowed in 1993. Consistent themes in the lectures that ensued include attention to (a) an accounting of the basis for urban children's school failures and successes; (b) a focus upon the sources of educational inequities, and appropriate forms of their resolution, whether in relation to class, race, or gender; (c) an emphasis on school improvement, even school restructuring, such that educational institutions are modified to address children's personal-social needs, cognitive capacities, and behavioral motivations; (d) an emphasis on the potential contributions of parents, families, even communities, to positive and constructive classroom and school change; (e) an almost unquestioned allegiance to the value of quality education for all of the nation's children; and (f) an expectation that teacher, and administrative, training/retraining are essential elements to realizing this educational aim. The lectures explore how these ideas have been presented, described, and rationalized over the past two generations when, in my view, the concept of urban education really emerged and evolved.

A word about how the annual Clayton lecturers were chosen by myself: I usually conferred very informally with members of a school-wide Clayton steering committee. Influential factors included persons I knew as significant mentors who also had national reputations; persons whose current educational research and policy interests significantly interfaced with themes linked to the ongoing life works and concerns of Dr. Constance Clayton; and my desire to vary the annual program so as to maximize the interests of different constituencies in our school and in the University. In the first year of the series, a school-wide Clayton steering committee was established that endured; members included myself, the current dean of the school, all African American faculty, and selected faculty with special interests in early childhood development and/or African American urban education. Co-sponsorships included other units in the University of Pennsylvania (e.g., Africana Studies, Engineering, History, Psychiatry, Psychology, and Sociology, the National Center for the Study of Fathers and Families [NCOFF], the Netter Center for Community Partnerships [NCCP]), and organizations outside of the University (e.g., Delaware Valley for the Association of the Education of Young Children [DVAEYC]).

A Brief Overview of the Clayton Lectures

Upon reflection, the above strategy worked well, and I believe readers will find the first 10 lectures reproduced in this volume in Chapters 3–12 very powerful and engaging. In addition, the Clayton Lecture series addressed many themes highlighted as important to the professional life of Dr. Constance Clayton in the Foreword to this volume written by Bernard Watson, her longtime colleague and friend. For example, Connie Clayton's emphasis in my interview with her in Chapter 14 on the importance of a supportive home environment throughout childhood and adolescence to her own development as a leading educator is echoed in Chapters 3 (Comer) and 8 (Slaughter-Defoe). Further, three lectures focus on early childhood intervention and development, complementing her early involvement and engagement of the Philadelphia Project Head Start program: Chapters 5 (Bowman), 10 (Schweinhart), and 13 (see Murray's discussion of the panel by Craig and Sharon Ramey, John Fantuzzo, and Vivian Gadsden in this chapter). Dr. Watson also observed that Dr. Clayton reached out to nourish and enrich curriculum in math and science; a similar outreach strategy is a primary aim of the GO GIRL intervention described by Pamela Reid in Chapter 11.

Two lectures focus on effective teaching and educational leadership, a lifelong preoccupation closely linked to her successful superintendence: Chapters 7 (Darling-Hammond) and 12 (Gomez). In the invited Chapter 15, Loder-Jackson addresses intergenerational mentoring and educational leadership issues. While all lecturers draw implications for school improvement and sustaining such interventions, this broad theme was a special focus of Chapters 3 (Comer), 6 (Fuhrman), and 12 (Gomez), each with different ideas about where to focus for enduring school change: school development, school accountability, and individualizing and enhancing instruction. Lecturers also address the continuing concerns of Dr. Clayton for positive public health, both physical and mental: Chapters 3 (Comer) and 13 (see Murray's summary and discussion of the lecture by Dr. Margaret Spencer in this chapter). Last, but definitely not least, three lectures address important aspects of African American history and culture, particularly as racial issues interface with educational practices and policies: Chapters 4 (Epps), 9 (Jones), and 13 (see Murray's summary and discussion of the lecture by Dr. V. P. Franklin). In Chapter 4, Epps evaluates school desegregation; in Chapter 9, Jones discusses factors linked to the intractability of racial inequalities; and in Chapter 13, Franklin's summary alludes to the implications of this cultural history for contemporary educational policies.

I began my career at a time when the nation had great faith in the promise of educational research and training institutions for making a real difference in the lives of school children and youth; today the nation's optimism has been challenged. Public schools, in particular, are challenged. Will they be the primary vehicle for teaching and learning among the nation's urban and "minority" youth in the 21st century? Can they be the foundation for equal opportunity in American society? Should they be? I hope that as we read and digest these urban education lectures, we keep the larger questions before us.

Production of the Clayton Lectures

My current administrative assistant, using available audiotapes and videotapes, immediately transcribed each one of the 10 lectures following the lecture. Over the years 1998 to 2010, respectively, these administrative assistants were Janean Williams, Jennifer Bateman, Donghui Zhang, Crystal Aderson, Erin Bogan, and Krystal Anderson. I am very appreciative of the dedication shown by these assistants; all but one assistant were graduate student workers. Like myself, the assistants were present at the lecture. Members of the Graduate School of Education editorial staff at the University of Pennsylvania rechecked the resultant transcriptions.

However, when I started publication plans in 2008, I supervised two graduate assistants who re-reviewed the earlier audio materials and transcripts. Therefore, I gratefully acknowledge the assistance of students in the Applied Psychology and Human Development Division, Andrea Coffin and Lapde So. Andrea especially devoted many hours during the Fall 2008 semester, and part of Spring 2009, to making each transcript, originally based upon a spoken lecture, ready for a reading audience. She was guided by my expressed wish to model the volume after the late Professor Allison Davis' 1948 published lecture on *Social Class Influences Upon Learning* at Harvard University. I also shared the transcripts on two different occasions between 2009 and 2011 with the first 10 lecturers. Thus, I think the lengthy and deliberate editorial process preserved the actual presentations, the spirited styles in which they were delivered, and the masterful links between the technical meaning of what was said and a delivery intelligible to everyday persons.

Concluding Comment

In the concluding chapter to this volume, Chapter 16, I discuss one area of Dr. Clayton's life noted by Dr. Watson but not addressed in the Clayton Lecture Series: the arts. With Dr. Clayton, I also believe children must discover through education the pleasures and joys associated with the humanities, both mainstream and intra-cultural, if they are to reach adulthood as whole persons. In contrast, the following Chapter 2 was originally drafted for Black History Month, 2002. It is an orienting chapter, written for newcomers like I once was, to the professional life and scholarship of Dr. Constance E. Clayton, Black Woman and Educational Leader in the metropolitan Philadelphia community.

References

Davis, A. (1948). *Social-class influences upon learning*. Cambridge, MA: Harvard University Press.

Davis, A., & Eells, K. (1953). *Davis-Eells test of general intelligence or problem-solving ability*. London, England: World Book Company.

2. Reflections on Dr. Constance E. Clayton, Urban Educator, Activist, and Humanitarian

DIANA T. SLAUGHTER-DEFOE*
University of Pennsylvania

I am pleased to speak briefly with you during Black History month about one of Philadelphia's most beloved native citizens, Dr. Constance E. Clayton. Dr. Clayton is a University of Pennsylvania alumna in the Graduate School of Education, and also a former member of the Board of Trustees of the University of Pennsylvania.

I came to Philadelphia in 1998 primarily because I knew that I would be helping to make American history: I believe Constance Clayton is the first African American woman to have an endowed chair named after her at any educational institution [major, predominantly White] in the United States.[1] I thought it quite an honor to be appointed to this position. Since 1998, other endowed chairs have been established. I believe there is one named after Sara Lawrence-Lightfoot, MacArthur Fellow, at Harvard, and another after Ida B. Wells-Barnett, journalist and anti-lynching activist, at DePaul University in Chicago.

Dr. Clayton was the Superintendent of Schools in Philadelphia from 1982 to August 1993. When she retired, an endowed chair was established in her honor at the Graduate School of Education where she had obtained her doctorate degree in educational administration in 1980. I am fortunate to be the first [inaugural] occupant of the endowed chair; so naturally, I was pleased to have an opportunity to research Dr. Clayton for this presentation. Dr. Clayton is a product of the city's public schools, and has spent her entire

---

* This chapter is based upon a lecture originally given to the Multi-National Luncheon at the Education Commission for Foreign Medical Graduates (ECFMG), 3624 Market Street, Philadelphia, PA, on February 28, 2002. Dr. Slaughter-Defoe was asked by this group to give background information about Dr. Clayton.

career in Philadelphia. She began her career as a fourth grade teacher in 1955, worked her way up through the ranks, and assumed the superintendence in 1982 (Schwartz, 1994, p. 111).

Three White men served on her dissertation committee: Dr. William Castetter, chairperson, and Drs. William Heisler and Edwin Hutchins, committee members. Of interest, Dr. Castetter, himself alum of the University of Pennsylvania, had been a member of the faculty of the School of Education since 1948, having joined the school when Emit Duncan Grizzell, the new dean, hired several faculty. In Dr. William Brickman's (1987) history[2] of the Graduate School of Education at Penn (affectionately known as GSE), Dr. Clayton's chairperson is described as having major responsibility for the Educational Service Bureau from the beginning of his appointment in 1948:

> Dr. Castetter, who immediately became associate director of the Educational Service Bureau and associate chairman of Schoolmen's Week, was in time to head the program of educational administration and to serve on two occasions as acting Dean. . . . The Educational Service Bureau continued its aid to various educational agencies and organizations toward the solution of their professional problems . . . the Bureau issued in 1950 financial and salary analyses of school districts in the four counties nearest to Philadelphia . . . it conducted several school building surveys . . . beneficial impact on teachers. (pp. 124,134)

I think Dr. Castetter was most definitely not an "ivory-tower" scholar disinterested in neighboring schools and school districts. In fact, he seems to have been a faculty leader in educational administration and policy studies, with high practical import for classroom teaching. He supervised Constance Clayton towards the end of what seems to have been a very long career at GSE, retiring during the second tenure of Dean Dell Hymes, a term that began in the 1980s. I also think Castetter must have served close to 40 years on the GSE faculty, a period in which the officially founded School of Education in 1914 became, as of 1961, a Graduate School of Education.

Dr. Richard Heisler is described in the history as being the dean's administrative assistant, and also as serving as Director of the Center for Field Studies, while Dr. Edwin Hutchins was a faculty member in psychology and evaluation, with a specialty in health professional education. This appointment was quite consistent with the interdisciplinary history of the Penn School of Education.

Dr. Clayton's doctoral dissertation was entitled *An Analysis of the Persistence of High Achievement Among Low Income Fourth Graders with Pre-kindergarten Experience*. Clayton described the problem of the study as follows: "to determine whether low-income children with pre-kindergarten experience differed from those without this experience in level of achievement (intercept), ongoing achievement trends (slope), and rate of change in both Total Reading and Total Mathematics" (Clayton, 1980, p. 5).

At that time, the Stanford Early School Achievement Test (essentially a school readiness test) was administered by the school district in February to kindergarten students, and the Calforina Achievement Test (inclusive of the Total Reading and Mathematics scores) to students in grades one to four. In articulating the rationale for her thesis, Clayton focused on the need for additional studies of the potentially favorable effects of structured early experience on young children's learning and development. Thus, this study of achievement test performance in a large, urban school district complemented the research of many others in the field who cited the critical importance of early childhood as a sensitive learning period in children's lives, and as a period with longer-term consequences for the youths' future growth and development.

For the study, primary grade children, half of whom attended the Get Set pre-kindergarten program, were selected. Get Set was apparently the original Head Start Program in Philadelphia; however, it was designed and operated as a full-day child care program for lower-income children under age 16. Children were selected from four different Philadelphia administrative school districts. Submitted October 1980, and approved May 1981, the dissertation analyzed the academic progress in reading and mathematics performance of 301 Get Set children (i.e., children with pre-kindergarten experience) by comparison to 301 children without pre-kindergarten experience.

Not surprisingly, throughout the primary grades, children with pre-kindergarten experience performed significantly better in reading than those without. In my opinion, this research reflects Dr. Clayton's earliest commitment to the school system. She was responsible, I understand, for bringing Project Head Start resources to the district, and also worked for the district in the Early Childhood Education Department immediately before assuming the superintendancy.

The dissertation was dedicated to her mother, Willabel Clayton. Acknowledgements apart from her committee members include Dr. Sadie T. M. Alexander, described by Connie Clayton as an "attorney, scholar, role model and family friend—the first Black woman in the U.S. to earn a PhD—insisted that I attend the University of Pennsylvania" (Clayton, 1980, p. 8), Dr. Bernard Watson, Mr. Chuck Stone, and "The Rockefellar Foundation for selecting my area of study—Early Childhood Education—for an urban education grant, thus making the dissertation a possibility" (Clayton, 1980, p. 9). I believe that shortly after concluding this thesis, Dr. Clayton assumed the beginning of an 11-year tenure as school superintendent of the School District of Philadelphia, from 1982 to 1993, at that time the longest superintendency tenure ever held by any superintendent in the nation.

Ruth Wright Hayre, distinguished in her own right as the first African American teacher in the Philadelphia public school system, the first African American senior high school principal, and the first woman president of the Philadelphia Board of Education, had the following to say about Connie Clayton's superintendency:

> I felt that no one could be better suited for the position than Dr. Constance E. Clayton, a product of the city schools, a lifelong educator and administrator right here in the Philadelphia system. The committee agreed and appointed her to an outpouring of accolades and acclamation. . . . Working with parents, teachers, and Administrators, she developed a standardized curriculum for kindergarten through twelfth grade. . . . Among her innovations were magnet school programs, desegregation programs. . . . For all eleven years of her tenure, the school district was free of labor unrest, and for the first time in many years the schools were financially sound. Philadelphia citizens, including a large cadre of businessmen, became strong supporters of the schools. There was a widespread feeling of trust, confidence, and admiration for this superintendent. . . . Schoolchildren called her "Miss Connie." Her motto, "The children come first," became a rallying cry for Philadelphia's educational efforts and was imitated in other cities. . . . She worked hard and supervised a tight ship. (Hayre, 1997, pp. 80–81)

In my opinion, this is especially high praise from an African American woman of similar social standing who was herself committed to "giving back" to her community something of the remarkable benefits she had experienced in her own good-quality life.[3] Later in the book, Hayre reported how Constance Clayton helped her to publically share her contributions, and to reinforce community awareness of Black philanthropic efforts in support of the educational aspirations of African American elementary and high school students. Dr. Clayton facilitated Dr. Hayre's housing of the program "Tell Them We Are Rising" at Temple University, and was, in 1994, the unanimous choice of the Riser students to give their graduation message, although by that time Dr. Clayton was the former superintendent.

During this period as an administrator engaged in educational practice, Dr. Clayton also published. For example, in 1991 she published an article in *Educational Evaluation and Policy Analysis* that discussed "Chapter 1 Evaluation: Progress, Problems, and Possibilities." In this piece, she evaluated the 1988 reauthorization of Chapter 1, from the perspective of its support and challenges to school-wide programs in Philadelphia. In 1996, she published "Children of Value: We Can Educate All of Our Children" in a book edited by William Ayers and Patricia Ford, *City Kids, City Teachers: Reports From the Front Row*. This article was originally published in 1989 in a special issue of *The Nation* that was devoted to redressing the American tendency toward engaging in "Scapegoating the Black Family." "Children of value" is the phrase Clayton prefers, according to Hayre, to "children at-risk" because the former term implicitly conveys the assumption that "Every human being has value" (Hayre, 1997, p. 188).

Just before she announced her retirement in August 1993, Dr. Clayton engaged in a lengthy interview with Robert Schwartz of the Pew Charitable Trusts and Dr. Michelle Fine, at that time a professor at the University of Pennsylvania. The interview was subsequently published in 1994 in the *Journal of Negro Education*. It is an important piece that points to the difficulties and challenges confronted by those who would restructure American high schools.

The article states that in 1988, the School District of Philadelphia established a separate, non-profit organization whose purpose was to lead the rethinking and restructuring of the city's 22 neighborhood high schools. This initiative was called the Philadelphia Schools Collaborative, and:

> took as its principal mission the development of multiple, autonomous charters within the neighborhood high schools. . . . Designed and led by interdisciplinary teacher teams, charters are small schools serving 200–400 heterogeneous students in grades 9 through 12, organized to meet the academic and social needs of students. Because Philadelphia pioneered the development of career academies in high schools beginning in the late 1960s, the school-within-a-school concept was already well-established when the Collaborative began its planning in 1998 . . . the district was confronted with a $60 million budget deficit, a recalcitrant teacher's union, and a massive turnover in high school principals due to a state-funded early retirement program. (Schwartz, 1994, p. 1121)

In the article, Clayton credits herself with deciding to focus the district on making a difference in its 22 high schools, particularly since things seemed to be going fairly well in the early childhood area by 1988:

> I thought if there was an opportunity to zero in on any grade organization, it ought to be high schools because those are kids who are most visible...in the community. I was tired of reading national data about high school graduates who couldn't read, couldn't fill out an application. . . . I must tell you that there were many who thought I was crazy to take on the high schools, that it was already too late. But since my position is I don't write off any child for any reason, it seemed imperative that we zero in on the high schools. (Schwartz, 1994, p. 112)

The remainder of the article, written in the form of an in-depth interview with Dr. Clayton and former University of Pennsylvania professor, Dr. Michelle Fine, outlined the challenges of the public high school charter concept. Dr. Clayton stressed that high schools must choose to be fully chartered and self-governing—in effect, such an organization cannot be effectively imposed from the "top-down." A consultant to the Collaborative,

Dr. Fine stressed that the "public sector can't wait" . . . with Clayton responding:

> Now I know the Collaborative feels that more functions ought to go right from the central office to the school. [But] I don't believe you can simply take functions from the central office and dump them into the schools and say, "Here, it's yours, run with it." Decentralization requires the same kind of staff and preparation that the Collaborative has been very good at providing to the schools to help them establish smaller learning communities. . . . If school staff are going to be given more control over resources, they will need help in decision-making, in understanding the tradeoffs, for example, in giving up counselors for social workers . . . those conversations between central and the schools need to continue. (Schwartz, 1994, pp. 121–122)

Of course, we know today that the recent state takeover of the Philadelphia public schools has pushed the concept of centralization to the extreme form and, from all indications, the superintendent succeeding Dr. Clayton has left this Philadelphia school district more vulnerable than ever before in the past quarter century.

Happily for me, in appreciation of Dr. Clayton's school superintendence, inclusive of her role as trustee of the University of Pennsylvania, and as a GSE alumna, the Clayton chair was established at the University, and a search conducted by GSE faculty and Dean Susan Fuhrman that culminated in my appointment in January 1998. I know for a fact that over 69 donors contributed to the endowment of this Penn chair. I have enjoyed the autonomy of being a faculty member at GSE, concluding and beginning projects that would not have otherwise been possible.[4]

Although she retired in 1993 from her Philadelphia school superintendency, today Dr. Clayton continues to lead a very full life. For example, since I have lived in this city, she has been acting dean at Hahnemann Medical College, School of Public Health, lectured at Harvard College in Boston, and operated Portobello Antique store in the Chestnut Hill area of the city. I also know that she is a member of the board of directors of the Philadelphia Museum of Art. During her short tenure on the board, the Museum has been showcasing its African American artists, inclusive of a recent exhibition of Dox Thrash's work (he was an African American master printmaker), and the important lecture and book signing of Camille and Bill Cosby's curator, Dr. David C. Driskell[5] on Friday, January 30. She also continues to be honored around the city, is a cherished member of the Philadelphia Alumnae Chapter of Delta Sigma Theta Sorority, Inc.,[6] which is celebrating its 75th anniversary this year, and participates actively in the local chapter of the Links. I am sure the legacy of Constance E. Clayton's commitment to Philadelphia's children will continue well into 21st century Philadelphian life.

Selected References of Dr. Constance E. Clayton

Clayton, C. (1980, October). *An analysis of the persistence of high achievement among low-income fourth graders with pre-kindergarten experience* (Unpublished doctoral dissertation). University of Pennsylvania Graduate School of Education, Pennsylvania.

Clayton, C. (1989, July 24/31). Children of value: We *can* educate all our children. In W. Ayers & P. Ford (Eds.), *City kids, city teachers: Reports from the front row* (pp. 137–146). New York, NY: The New Press. (Reprinted from *The Nation*, 132–135, 1996).

Clayton, C. (1991). Chapter 1 Evaluation: Progress, problems, and possibilities. *Educational Evaluation and Policy Analysis, 13*(4), 345–352.

Schwartz, R. (1994). Restructuring Philadelphia's neighborhood high schools: A conversation with Constance Clayton and Michelle Fine. *Journal of Negro Education, 63*(1), 111–125. Reprinted as ProQuest Document: 7212213. Retrieved from http://proquest.umi.com/pqdweb?did=7212 213&Fmt=3&clientId=12526&RQT=309&VName=PQD

Notes

1. By 2007, 22 chairs had been identified as endowed and named for African American men and women. Apart from Constance E. Clayton, two others were named for women: Willa B. Player and Grace Towns Hamilton. (For details about the source of this information, see the footnotes to Chapter 12 in this volume.)
   Dr. Willa Player's chair was endowed at Bennett College. In 1956, Dr. Player was named President of Bennett College in North Carolina, becoming the first Black woman president of a four-year college in the United States. Dr. Player graduated from Ohio Wesleyan in 1929 and earned a master's degree the following year at Oberlin College. From there, at age 21, she was hired to teach French and Latin at Bennett College in Greensboro, NC. Bennett was then a new Methodist-affiliated school oriented toward the education of African American women. At Bennett, Willa Player rose through the college's administrative hierarchy, holding the posts of director of admissions, dean, coordinator of instruction, and vice president. She added to her educational credentials, studying on a Fulbright fellowship in France in 1935, did graduate work at the Universities of Chicago and Wisconsin, and earned a doctorate in education from Columbia University in 1948. In 2007, Linda Beatrice Brown held the Willa B. Player chair in the Humanities at Bennett. The Grace Towns Hamilton chair was created at Emory University in Atlanta in 1990. Not an academic professor herself, Grace Towns Hamilton had been the first Black woman elected to the Georgia Legislature and the first Black female to serve as a state legislator anywhere in the Deep South.
2. According to Brickman, GSE traces its history to the establishment of a professorship in pedagogy in 1884. The book is entitled *Pedagogy, Professionalism, and Policy: History of the Graduate School of Education at the University of Pennsylvania,*

by William W. Brickman, 1986. It was published with the support of Dean Dell H. Hymes of the Graduate School of Education, in honor of GSE's over-65-year existence.

3. Dr. Ruth Wright Hayre (with Alexis Moore) is the author of *Tell Them We Are Rising: A Memoir of Faith in Education*, published in 1997, by John Wiley and Sons, Inc. CBS Broadcaster, and one of Ruth Hayre's protégés, Ed Brodley, commented in the book's preface about Dr. Hayre:

> This book focuses on her life and education and a career that has spanned the remarkable as well as the terrible changes in our inner cities and the children who live there. Giving back became an obsession for her. *Tell Them We Are Rising* is the inspiring story of how one woman gave back. (Hayre, 1997, pp. 11–12)

4. I am eager to collaborate with those prepared to document the circumstances surrounding the next few years of the Philadelphia School District's immediate future attempts to educate her children. I have been privileged thus far to study two schools that are reputedly doing quite well in this regard, and I hope to expand the study to include others.

5. Dr. Driskell is author of *The Other Side of Color: African American Art in the Collection of Camille O. and William H. Cosby Jr.*

6. Dr. Clayton and I were featured in the *National Delta Newsletter* soon after I arrived to assume the Clayton professorship, thanks to Soror Gloria Akers.

3. Waiting for a Miracle: Why Schools Can't Solve Our Problems and How We Can

JAMES P. COMER

Yale University School of Medicine—Yale Child Study Center

After twenty-five to thirty years of work, I really became concerned and began to reflect on what was going on, and why it was so difficult to change schools. *Waiting for a Miracle*, my latest book, is just that: a first-step reflection on the resistance and difficulty in changing schools.

I remember that in my first year of work, I was invited to give a talk. The sponsor invited me to go to lunch with him. He listened to my spiel about the importance of education and the importance of educating all children, from all backgrounds, especially low-income minority children. He had been around supporting civil rights for a long time. He listened and finally said, "What makes you think that everybody wants to see low-income Black children succeed?" That was a surprising, new thought to me. It never occurred to me that anybody would not want to see all children succeed. Society was changing rapidly and needed everybody to succeed in school. I realize now that he was right. But it was more complicated than racial prejudice alone. The problems in the urban educational setting mirrored the problems in our larger society, and the problems in society and school stem primarily from a very deep-seated cultural belief. That belief is that success is determined by your genes, your inborn intelligence, and your will.

This idea justifies the extreme individualism we have and leads to notions that we hold about the economy and the status quo. The entire educational enterprise—institutions, people, even research, curriculum, instruction, assessment, and technology—is affected by this underlying belief. Children from families under economic and social stress are hurt the most by this belief, and until we change that cultural belief, thinking that the schools will solve our problems and prepare children to solve the problems of society is, I think, waiting for a miracle.

There is a special complication in our society. Because it is a competitive society, we need winners and we need losers. We have scapegoated every new group to arrive in America to produce these winners and losers. Yet, for historical reasons, Blacks in particular, but other minorities too, have become the designated scapegoats, and that makes it all the more difficult to face up to the complexities of today's educational problems and today's societal problems because you can always blame it on the group that is currently the losers.

What the work of our program at the Yale Child Study Center and the work of others have shown is that a large group of children, disproportionately urban, disproportionately minority, come to school unprepared to learn. This leads to a difficult interaction between home and school that is troublesome for the children in schools. Staff in many schools are products of a training model that ignores the importance of child development. Additionally, organization and management of these schools prevents the staff from successfully addressing the school challenge.

We have also shown that you can change the schools by giving parents and staff a developmental focus and emphasizing that helping children develop well can lead to better teaching and better learning. These are attitudinal and structural changes that are difficult to bring about, and they prevent the large-scale changes that we need to improve our educational system. I hope I have been provocative enough. What I want to do now is to make a case to support what I have said. Let me do this by talking about my own background, because my own background is the source of much of my insight.

Autobiographical Reflections: The Context and Impetus for the School Development Program

I am from a low-income family. My mother was born in rural Mississippi, the child of a sharecropper. Her father was a good man who cared about his family but he was killed by lightning when she was about six years of age, and because there were no support programs around during that period, a cruel stepfather came into the lives of my mother's family. He was abusive in every way. He would not allow the children to go to school. My mother decided when she was about eight years of age that the way to a better life was through education. So when she was sixteen, she ran away to her sister in East Chicago, Indiana, and tried to go to school. But when her sister did not support my mother's dream, she had to leave school and become a domestic worker with no education whatsoever. When she left school, she declared that if she ever had children, she was going to make certain that every one of them got a good education, and then she set out to very, very, very, carefully find my father!

My father had been married once before, and she was not absolutely sure he was the right one, so she insisted that he bring a letter of recommendation from his ex-mother-in-law (but it worked out). My mother, with no education at all and working as a domestic, and my father, with a rural Alabama sixth grade education and working as a steel mill laborer, sent my four siblings and me to college for a total of thirteen college degrees among us.

While that was happening in my family, I had three friends who went off to elementary school with me, and while they were just as bright and just as able as anybody in my family and anybody in our predominantly White, middle-and upper-income school, they all went on a downhill course. One died early from alcoholism; one spent a good part of his life in jail; and the other was in and out of mental institutions all his life until he died recently. Society cannot afford that kind of lost potential on an ongoing basis and expect to survive and thrive. And so the question became for me: what happened to them? That was the question that began to percolate in my mind. It eventually changed my plan to become a general practitioner in my hometown and led to my career in child psychiatry and education.

My friends and I went to the same schools, our parents worked the same jobs—steel mill laborers and domestics—and yet I experienced such a different outcome. I realized eventually that the difference was in the quality of the developmental experience in my home compared to the homes of my friends. I want to talk a little about that developmental experience because I think that it is critically important and it is also what has guided my work all these years.

First of all, my siblings and I were very much wanted. My parents had goals for us and they did everything they possibly could to promote our growth and educational interests. Every Sunday, the four younger children would gather around my mother and she would read us the funny paper. Now the funny paper is not great literature, but the important thing was the nurturing, the closeness. We would have her read our favorite column over and over again, giving us more time together.

Also, there was the malted milk, the popcorn, the play at the lake front park on many evenings. There was time spent on the porch together with our parents. I remember many occasions on that porch, when one of my three friends who went on a downhill course would come by and ask, "Mrs. Comer, can I come up and play?" (He was known to be a bad boy in school.) My mother would spell out the rules of the porch and the rules of play, and if he could live by that, he could come up. So he came up and I never remember a fight the entire time. He was not a bad boy; he was simply an underdeveloped boy who was mismanaged in a variety of settings.

Also, dinnertime was important. Every evening we had dinner at the same time. There was always discussion at the table. We were expected to talk about what went on during the day, and as we talked, we learned all of the rules of conversation: not to talk too much, not to talk too little, not to interfere with others' points, and to always listen carefully to others. Those discussions would spill over into debates after dinner, and we would debate everything and anything. There was a rule that no matter how badly you were losing your debate, you could not fight. Therefore, you had to learn to make your points very well. I would come home from school already thinking about how I was going to make my points. All of that thinking and reflection was preparing me for good performance in school.

Then, there was exposure to experiences outside of the home. For example, when President Roosevelt's caravan came through town one winter, my mother bundled us all up and took us out to see the President. On another occasion, when my mother was working at the polls, she invited me into the polling place (which was probably against the rules), and actually let me pull the lever (which was definitely against the rules). The important thing was the emotionally powerful introduction I got to mainstream, adult activities.

Equally important was the protection of my aspirations and ideas. I remember, well at least I was told, that when I was about four years old, I said that I wanted to be a doctor, and my parents encouraged that dream. They bought me a toy doctor's kit. One day, a visitor said to my parents, "Why are you encouraging him to be a doctor? We are poor people. You know that he will never be a doctor." My mother said, "If you say that one more time, you will have to leave this house!"

On another occasion, when I was in about fifth grade, a student transferred into our school. She said that she knew my mother. I was curious, so when I got home, I asked my mother how the girl knew her. My mother said, "I worked for her mother many years ago." She could immediately see that this was a problem for me. She said, "You know, you are just as clean as she is, you are just as smart as she is and you can do just as well." And then she looked at me as only my mother could do and said, "And you had better!"

We were also part of a church community, which was warm and supportive, like my home. There, my father, the Sunday School Superintendent, expected everyone to arrive on time. People would run to make sure they got there on time. My father refused to give us special treatment. On one occasion, he was the Baptist Young Peoples' Bible Drill moderator. The idea behind the drill was to find the verse first. My sister had found the verse, was about to give it, and somebody whispered the answer. My father disallowed her answer. My sister thought that she should get a break because he was her father. Not my father. What is fair is fair, is fair always. My point is that we caught the values that were modeled in that environment. It was not taught, it was caught. This is critically important for children.

Yet, I was like most eleven year olds. In spite of all that support, I would get in trouble. Once, I was curiously exploring my environment and was about to get into trouble. Before I got home, my father knew what I was up to. I was fortunate that I had one of those progressive fathers, who did not spank me, but said to me, "You know if you want to be respected by the people in your church and the people in your neighborhood, there are certain things you can do and there are certain things you just cannot do." So because I wanted to be respected, I did not do those things—well, at least not where anybody could see me! The point I am making is that the entire community was locked into a conspiracy to make certain that I grew up to become a responsible, contributing citizen.

The school was a natural part of the community because school people could be seen in the grocery store, post office, and other local public places. Because of my pre-school experiences at home and in the community, I was prepared to go to school ready for learning and able to elicit positive responses from school staff. I got some support for this notion when I went home a few years ago to visit my mother in the hospital. There, I encountered my first grade teacher, then a spry 80-plus-year-old volunteer at the hospital. She threw her arms around me and she said, "Oh, my, Little James!" I was 55, but of course you are always "Little James" to your first grade teacher. Then, she stepped back and said, "Oh, we just loved the Comer children. They came to school bright-eyed and eager to learn."

Now, this type of response is exactly what my friends did not receive. They had not been given the support at home that enabled them to elicit such responses, and as a result, they had difficult interactions in school. I remember one occasion when the school had a contest intended to teach us how to use the library. It was a reading contest, in which we had to read as many books as we could. I won the contest by reading the most books, but my three friends, the only other Black youngsters in the class, did not read any books. My teacher was so frustrated and disappointed that she said, "If you three little colored boys do not want to be like the rest of us, you should not come to our schools." My friends felt rejection as a result of that, I am sure.

My teacher was not a diehard racist. She used to walk to school with me hand-in-hand every day. But she was simply not prepared to respond to that situation. If she had known that these were the grandchildren of sharecroppers and tenant farmers who were intimidated by mainstream institutions, systems, and ways, she would have taken them by the hand to the library and helped them succeed.

I was vulnerable when I went off to college and experienced significant racial prejudice. For example, in English Composition the professor would grade the exams anonymously and then read the best paper at the beginning of class. Once, he was reading my composition as the best. Midway through, he questioned, "Whose paper is this?" I was the only Black kid in the class. I raised my hand, and from that point on he ripped it apart, line for line. As a result of this and other incidents, I made almost all Cs the first year, which was not good enough to remain a pre-med student.

My response demonstrates the importance of family and community and the strength that they provide. I was devastated because my family expected me to succeed, but I did not fall apart. That summer I went back home and visited every "sister" from our church who had helped to rear me. I was tapping the good feelings and good experiences of my community. When I went back to college I stayed on the Honor Roll from that point on.

Also at college, I noted that there were a number of successful Black students, despite the fact that other Black students of the same ability level avoided the classroom setting, played cards, flunked out, and went home. Many of those in my Black fraternity were among this successful group. I also noticed that many of the men in my fraternity were from the same kind of background as myself—from strong families and a warm supportive church culture that was important to them. Young people need a supportive culture around them in order to succeed in school. The kind of community that I grew up in has all but disappeared, and it has disappeared because of changes that have taken place in our society very rapidly and very recently.

Let us focus on change. Human beings have been on earth more than five million years and there has been very little change from generation to generation until the last one hundred and fifty years. Within the last century, we have gone from horse and buggy to automobile, jet plane, and interplanetary-rocket levels of technology. Yet, the needs of children have not changed at all. They still need to be protected, supported, and guided in order to succeed.

In recent times, more than ever before, we need our children to achieve high levels of education. In the past, only a few needed to succeed at a high level because most people could be swept into an economy that did not require an education: the farm, the factory, the waterfront, and a variety of other jobs that no longer exist. Today, ninety to ninety-five percent of young people must be able to get a good education in order to earn a living, take care of themselves and their families, and meet all of their adult responsibilities. In order to do that through education, children need a higher level of development.

The experiences young people have today are very different from the ones that I had. For example, when my daughter was about four years of age, my wife and I were both working and we had a housekeeper who liked to watch the soaps with her daughter. I was packing one day to leave for a trip and my little four-year-old very solemnly shook her finger at me and said, "Now don't you have an affair!" She was four; I was sixteen before I knew what an affair was! (It is ironic that she is now an actress, and her first small part in Hollywood was on "Days of Our Lives"). The point I am making is that today's children see more, hear more, and know more than ever before, and yet they are no more mature than the children before them. This is the first time in history that information goes directly to children, rather than through the important authority figures who can censor the information and censure them for acting inappropriately on that information.

Because of family breakdown, poverty, and the fact that many people are busy, many children are not receiving the kind of support that they need during this time when high-level development is essential. Many children come to school unprepared for the challenge, and too many people in school are not prepared to support their development. In fact, the whole school structure is not set up to support development.

A Program Supportive of Children's Development: The School Development Program (SDP)

Let us now focus on our work in the School Development Program, started 43 years ago as a response to the underdevelopment of our children. As part of an intervention project, we went into schools that were not functioning well and we realized that the major reason was a difficult interaction between home and school due to underdeveloped children and unprepared staff. Everybody was defeated—parents, teachers, children—and everybody was defensive. At the same time though, everybody wanted to succeed.

We had explosions. We were almost blown out of the school. In order to survive, we created a governance and management team that was representative of all the players: parents, teachers, administrators, and students.

The nine elements of the School Development Program grew out of the needs that we observed. The School Planning and Management Team (SPMT) was charged with the responsibility of developing a Comprehensive School Plan that covered both social and academic areas, as well as coordinating staff development to achieve school goals. Assessment and Modification took place on an ongoing basis. The Parent Team was a mechanism through which parents could support the school plan, and the Mental Health Team, now called the Student and Staff Support Team, in addition to helping individual children, was given the role of reminding everybody to "think development," and focus all on important questions, such as: What do children need to succeed in school, and what do their behaviors mean?

Beyond delegation of responsibility to teams, we had to change the culture of the school—the way people behaved and the way that they thought. In schools that are not going well, there is a lot of fighting and conflict; everybody blames everybody else, so we came up with the idea of the "no-fault" environment. You do not blame anybody; rather you find solutions to the problems. We also implemented consensus decision-making rather than voting. When you have a vote, you have a winner and a loser and the loser says, "You won, you do it." This causes lack of support and leads finally to paralysis, preventing collaboration.

What we did, in short, was to re-create community in school—one like the community which existed in a natural way outside of school thirty years before—and it was this restored community that supported the development of children, permitting teaching and learning at a much higher level.

Over time, the School Development Program has had very good outcomes. When we first entered two New Haven, Connecticut schools, they were 32nd and 33rd in academic achievement out of 33 schools, and had the worst attendance and behavior in the city. After our intervention, the schools rose to be tied for 3rd and 4th in academic achievement. They were first in the city in attendance and had no serious behavior problems.

In recent years, we have had similar successes in other cities. For example, one school in Virginia went from 24th to 1st in academic achievement in their district. Unfortunately though, these successes are not always sustained if problematic action is taken by the district. In the case of Virginia, the central office did not believe the test scores. "Those students" were not supposed to do better than doctors' children and other professionals' children in the city. So they tested them again. The children did better the second time than they did the first. Then the tragedy occurred; they took 12 senior people from that school, moved them all over the place, and sent in a principal who was not trained to implement the model. Of course, the scores went down.

An example of a better transition is a school that rose from 34th to 1st in academic achievement. In the case of this school, the district leadership moved the principal who had helped make success happen to work with many other schools, but they also properly trained a new principal and did not turn over the staff. That school was number one again this past year, so it can be done.

But, the point I am making is that our institutions have not adjusted in the way that they can and must in order to make it possible for all children to learn. This is due, in my opinion, to the fact that schools reflect the attitudes of the larger society, especially the popular attitude that success is a matter of intelligence, not a matter of development. Our culture still believes that if you pour information into the heads of children, those with the best brains will get it. We also believe that anybody who is bright enough can teach, that teaching is no more than passing on information, and as a result of that, we do not adequately invest in our schools. We do not train, select, or support teachers well, and we do not give them the time to work together collaboratively.

As a young psychiatrist, I was in the playroom with a youngster that we called the "wild child," because she was absolutely impossible. One day, she threatened to throw paint on my suit. It was the only suit I had, so I rushed to my supervisor to try to figure out what to do. He said, "She likes you." I could not imagine how she could show that she liked me by throwing paint on me, but I had to save my suit, so I did what he said. He had suggested that "the next time she threatens, you might say, 'You know, if you throw that paint, I will be so angry that I won't want to play with you.'" I could not see how that would stop the wild child, but I said it, and sure enough, her arm came down very gradually and she never tried it again.

It is important to note here that I had a supervisor. I had a senior mentor out there supporting me; someone who could help me understand what was going on and how to handle the situation so that I survived and was able to help the child. Teachers are out on the front line every day with all kinds of problems and there is nobody to help them. That is why so many leave the profession. It is a very serious situation that we must change.

There are people who are doing a great job in schools. At the same time, there are people doing a terrible job—some because they have not been trained, and some because they have the wrong attitude and simply should not be in education in the first place. We must address both situations.

Better support for education would help, but there is another great problem—the one I keep talking about—that is the absence of child development knowledge in the hearts and minds of so many teachers simply because it was not a part of their training, and it was not a part of the way they grew up. They reflect that lack of knowledge when they are there on the front line. In many schools of education, even today, you can graduate with just one course in child development. Often, that course is taken on campus in the school of education, not involving any applied work in schools. Some teachers receive no child development training at all.

Recently, I spoke at a school of education and a child development professor told me that a principal came to her and said, "Why do I have to take this course? I'm going to be a principal?" The professor said, "If it were up to me, this would be the only course that you would take." The lack of understanding of how important child development really is, and how much we need to know, and how we need to be able to apply it to everything that goes on in schools, is a huge problem. The adjustment and the changes needed are very difficult, not only because of the economic, political, and organizational interests, but primarily because of our cultural beliefs.

The competitive and defensive blaming postures that we get into in our culture complicate this situation even further.

I discovered when I was writing my book, *Maggie's American Dream*, that the schools in Denmark were based on knowledge of development. I went to Denmark to observe. When I came back, I realized that I had not asked one important question: What do you do with bad teachers and how do you get rid of them? I asked the people I had observed to write to me with an answer. After a long period, they finally called and explained that the process was too difficult to explain in writing. We arranged a telephone call.

In short, what the people in Denmark said was that a cultural difference makes it difficult to explain. The caller said, "We do not have many bad teachers." I asked, "How is that?" She replied, "Because the union selects the teachers and they would not want to do anything harmful to the children. That would give them a bad reputation. They make the recommendation to the city council and the city council appoints the teachers." I said, "But somebody's mother or sister or somebody needs a job, doesn't that happen?" The caller replied, "The city council would not hire a weak teacher. They would not want to harm the children." I said, "But what happens when somebody manages to get through and is not effective?" She said, "All the other teachers who work in the group will work together to help that teacher. They want every teacher to be successful because they do not want to hurt the children."

Over and over, the focus was on the children—no nepotism, no blame, no power struggles. And over and over in the United States, the focus is on what the parents want, what the teachers want, what the union wants, and on and on.

Concluding Observations

Let me close by outlining three thrusts that we must make. First of all, we must address the problems of marginalized children, families, and communities in our society. Secondly, we must change the structures and processes in school that create the negative conditions that I am talking about. And finally, we must change our cultural beliefs.

How do we help the children who have been marginalized? Many middle-income children gain what they need to succeed in school simply by living with, and growing up with, their parents. Many low-income children in particular are marginal to the mainstream. We can change that by giving children mainstream experiences in school. To do so, we must develop what I call the *new school*, where we focus on physical health, mental health, and child development in the service of academic learning. We must protect programs that we now call recreation (such as the arts and athletics), but that really provide constructive self-expression opportunities. We must bring all of these programs and services together in the school in order to connect children to the mainstream. We can then teach the social skills necessary to prepare them for mainstream participation. We, of course, must not just accept the mainstream as it is, but change it if necessary so that it works for everybody.

How do we enable our institutions to promote child development? I suggest that we need an Education Extension Service very much like the Agricultural Extension Service of a hundred years ago. Education is today to the economy what agriculture was to the economy a hundred years ago, and if we really want to move ahead, we have got to help people change those who are out there working in ways that are destructive and harmful.

We must also change our leadership training. In Denmark, you cannot elect to get a degree that makes you eligible to become a principal. You are selected because you have shown leadership talent as a teacher. Then, you go to be trained. We have too many going into educational leadership because they are not successful teachers. We have got to change leadership, and leadership academies, so that they are focused on helping educators learn to help children develop.

Authorities charged with the responsibility for improving schools need more clout. School functioning should become the responsibility of the courts. We should have a system where the courts can insist that schools will change and begin to use the methods and practices that have been demonstrated to bring about that change. There are many things going on in schools that work. We must use these best practices.

Today, there are many teachers in schools, especially those teaching math and science, and those in poor communities, who are not qualified to teach, or who are teaching outside their discipline. Nobody should be teaching in an area in which they were not trained to teach. Until we vigorously expose and address this and other problems, we are going to continue to have underachieving schools. This denies children their civil rights. That is why we need to have the courts involved.

Finally, we cannot bring about these changes unless we counter the culture that makes it all right to have poor Black kids, poor Hispanic kids, and isolated White kids underachieve, and create a culture where they are expected to do well. Until we change the belief that "these kids can't"—which many people still hold—we are not going to get the kind of changes in schools needed for all children. We need what I call a "Human Capital Development Movement" to really bring about change. Change is difficult, but it has been brought about before in our society in very resistant areas: racial segregation, smoking, and other areas. We must help all children to gain a good education.

It takes time. But we must hurry because time is running out, believe it or not. We cannot continue to have the "haves" and "have-nots" move farther and farther apart. In these days of media communications, where the "have-nots" can see what the "haves" possess, they are not going to tolerate it. The more dependent we are on technology, the more vulnerable we are to expressions of discontent. If we do not change now, in 30 years we are going to be in a condition that none of us would like to see. The only solution to the "have versus have-not" problem is education.

References

Comer, J. P. (1980). *School power: Implications of an intervention project.* New York, NY: Free Press.

Comer, J. P. (1988). *Maggie's American dream: The life and times of a Black family.* New York, NY: New American Library.

Comer, J. P. (1988, November). Educating poor minority children. *Scientific American, 259*(5), 42–48.

Comer, J. P. (1997). *Waiting for a miracle: Why schools can't solve our problems—and how we can.* New York, NY: Dutton.

Comer, J. P. (2001, April 23). Schools that develop children. *The American Prospect, 12*(7), 30–35.

4. Race and School Desegregation: Contemporary Legal and Educational Issues

EDGAR G. EPPS
University of Chicago
University of Wisconsin, Milwaukee

I will begin with a quotation by W. E. B. Du Bois, who wrote in 1936, the following:

> Theoretically the Negro needs neither segregated nor mixed schools. What he needs is education. But he must remember that there is no magic either in mixed schools or in segregated schools. A mixed school with poor and unsympathetic teachers with hostile public opinion and no teaching concerning Black folk is bad. (Quoted in Woodson, 1977).

Unfortunately, the experiences of our children in public school desegregation have often been very bad.

The Economic Basis of Race Relations and Racial Discrimination

This lecture is being presented 45 years after the passage of the historic *Brown* decision. Also, it is 55 years since the publication of Myrdal's (1944) monumental study of American race relations, *An American Dilemma*. Myrdal's study dominated the discourse on race relations for almost a generation. His most ardent critic was the sociologist Oliver Cromwell Cox (1948) who earned his PhD in sociology at the University of Chicago. And, as an aside, I must point out that Professor Cox entered the University in 1928 to study economics. In 1929, the Great Depression caused him to change his major; he decided that any discipline that could not predict an event as monumental as the Great Depression was not worthy of study, therefore he changed to sociology. However, sociology, my own discipline, was not much better because neither sociologists, nor psychologists, nor anthropologists, nor economists, none of us predicted the Civil Rights Revolution.

The contemporary wisdom when I was in graduate school was that it was impossible to legislate social change in attitudes, behaviors, and customs regarding segregation in a society such as the United States that had accepted legalized and de facto segregation in most of the nation for several generations. Social scientists contended that change had to come gradually and, following Myrdal's lead, that it had to come about by changing the hearts and minds of White Americans. You all know that history and you all know how wrong all of us social science experts were about that. Cox, for example, critiqued Gunnar Myrdal's ideas about White prejudice. According to Cox (1948), "[Myrdal states] . . . the vicious circle runs as follows:

> 'White prejudice . . . keeps the Negro low in standards of living. . . . This, in turn gives support to white prejudice. White prejudice and Negro standards thus mutually "cause" each other.' [Cox observed] these two variables are interdependent, but neither is consistently dependent; a change in either will affect the other inversely. If we initiate a change in Negro standards, say, by 'giving the Negro youth more education,' white prejudice will go down; . . . It is this kind of mystical dance of imponderables which is at the basis of the system of social illusions marbled into Myrdal's discussion. In the first place, Myrdal does not develop a careful definition of race prejudice . . . for race prejudice is a social attitude, an acquired tendency to act; it is not some act or actions which is the meaning of discrimination. . . . The point which the author [Myrdal] seems to have avoided is this: that both race prejudice and Negro standards are consistently dependent variables . . . produced by the calculated economic interests of the Southern oligarchy." (Cox, 1948, pp. 529-530)

Cox noted Myrdal overlooked that both prejudice and the status of African Americans are dependent variables, not independent variables. Both are dependent on a set of powerful economic interests. In my opinion, it is surprising that Myrdal, an economist, ignored the economic basis of race relations and racial discrimination.

The decision by the United States Supreme Court in *Brown v. Board of Education* (1954), which ordered the dismantling of the legal system supporting segregation of schools, largely in the South and Border States, marked the beginning of a new era of American race relations. The American dilemma would be confronted head on. No longer could the gap between the American Creed and the reality of racism be ignored. However, 10 years later, Charles Silberman (1964), in *Crisis in Black and White*, wrote:

> There is no American dilemma. What we are discovering, in short, is that the United States, West as well as East—North as well as South, is a racist society in a sense and to a degree that we have refused so far to admit, much less face. Twenty years ago Gunnar Myrdal concluded that the "American Negro Problem was a problem in the heart of the American," Myrdal was wrong. The tragedy of race relations in the United States is that there is no American dilemma. White Americans are not torn and tortured by the conflict between their devotion to the American Creed and their actual behavior. They are upset

by the current state of race relations not because of justice being denied, but because their peace is being disturbed and their privileges challenged. (p. 10)

Now, that was written in 1964, but it could have been written yesterday. In a similar vein, the *Report of the Riot Commission (National Advisory Commission on Civil Disorders)* in 1968 was produced by a group of scholars (informally known as the "Kerner Commission") almost as impressive as the group that did the research reported in *An American Dilemma*. The Commission concluded, rather grimly, "that our nation is moving toward two societies, one Black, one White, separate and unequal. Discrimination and segregation have long permeated much of American life. They now threaten the very future of every American." Another conclusion of the Kerner Commission Report was:

> What White Americans had never fully understood but the Negro can never forget, is that White society is deeply implicated in the ghetto. White institutions created it; White institutions maintain it, and White institutions condone it. In a country where the economy, and particularly the resources are predominately White, a policy of separation can only relegate Negroes to a permanently inferior economic status. (Summary Introduction, 1968)

However, the Commission stopped short of a recommendation for the integration of American society. It recommended a policy that combined "ghetto enrichment" with gradual and selective integration into the mainstream. Again, these comments could have been written yesterday.

In a 1969 book, *Beyond Racism: Building an Open Society*, author Whitney Young, stated that racial concentrations of Black people in segregated, impoverished ghettos leads to emotional tensions that could ultimately explode into riots and violence. His views could have been written very recently.

Legal Foundations of School Desegregation

Now, on to desegregation. Thanks largely to the work of the National Association for the Advancement of Colored People (NAACP), a series of court cases from 1966 to 1971 established the legal foundation for desegregation. Remember that the first *Brown* decision was passed in 1954, and the second decision (*Brown II*) in 1955. The second decision said "desegregation must progress with all deliberate speed." We know that "all deliberate speed" had progressed for 10 years with almost no desegregation (see, for example, Clark, 1969). It was not until 1966 that the Federal enforcement apparatus became serious and said, "the desegregation plan has to take steps that will make it work. If the plan does not yield results, it is not an acceptable plan." It was only at that point that desegregation actually began. We had more than 10 years from the decision to the serious beginning of school desegregation.

In subsequent cases, the Supreme Court ruled that desegregation plans must be realistic and guaranteed to work. Only unitary systems without vestiges of the historic dual system could meet the standard. The final obstacle to desegregation of schools was residential segregation. In *Swann v. Charlotte-Mecklenburg Board of Education* (1971), the Supreme Court ruled that desegregation plans could not be limited to neighborhood schools. Mandatory transportation could be used by school districts to bring about a unitary system. Busing was born. Following this ruling, desegregation in the South proceeded rapidly. Outside the South, not much was happening. Northern districts claimed that the segregation that occurred in these systems was natural because of housing problems and personal preferences. Since de facto segregation existed because people of different races lived in different neighborhoods, the *Brown* decision did not apply. However, in *Keyes v. School District No. 1* (1973), the Supreme Court ruled that Denver had assigned teachers and students to schools on the basis of race. The finding that a pattern of "intentionally segregative school board actions in a meaningful portion of a school system . . . creates a presumption that other segregated schooling within the system is not adventitious" paved the way for desegregation litigation in Boston, Chicago, Cleveland, Columbus, Dayton, Indianapolis, and so forth (p. 210). So Northern school desegregation became subject to the ruling of *Brown*. Where resistance was strong, in Boston, for example, federal judges appointed monitors to administer desegregation plans for school officials who were unwilling to comply with desegregation orders.

In 1975, Lewis Killian, a sociologist, in a book called *The Impossible Revolution Phase II*, concluded that, "To subscribe to the general principle of racial equality is one thing, to pay the personal price in terms of sharing traditionally white held advantages is quite another" (p. 175). In countless instances White people proclaim dedication to the abstract principle of racial equality but resist application of this principle when they perceive that their own neighborhoods, their children's schools, their job opportunities, or their political power or tax bills will be affected.

The general consensus of scholars by 1970 was that the courts and the enforcement apparatus had done their job. However, the resistance to school desegregation was followed by White flight in the 1970s and 1980s, leaving the majority of African Americans and Hispanics attending segregated public schools. As Gary Orfield and his colleagues at Harvard point out annually, schools today are more segregated than they were 25 to 30 years ago (e.g., Orfield & Eaton, 1996). The only remedy that might make a difference would be a desegregation plan that included all of the contiguous suburbs of a metropolitan area. That remedy was essentially made impossible for most urban areas by the Supreme Court ruling in *Milliken v. Bradley* (1974, 1977), the 1974 decision pertaining to Detroit, because it required plaintiffs to demonstrate that the state, county, or other school districts were involved in actions that contributed to the segregation of the system. A few districts were found guilty even with that restriction, for example, Indianapolis, Indiana; Wilmington, Delaware; Louisville, Kentucky; St. Louis and Kansas City, Missouri.

To give an example, the Louisville case was quite simple because Jefferson County, in which Louisville is located, had a long-standing practice of sending its African American high school students into Louisville to attend Central High School rather than provide a high school for them in the county. There was clearly collusion between the county and the city to provide segregated schooling; therefore, it was an easy case for the justices to decide. The others were not quite that simple. The St. Louis and Kansas City cases were based on the fact that the state of Missouri had required legal segregation of schools before 1954. Therefore, the state was directly involved in creating the segregated condition of the urban school systems. So, in both St. Louis and Kansas City, the state of Missouri was required to pay substantial amounts of money in support of desegregation plans.

The Contemporary Status of School Desegregation
Legislative Retreat From the Mandates for School Desegregation

Leaving history and getting to the present status of desegregation, in the 1990s school districts are going into court asking for release from desegregation plans based on the claim that these school systems now meet the requirements of unitary status, therefore exempting them from court-ordered desegregation. These claims are made even though the majority of African American students still attend racially isolated schools. The Supreme Court decisions in *Board of Education v. Dowell* (Oklahoma City, 1991) and *Freeman v. Pitts* (1992) have enabled school systems to return to segregation without violating the law. Following *Pitts*, it is only necessary for school districts to demonstrate that they have shown "good faith effort," and have attempted to comply with the requirements of desegregation plans to the extent that they have done everything "practicable" to remedy the effects of a dual system of segregated schools. Isn't that interesting? If the school district has decided that it has done all that is practical, it can now be excused from the desegregation plan, even *if there is no desegregation*. That is amazing!

These decisions set the stage for resegregation of America's public schools. Just last month, a federal judge concluded that the Charlotte-Mecklenburg district, the district of the historic *Swann* (1971) decision, has fulfilled the purpose of its desegregation order and declared the district unitary. The district did not ask to be released from this order. This case came about because disgruntled White parents felt their children were being denied access to high quality education because the district had a pupil assignment plan for certain magnet schools that relied on racial quotas to assure adequate representation of African American students. The judge ruled (*Belk et al. v. Charlotte-Mecklenburg Schools*, September, 1999), in spite of the evidence provided by the school district that there was still the need to maintain the desegregation plan because Black students were still not receiving equal education, that the district was "unitary." In other words, the judge said, you do not have to do it any more. In fact, if you do it, it is illegal. This decision removed the district from costly busing provisions and ended race-based admission to the district magnet school. And this is not an isolated case.

In Boston, the First U. S. Circuit Court of Appeals, in a case called *Wessmann v. Gittens* (1998; see also, *Wessman v. Boston Sch. Comm.*, 996 F. Supp. 120 [D. Mass. 1998]), reversed a lower court decision that upheld the Boston School Committee's policy of using race as one of the criteria for admission to Boston Latin School (and two other "examination" schools). "Thus, the majority decision in *Wessmann* seeks to make illegitimate nearly every concept and tool devised since *Brown* to fashion a remedy to racial and ethnic student assignment discrimination" (Dentler, 1999, p.16). Dentler also reported that:

> [t]he Boston School Committee voted unanimously on February 3, 1999 to not ask the United States Supreme Court to decide on its Latin School assignment procedure in an appeal from the First Circuit decision . . . [in order to avoid] the making of bad law by a court known to be hostile toward affirmative action policies in general. . . . At the same meeting, the committee chose by a vote of 4–2 to discontinue the use of any factor except achievement test scores in the selection of students for Advanced Work Classes, Boston's method of prepping students for competitively high secondary school achievement after elementary school. (p. 17)

The [Boston] mayor then announced his intentions to return the system to neighborhood schools within 6 years. That is where we are today. The Boston School Committee did not appeal the decision because several legal scholars argued that this is not a good case to send to the Supreme Court, and that they did not want the decision in this case to become a precedent for future decisions on affirmative action. They decided that it would be wiser to wait for a better case. I think this was a wise decision.

One final example of the retreat from desegregation; this one is from Rockford, Illinois, which has a controlled-choice desegregation plan (*People Who Care v. Rockford Board Education School District No. 205*, 1994). During the first 2 years of this court-ordered, controlled-choice plan, segregation was reduced at the elementary school level from 15 schools to 4 schools, and 1 secondary school was resegregated. If this controlled-choice plan is rescinded and the district is returned to neighborhood schools, Rockford would have at least 26 segregated elementary schools. If Rockford, then, appeals for relief and becomes a unitary district, it will resegregate more than a dozen elementary schools. In essence, beginning with the Reagan Presidency and continuing through the 90s, the federal government and federal courts as well as state courts and legislatures have proceeded systematically to dismantle the legislative and judicial protections gained by African Americans and subsequently other people of color, women, and the handicapped. Conservative politicians, judges, and the intellectuals who provide them with the conceptual and empirical support for their views, take great delight in "turning the tables on the liberals."

I am reminded of what I learned from my sociology professor, Butler A. Jones, at Talladega College in 1946. He said, "Americans are more concerned with form than with substance, and empirical evidence does not convince self-righteous people." The myth of equality overshadows all evidence; we read that White males are losing jobs because of affirmative action, yet Black unemployment rates have consistently remained twice as high as those of Whites, and rates for Hispanics are almost as high as those for Blacks. We are now told that affirmative action hurts those that it was designed to help in spite of the wonderful book by Bowen and Bok (1998), *The Shape of the River*, which contradicts that statement: "you can't change the minds of self-righteous people with evidence." We were told that social class is more important than race in determining life chances of Blacks (Wilson, 1978, 1980). That was 20 years ago, and the author of that proposition has now decided that, yes, there is still discrimination against Black people, especially in employment. Black people are discriminated against when they apply for jobs; he found that out while studying the ghetto of Chicago, and for that, I admire him. It took 20 years, but he changed his mind. . .

The Gains and Losses From School Desegregation

So, what have we learned? What have we gained? What are the gains and losses of desegregation in the last 45 years? Well, the end of integration is in sight. This was the title of an article in *Time* magazine in 1996. Let's assess the consequences of the desegregation effort. For me, the important question is how desegregation affects student achievement. Maureen Hallinan, a sociologist at Notre Dame, agrees. She reported in an article she published in the *Ohio State Law Journal* in 1998 that assessment of the results of large-scale studies of the effects of racial composition on student achievement supports the following conclusions:

Children's academic achievement in desegregated schools First, Black students attain higher academic achievement in majority White schools than in predominantly Black or all-Black schools. Second, Black students attain higher academic achievement in majority White classrooms than in majority non-White classrooms. Third, the earlier a Black student is placed in a majority White school or classroom, the higher the academic achievement. Fourth, Hispanic students attain higher academic achievement in majority White schools than in minority White schools, and (this is most important, but you cannot convince White parents that it is true), fifth, White students do not suffer from lower achievement when they attend schools with Blacks or Hispanics. (But now try and convince a mother of a White child of that.)

I am sorry; I should not indict all White mothers. Many White mothers are quite comfortable if their child is attending an integrated school. What we have to understand, though, is that White mothers' definition of an integrated school is quite different than a Black mother's definition of an integrated school. To the White mother, the school is integrated if it has 10 percent or fewer Black students. It is viewed as becoming threatening when that number rises to 20 percent, and it is intolerable if it reaches 40 percent. At that point, the school rapidly becomes all Black. That is what is called "the tipping point." Now to Black mothers, the comfort level is right at about 40 percent and it is even better if it is 50 or 60 percent Black. Black mothers are a little uncomfortable at 10 percent Black (the White comfort level), and many are quite uncomfortable with less than 10 percent Black. So, you can see that we have different perceptions of what integration means. Thus, it is not surprising that social science surveys report that 80 to 90 percent of White Americans agree with the principle of integration of public schools and most say they would not object to their child attending a public school that is racially integrated. However, when you begin asking White parents how they would feel about certain percentages of Black children in schools or classrooms you begin to get the perception that their tolerance for the presence of Black children in their children's classrooms is relatively low.

There is a psychologist named John Dovidio who (with S. L. Gaertner) has coined a phrase that describes this phenomenon: "aversive racism." By aversive racism, he means that Whites who are not overtly prejudiced or racist, or who do not consider themselves to be prejudiced or racist, have varying tolerances for contact with people of color. Those who can't tolerate any contact, you could say are the most extremely aversive racists, while those who can tolerate a little contact are less extreme, and so on and so forth until you finally get to the tolerant end of the continuum where you find people who can tolerate a lot of interracial contact. The problem, of course, is that comfort zone of 10 percent; and this applies not only to schools, it also applies to housing, and this is very important, as we shall see. The idea here is that as long as Whites have low tolerance for social contact with members of the African American racial group, the outlook for support of desegregation of public schools in any community where the school population of minority students is greater than 15 percent is not very good. To some extent, this applies to desegregation of Hispanic schools as well. The tolerance for Hispanics may be somewhat greater than that for African Americans, but I'm convinced there is also a tipping point for Hispanics. Even in affluent Chicago suburbs where the average home price is $250,000.00, if the schools become 40 percent or more African American, White families start moving out to neighborhoods where the home prices are even higher, and the schools rapidly become predominantly Black; a "majority minority school."

The development of interracial and interpersonal skills in desegregated schools Following up on the gains or losses theme, and still looking at the gains for African American children, according to Dawkins and Braddock (1994), desegregated school experiences provide for the socialization—the development of the interpersonal skills useful in interracial contexts—and reduce social inertia, leading to increased tolerance and willingness to participate in desegregated environments (p. 396). Elementary and secondary desegregated school experiences affect not only social, psychological, and academic achievement outcomes, but also such crucial factors as college attendance and access to broader social networks (social capital) that provide job information, contacts, and sponsorships necessary for career advancement (p. 395). These results are similar to those reported by Wells and Crain (1994) who concluded that the long-term outcome of desegregated educational experiences is to increase the ability of Blacks to work effectively with Whites, live in racially integrated neighborhoods, attend predominantly White institutions of higher education, etc. It appears that early racial integration (pre-school through elementary school) has an inoculation effect; that is, it increases the ability of African American children to cope with the tensions and stresses of day-to-day contact with Whites. Put in a different way, results from longitudinal studies show that Black students who attend desegregated elementary and secondary schools are more likely to enroll in 2- or 4-year predominantly White colleges and to have White social contacts in their integrated neighborhoods. Wells and Crain also concluded that

Black students who have had substantial experience in desegregated schools are more likely than comparable students (who have not had such experiences) to have desegregated social and professional networks in later life, and are more likely to be working in white-collar and professional jobs in the private sector. It is important to note that these effects are not a direct result of sitting a Black child next to a White child or the racial composition of a school or classroom, but rather the result of the exposure to the "social networks" or social capital that African Americans may not have access to in their home environment. In essence, research suggests that aside from any academic gains, there are social capital and human capital assets to be gained from long-term matriculation in racially integrated schools for Black students.

The development of racial self-concept and self-esteem in desegregated schools In another area of interest, the results are mixed. In my reviews of research on racial self-identity, self-concept, and self-esteem (e.g., Epps, 1981), some studies find higher levels of self-esteem for Black students in segregated schools, others report higher scores in integrated schools, and still others report no difference. These conflicting reports can be attributed to methodological differences, including the use of many different instruments to assess personality characteristics, comparisons of different age, sex, and geographic groups, and comparisons of results from different time periods. However, a few conclusions are warranted.

First, there is fairly consistent evidence that Black students' sense of personal control is higher in desegregated schools than in segregated schools. Second, Black students' educational aspirations are usually high in both segregated and desegregated schools, and to the surprise of many researchers, they tend to be as high as, or higher than, the aspirations of White students (however, the actual college attendance rates favor Whites by a larger margin). Third, self-concept of academic ability is also surprisingly high in both types of schools in view of the relatively low performance on standardized achievement tests of Black students. Fourth, Black students' general self-esteem is equal to, or higher than, that of White students in both segregated and desegregated schools. (You might ask how this is so since Blacks are not held in high esteem by the general population. The simple answer is that Black students do not look to the general society for approval; they look to their families, to their communities, and to their peers.) Fifth, the self-esteem of Black students is only weakly related to their academic performance (for the same reason, they look to their peers for validation). And sixth, student perceptions of positive interracial classroom climate are associated with higher self-esteem and better academic performance. I think this is a very important finding. It is supported by a recent study by Marcus-Newhall and

Heindl that appeared in the *Journal of Social Issues* (1998). It is important because if we are looking for a clue about how to make classrooms effective for Black children (and other minority children), then this idea, this perception of *positive interracial classroom climate*, is, I think, something we can focus on.

Challenges to Black educators as a consequence of school desegregation   Finally, let's look at the losses and costs of desegregation. Desegregation, especially in the South, was achieved largely by closing Black schools and busing the students to predominantly White schools. This resulted in many Black teachers and administrators losing their jobs and being demoted. It is estimated that 38,000 African Americans in 17 states lost their positions as teachers and administrators between 1954 and 1965. The result for many African American children is the loss of an important social resource. African American teachers often represent surrogate parent figures, firm disciplinarians, empathetic counselors, positive role models, and advocates. Current research suggests that lower-achieving African American students benefit most from relationships with African American teachers. These results are particularly disturbing because the proportion of all teachers who are African American has steadily declined in the last 35 years to less than 10 percent. The proportion of Hispanic teachers is even lower.

Challenges of school desegregation to Black students and families   Among the costs of desegregation is the overwhelming burden placed upon Black students and families. Most desegregation plans were constructed with the view of making it as painless as possible for Whites in order to keep Whites from leaving the public schools. What this means, then, is that African American students typically have to travel longer distances than White students (via busing), and that within the schools, they are often segregated through the processes of ability grouping and tracking. There is an interesting story-within-a-story about busing programs. For example, students might be bused into a school, and then assigned to classrooms on different floors of the building than those to which neighborhood (White) kids were assigned; they might also be assigned different lunchrooms or playground periods. The contact between White students and Black students is, therefore, minimized; White students see the Black students only when they arrive on the bus and when they get on the bus to return home. We should not be surprised that in such extreme situations racial integration has not been entirely successful.

In addition, Black students have experienced different patterns of discipline, including disproportionately high suspension and expulsion rates. In some nominally integrated schools, Black students have been denied access to higher-level courses, including AP classes. Tracking, ability grouping, and disproportionate assignment to special education are examples of the processes by which Black students are denied equal access to high-quality education even when they attend the same schools as Whites. In essence, when Black students have been assigned to predominantly White schools they have not received equitable treatment and have not had access to the quality of resources that were available to White children. Let us be clear: What desegregation was supposed to be about was making the same quality of educational resources available to Black children as were available to White children. This simply has not happened in most instances. For the most part, when Black children were put into the same schools as Whites, arrangements were made to deny them access to the best education that was available to Whites, and the most efficient way of doing this, of course, was by ability grouping and tracking. And, lest we forget, the use of special education as a "dumping ground' for many Black children has been very prevalent. So, where does that leave us in our assessment of 45 years of experience with school desegregation?

Assessing 45 Years of School Desegregation

In recent years, opposition by both Black and White parents has resulted in a political climate in which alternatives to busing and other mandatory desegregation measures are being promoted and implemented. Among these are magnet schools, voucher programs, and charter schools. The voucher programs and charter schools have not been studied extensively, but the available evidence suggests that they, too, will leave low-income, low-achieving students behind. What all of these programs have in common is the tendency to separate children or sort them according to social class. Middle-class parents of all racial and ethnic groups have access to better information than lower-class parents, and they have the resources to persist in the application process until they have arranged for their children to be accepted at a "selective" school. Therefore, most racially diverse magnet schools have disproportionately high ratios of middle-class and White students. Critics also contend that magnet and other special admissions schools siphon both human and financial resources from neighborhood schools, thereby creating a form of dual education system within the public schools of a district.

The Case of Magnet Schools: Chicago as Exemplar

I will give a couple of examples from Chicago. The Chicago magnet school program is a part of its desegregation consent decree. There are 29 magnet schools in Chicago attended by 17,000 students (of approximately 400,000). Of the students enrolled in magnet schools, 19 percent are

White, 50 percent are African American, 24 percent are Hispanic, and 7 percent are Asian. Note, however, that Whites make up only about 9 percent of the public school students in Chicago. In addition, there are 93 integrated, desegregated schools in Chicago serving 14,500 students. Of these, 37 percent are White, 16 percent are African American, 34 percent are Hispanic, and 12 percent are Asian. Keep in mind, however, that this is a school district in which African Americans make up two-thirds of the student body; yet, in these integrated schools they comprise only 16 percent of enrollment.

Why is this lack of proportionate representation important? Overall, magnet and integrated schools are the highest achieving schools in the district, based on standardized achievement test scores and college attendance. What some critics would say is, "of course they have higher test scores; after all, the best students were selected to attend these schools." Thus, the higher test scores cannot be attributed to better quality instruction or curricula; it is simply the case that if students are selected on the basis of test score performance, their test scores will continue to be high (even with mediocre instruction and programs). In essence, the magnet schools are not (necessarily) doing a better job of teaching; they are just getting better students. Why should they not do better on the test? Of course, magnet school teachers and administrators reply that it is not that simple; magnet schools are actually doing a better job through better teaching and better programs. The critics' response is that magnet schools get the best teachers by causing a "brain drain" from the neighborhood schools. These schools get both the best students and the best teachers. Any comparisons with neighborhood schools are, therefore, inappropriate.

In Chicago, it is estimated that magnet schools spend considerably more dollars per student on average compared to dollars per student spent in neighborhood schools. (The exact amount of the disparity is in dispute and I cannot verify the figures.) Thus, overall, magnet schools offer specialized curricula as well as a broader range of educational enrichment programs than neighborhood schools. In addition to more resources, magnet schools can select their teachers and students. And they do not have to accept special education students or students who have behavior problems. Therefore, we should not be surprised that magnet schools have better achievement. With these advantages, why should they not be superior?

The Case of Charter Schools:
With Special Attention to Afrocentric Charter Schools

Now, let's look at charter schools. There are lots of different kinds of charter schools that provide a wide range of educational alternatives. There are 15 charter schools in Chicago now, which provide additional choices for students. The programs range from Afrocentric to technocentric. I will describe only the Afrocentric school because it represents a vision that is very attractive to some parents and educators, and it is less familiar than other types of charter schools.

The Betty Shabazz International Charter School has an interesting history. Shabazz was created by poet and educator, Haki Madhubuti, and his wife, Safisha (who is also known as Professor Carol D. Lee of Northwestern University; she received her PhD in education with honors from the University of Chicago). They started this institution as a private school 25 years ago, and ran it out of their own pockets with whatever resources they could beg and borrow from their friends and supporters. It was known as the New Concept Development Center, an Afrocentric school based on African principles. In a fortuitous turn of events, at the time they began to have difficulty raising sufficient funds to keep the school afloat, Chicago implemented its charter school program. This school had earned considerable favorable publicity that came to the attention of the Chief Executive Officer of the Chicago Public Schools, who suggested that they should turn this Afrocentric institution into a charter school. After investigating the feasibility of becoming a charter school and still maintaining its visionary integrity, the New Concept Development Center became the Betty Shabazz International Charter School, publicly funded, but still an Afrocentric school located on the Southside of Chicago. They still call the women teachers "mama" and the male teachers "baba." They also have Swahili names for the students and parents as well as rituals signifying passage from one grade level to another that are based on African traditions. What fascinates me about this school is that the one bright spot that I see about the voucher and charter movements is that African Americans who have the insight and the determination can create their own schools in their own image (or any other they choose). They can use the schools as examples to show the rest of us how to produce achieving students with high self-esteem who have high political consciousness, and who are self-directed independent learners, on the Southside of Chicago, in the heart of the ghetto.

Now, I am not naïve. Clearly, a school that is self-consciously Afrocentric will have a self-selected clientele that is not likely to be comprised of the most "truly disadvantaged" children on the Southside. That is, the students who are most difficult to educate, whose parents are the most uncommitted to education, will in all likelihood remain in neighborhood, racially isolated schools with high concentrations of poverty-level students. The clients of Betty Shabazz are likely to be the same types of parents who put their children in magnet schools and private schools except for their commitment to Afrocentric principles of education.

Therefore, I would be very surprised if this school and others like it are not successful. I won't give other examples, but the important fact about charter schools—and some voucher schools, for example in Milwaukee—is that the African American community has the opportunity to become a major player in the charter, voucher, private school game. And, if I were a dreamer, I would ask that every Black church of every denomination develop its own school. Perhaps we would no longer need the public schools. But that is a pipe dream. On a serious note, given the opportunity, community people, not only Black community people, but community people of all races and ethnic groups, could create schools in their own image and, therefore, if the public schools have not been serving them well—and we know they are not serving Black people well, they are not serving Hispanic people well, and they are not serving poor people well—could take advantage of this opportunity to take control of their children's education and show us experts how it should be done.

Sources of Black Resistance to School Desegregation

Nostalgia about Black history. I would like to focus on another aspect of resistance to desegregation that has come from Black folk—scholars who are nostalgic about the past. One of my former schoolmates at Dunbar High School in Little Rock, Arkansas, Faustine Jones (Wilson), has written a book that highlights the positive characteristics of this segregated institution. I remember Dunbar as a truly magnificent school (I had little to compare it with at the time). It was arguably the best "Negro" high school in the state of Arkansas, but we now know that it was not equal to Central High School (the White school that later became the focus of a famous desegregation movement) in facilities, science equipment, curriculum, etc. In the dual system of pre-*Brown* segregated education, separate was never equal; even the best Black school was not equal in resources to its neighboring White school. That is the aspect of the history of segregated education that the historical revisionists ignore. They also ignore the fact that in many communities, such as the rural village in which I attended elementary school (Woodson, Arkansas in Pulaski County of which Little Rock is the county seat) *there was no high school for Negroes*. School for us ended in ninth grade unless our parents arranged for us to attend private schools or public schools in other school districts (e.g., Little Rock). My parents had to bus my siblings and I to Little Rock, paying the Greyhound Bus Company for transportation, and then paying tuition to the Little Rock Public School district so that we could attend Dunbar High School. Without that kind of parental commitment, most rural African American students never attended high school during that era. Is that what these scholars want to go back to?

People forget   Time and distance erode memory. Yes, there were some bright spots. There were schools such as Dunbar in Little Rock, Dunbar in Washington, D.C., Stanton in Jacksonville, Florida, Booker T. Washington in Memphis, the laboratory schools at historically Black colleges, and many others that were doing a good job. These were the places that produced most of the Black doctors, lawyers, and other professionals. But focusing on these beacons of light ignores the vast wasteland of public education experienced by the majority of African Americans under the legally segregated dual system that *Brown* attempted to destroy. For those who are tempted by the revisionist picture painted by the nostalgia buffs, I recommend that you read the dissertation by Dr. Sylvia Gist, entitled "Educating a Southern Rural Community: The Case of Blacks in Holmes County Mississippi, 1870 to the Present." Gist concluded that between 1870 to the late 1960s, Whites denied Blacks access to comparable educational facilities (Gist, 1994). Read the dissertation if you want to know the magnitude of the disparities. Now, ladies and gentlemen, when anybody starts telling you how good things were during segregation, tell them to read this dissertation. Or tell them to talk to me. Because anybody who believes things were good was not there! Perhaps those who were there are becoming senile by now.

The Currency of Selected Afrocentric Schools

Returning to an earlier theme, a part of the response to the non-segregation of schools in places such as Detroit and Milwaukee has been the development of Afrocentric schools within public school systems. In both Detroit and Milwaukee, such schools have been in operation for more than 5 years. These schools developed as a response to the frustration that Blacks have experienced with urban school districts that have been unwilling to allocate sufficient resources to the reformation of central city schools.

Evaluations of these schools have been mixed. I will give you an example from Milwaukee where two Afrocentric public schools were created: an elementary school and a middle school. The elementary school, by all accounts, has been an outstanding success. The middle school has been declared a disaster. It was a clear failure of implementation. When the middle school was transformed into an Afrocentric school, neither visionary leadership nor a committed teaching force guided the effort. Because of seniority provisions in the teacher union contract, senior teachers who wanted to remain in the school could not be removed if they did not endorse the program. Racial balance provisions of the desegregation agreement also prevented the recruitment of African American teachers. The school also experienced high turnover among teachers and administrators as well as interference from the central office. Putting these problems together, it is not surprising that this school is not doing well. The elementary school, on the other hand, had a principal who was dedicated; a visionary, a true believer. This principal selected teachers who shared the vision; of course the parents were believers. The combination of strong leadership from the principal, a supportive and stable faculty, and strong parent support (as well as "benign neglect" from the central office) resulted in this school becoming a supportive and effective learning environment.

Future Prospects for African American Equal Educational Opportunity

Let me end by saying that we are trying many alternative paths to achieving equality of educational opportunity, primarily because the dream of desegregation has not been fulfilled. We went into school desegregation expecting to get access to the same quality of education that White kids were getting, but it has not come to pass. It does not appear likely given the current political climate that it will happen in our lifetimes. How did I come to this conclusion? One reason is that in many states, 98 percent of the voters have no children in urban public schools. There is little incentive for state legislatures to pass legislation that is friendly to Chicago, Philadelphia, or other large urban school districts. The resource rich districts get richer, and the resource poor districts get poorer by comparison. That is a political reality. Even in those states that have been required by state courts to devise more equitable systems for financing public education, the resource gap remains huge. New Jersey has been involved in the process of finance equalization for more than 15 years and still has not been able to eliminate such resource gaps.

All of this makes me a little bit pessimistic. What is the current state of race relations in the United States? I'll just read the titles of a few recently published books: *American Apartheid; The Rage of a Privileged Class; The Black-White Test Score Gap; Black-Wealth, White-Wealth*. These are just a few of the revealing titles. What do these books tell us? First, the country is still divided on racial issues. Second, Blacks and Whites still live their lives largely in separate communities. Third, the institutions serving Blacks and Hispanics and children in urban schools are vastly inferior to those serving Whites. Fourth, Blacks and Whites focus on different aspects of the racial divide. Fifth, the median income of Blacks is substantially lower than that of Whites, but pales in comparison to the wealth gap: Whites have substantially greater assets. Sixth, even those Blacks who have followed Myrdal's advice by becoming educated and acquiring the customs and values of the White mainstream are not immune from racism. . . . If any of you believe, like the majority of White Americans, that America is a "color-blind" nation, you are in for a rude awakening (especially) if you happen to be a person of color.

What is the outlook for the future? As the nation becomes more diverse ethnically, some groups are becoming increasingly isolated. According to

Gary Orfield and his colleagues (1996), Latino students will soon become the largest non-European racial/ethnic group in the public schools and, like African Americans, they tend to be urban dwellers and disproportionately from lower-income families. In addition to all the disadvantages associated with concentrated poverty, these students also encounter language discrimination. Latino segregation is currently more severe than African American segregation. And the relationship between segregation by race and segregation by poverty in public schools is very strong. High poverty schools will have to acquire many additional resources in order to address family crises, safety, and other neighborhood problems. These schools also tend to be served by less-qualified teachers, and have greater problems of student and teacher mobility. Schools with high concentrations of poverty- level students present the greatest challenge to educational reform. They have very low average academic achievement, and are perceived negatively by the general public (although less negatively by the parents of students attending the schools).

Concluding Recommendations

In conclusion, let me make a few recommendations. I have to admit these are puny, trivial recommendations because I am having trouble finding something positive to say. Let's put it simply, very simply. A serious recommendation would require restructuring the economic system and the reallocation of resources. We would have to start there, and we would have to talk about a massive redistribution of wealth, and a massive redistribution of power. We would have to change the system fundamentally if we were trying to create a system in which there would be no connection between educational outcomes and race, class, or gender.

Realistically, I know that is not politically feasible in the current climate. Therefore, I will talk about a few things that might make life in schools a little better for children.

1. Research supports the proposition that children's relationships with others are important for learning in schools. Thus, programs such as the Comer School Development Program (SDP) can help to improve relationships involving students, teachers, parents, and administrators within schools, and eventually, student achievement. There is fairly strong evidence that the Comer Program works.
2. Develop programs and curricular strategies that build upon the cultural backgrounds and strengths of the students served by the schools. Building on the cultural strengths of students and seeking to bridge the gap between the schools and the community is another promising strategy.

3. Finally, we should develop and mobilize the political and economic resources of communities served by the schools. The schools could become part of an integrated community development effort. You cannot really reform the schools by focusing only on schools. Strategies are needed that will improve employment opportunities, reduce concentrations of poverty caused by segregated housing, and provide opportunities for heads of low-income families to upgrade their educational and occupational skills. Only then will schools be able to make a significant impact on the historical inequalities in education that African Americans continue to experience.

References

Belk et al. v. Charlotte-Mecklenburg Schools, 99–239 (1999).

Board of Education of Oklahoma City v. Dowell, 498 U. S. 237 (1991).

Boston's Children First v. City of Boston, 62 F. Supp. 2nd 247 (D. Mass. 1999).

Bowen, W. G., & Bok, D. (1998). *The shape of the river: Long-term consequences of considering race in college and university admissions.* Princeton, NJ: Princeton University Press.

Brown v. Board of Education of Topeka, 347 U. S. 483 (1954).

Brown v. Board of Education of Topeka, 345 U. S. 294 (1955).

Clark, K. B. (1969). Fifteen years of deliberate speed. *Saturday Review, 52,* 59–61.

Cox, O. C. (1948). *Caste, class, and race: A study in social dynamics* (1st ed.).Garden City, NY: Doubleday.

Dawkins, M. P., & Braddock, J. H. (1994). The continuing significance of desegregation: School racial composition and African American inclusion in American society. *Journal of Negro Education, 63*(3), 394–405.

Dentler, R. A. (1999). Special report: A critical review of *Wessmann v. Gittens,* the U. S. First Circuit Court of Appeals decision in the Boston Latin School admissions case. *Equity & Excellence in Education, 32*(1), 5–17.

Dovidio, J., & Gaertner, S. L. (Eds.). (1986). *Prejudice, discrimination, and racism.* Orlando, FL: Academic Press.

Du Bois, W. E. B. (1936). Does the Negro need separate schools? Quoted in Woodson, C. G. (1977). *The mis-education of the Negro* (2nd ed.). New York, NY: AMS Press.

Epps, E. G. (1981). Minority children: Desegregation, self-evaluation, and achievement orientation. In W. Hawley (Ed.), *Effective school desegregation* (pp. 85–106). Beverly Hills, CA: Sage.

Freeman v. Pitts, 118 L. Ed. 2nd 108, 137 (1992), 112 S. Ct. 1430 (1992).

Gist, S. R. (1994). *Educating a southern rural community: The case of Blacks in Holmes County, Mississippi, 1870 to the present.* Unpublished doctoral dissertation, The University of Chicago, Chicago.

Hallinan, M. T. (1998). Diversity effects on student outcomes: Social science evidence. *Ohio State Law Journal, 59,* 733–54.

Jones-Wilson, F. C. (1981). *Traditional model of educational excellence: Dunbar High School of Little Rock Arkansas.* Washington, DC: Howard University Press.

Keyes v. School District No. 1, 413 U. S. 189 (1973).

Killian, L. M. (1975). *The impossible revolution, phase II: Black power and the American dream* (2nd ed.). New York, NY: Random House.

Kunen, J. (1996, April 29). The end of integration. *Time.* http://www. time.com/time/printout/0,8816,984466,00.html

Marcus-Newhall, A., & Heindl, T. R. (1998). Coping with interracial stress in ethnically diverse classrooms: How important are Allport's contact conditions? *Journal of Social Issues, 54*(4), 813–830.

Milliken v. Bradley, 418 U. S. 717 (1974).

Milliken v. Bradley, 433 U. S. 267 (1977).

Myrdal, G. (with Sterner, R., & Rose, A.). (1944). *An American dilemma: The Negro problem and modern democracy.* New York, NY: Harper.

Orfield, G., Eaton, S. E., & The Harvard Project on School Desegregation. (1996). *Dismantling desegregation: The quiet reversal of* Brown v. Board of Education. New York, NY: New Press.

People Who Care v. Rockford Board of Education School District No. 205, 851 F. Supp. 905 N.D. Ill. (1994).

Silberman, C. E. (1964). *Crisis in Black and White.* New York: Random House.

Swann v. Charlotte-Mecklenburg Board of Education, 402 U. S. 1 (1971).

U.S. Riot Commission (Kerner Commission). (1968). *Report of the National Advisory Commission on Civil Disorders.* Washington, DC: U.S. Government Printing Office.

Wells, A. S., & Crain, R. L. (1994). Perpetuation theory and the long-term effects of school desegregation. *Review of Educational Research, 64*(4), 531–555.

Wessmann v. Gittens, 160 F. 3d 790 (1st Cir. 1998).

Wilson, W. J. (1980). *The declining significance of race: Blacks and changing American institutions* (2nd ed.). Chicago, IL: University of Chicago Press.

Young, W. M. (1969). *Beyond racism: Building an open society.* New York, NY: McGraw-Hill.

5. Teaching Young Children Well: Implications for 21st Century Educational Policies

BARBARA BOWMAN
Erikson Institute for Advanced Study in Child Development

In this talk, I will address three things. First, I will provide a brief historical perspective on the care and education of young children. Second, I will describe some of the factors that have changed our thinking about the needs of young children and their families. And third, I will suggest some steps we might take to respond to the challenges we face in improving young children's care and education.

Changes in the World of Early Childhood

The world has changed a good deal since I began working with young children almost a half century ago. Then, there were two separate systems for the care and education of young children: full-day childcare for children of working parents (usually low-income children) and half-day nursery schools for middle- and upper-income children. Today, most early childhood educators agree that the care and the education of young children should go hand-in-hand, since both are needed if children are to develop and learn well. Programs for young children are coming together; increasingly, they have overlapping goals, use the same developmental knowledge base and similar pedagogical methods, and have increasingly integrated systems. So today we can talk about the early childhood field as if it is a single entity.

When I began teaching almost 50 years ago, hardly any young children were enrolled in center-based programs. In the 1970s, only 13% of all three-year-old and 28% of all four-year-old children attended preschools of some type, a significant, but still small, portion of the U.S. population. By 1997, however, 65% of four-year-olds and 40% of all three-year-olds were in some form of early childhood program (Bowman, Donovan, & Burns, 2001). This has led many experts to predict that preschool will soon be as ubiquitous as kindergarten, even though currently, early childhood programs lack the systemic support from the public schools that kindergartens enjoy.

But, this too is changing. Twenty years ago, few public schools considered early childhood as relevant to their interests. Now there are early childhood specialists in state departments of education; many schools have preschools and standards for achievement, and most are collaborating with Head Start, childcare centers, and other early childhood programs, to ensure a smooth transition of children into kindergarten.

When Head Start began in 1965, there were few opportunities for parents, particularly low-income parents, to get education and support. Today, parent programs are as diverse as Missouri's *Parents As Teachers*, (a program for parents of infants and toddlers to help them prepare their children for school), family support programs (to help parents organize their own lives as well as those of their children), and a literacy program sponsored by pediatricians to get parents to read to their children. Churches, government agencies, schools, social service agencies, and the media are all working to educate and support parents (Powell, 1991).

Colleges and universities have also felt the change. When the Erikson Institute began 35 years ago there were very few higher education institutions that focused on preparing professionals to work with young children and their families. Today, almost every college and university has a program to prepare students to work with children from infancy through the preschool/primary years. Finally, Congress has declared that having all young children ready to learn in school should be our first educational goal.

Factors That Have Changed Our Thinking

What has changed our thinking so radically? A number of things: changes in our knowledge about child development, changes in our expectations for children—particularly those who traditionally have not done well in school—and changes in family life. These changes have much to say about how we need to care for, and educate, young children.

Changes in the Knowledge Base

Probably the most profound change over the past 50 years is in our knowledge base of child development and learning. The evidence has altered our thinking about young children in a number of ways, particularly in how early learning begins, the capacity of young children to learn, the importance of relationships to development, the role of culture in framing development, and the precursors of school success. Let me give you some of the evidence on each of these points. Most of this research can be found in the reports of the National Research Council, *Eager to Learn* (Bowman, Donovan, & Burns, 2001).

One set of findings highlights how early children begin learning. It seems that infants do not just passively wait around for the world to teach them things. At birth, they begin to reach out and learn about their world of people, objects, and events, using their natural learning systems. For example, babies will usually suck on a nipple to increase visual stimulation, or turn their head to hear music or speech sounds, or shift their eyes away from a familiar stimulus and toward a novel one. Probably the most interesting of these findings is that children as young as a few months old notice changes in the number of objects in an array that they are paying attention to. With so much potential available so early, our challenge is to provide programs that are stimulating, interesting, and responsive to children— beginning at birth.

Another set of findings has pointed to the importance of early learning to subsequent learning. The research in neurobiology, for example, has literally revolutionized our thinking about the brain and learning. Instead of the brain's capacity being fully set at birth and the only factor driving learning, we find that as children learn, the learning itself develops or constrains the brain's capacities as much as the other way around. The classic example of this is the fact that young children only keep the babbling sounds they can make during infancy if these sounds are heard in their language community. If they do not use particular sounds in the language they hear, they lose the capacity to make them. Eventually, as many of us have found out when we have tried to learn a foreign language later in life, our brains no longer let us hear or make unfamiliar sounds. So, there seem to be critical or sensitive periods for learning different things.

Other studies show that when children know a great deal about a subject, they can operate on a higher cognitive level than we would expect. For example, it is generally assumed that young children cannot sort objects using multiple criteria. Yet Gobbo and Chi (Bowman, Donovan, & Burns, 2001) found that children who knew a great deal about dinosaurs were able to demonstrate much higher levels of classification ability than we would expect. So, although Piaget (1952, 1958 [with Inhelder]) alerted us to the difficulty that young children have in taking the perspective of another person, for example, we have learned that, given enough background, children can do some things we used to think they could not.

Information like this has made us very aware of the importance of learning during the early years, not because children can *never* learn if they miss a critical or sensitive time, but because it is so much more difficult to learn later. We also do not know exactly what kinds and quantities of experience children need to maximize their capacity to learn. Children learn different things at different times and new experiences must be within their zone of proximal development if they are to have an effect. Nevertheless, it is clear that early childhood is a time of rapid development, and that deprivations and opportunities during this period can have long-term effects on children's learning.

Children who have a broad base of experience in domain-specific knowledge move more rapidly toward acquiring more complex skills. It seems that when children know something well, they can build on it to learn even more complex ideas. This new research has made it essential to reconsider many traditional beliefs about what young children can and cannot do or learn during their preschool years. Our challenge is to make sure our programs provide children with the kinds of experience that promote school learning.

Another set of new findings points to the importance of early relationships to development. Children's brains are evidently pre-wired to encourage them to engage in social interchange; infants are primed to gaze at their caregiver's face, they respond to cuddling by calming down, they seek out social interaction and will smile or look sad in response to the expressions of others. But if no one provides attentive and responsive care, children's capacity to love and care about others does not develop. There are numerous examples of this, including studies of hospitalism (Spitz, 1973), Romanian orphans (Carlson & Earls, 1997), and the effect of depressed mothers on children's development (Sameroff, 1981). All of these studies suggest that if children do not have responsive and caring interactions with caregivers during early childhood, they are apt to have great difficulty forming satisfactory social relationships later.

In addition, positive relationships predict later learning. Presumably this is because children attend better to objects that the caregiver shows interest in, are freer to explore when their caregiver is present, learn to control their feelings better when their caregiver is available, and are more willing to accept help from people they know and care about. Adults, through their care giving—by looking, touching, talking, feeding, and changing clothes—and by doing the ordinary things adults do, stimulate children's interest and learning. Through children's enjoyment of social relationships and through social mediation we help children create their intelligence.

And finally, studies have noted the connection between children's relationships with their teachers and how well they learn in school. Children with positive relationships with their preschool teachers are more apt to learn better in kindergarten, and children with good relationships with their kindergarten teachers learn to read faster (Pianta & Cox, 1999). During the preschool years, adults bring new experiences to children that challenge and excite them, thereby helping them learn. Our challenge is to provide for children's need for responsive relationships throughout their preschool years.

Another set of research findings has focused us on the role that culture plays in what and how children think and learn. Children's experiences are defined by cultural definitions of appropriate goals and aspirations, as well as by the kinds of experiences that are provided for them. Development and culture are two sides of the same coin, interacting to set parameters for individuals (Bowman & Stott, 1993). For instance, acquiring language is a developmental accomplishment, and it does not matter developmentally whether children speak Standard English, Spanish, Black English, or Chinese. A developmental capability may have many different forms, all of which represent competence.

Despite the fact that all children have learned a great deal before they come to school, not all environments prepare children equally well for school. For example, when children are exposed to environments that are rich in verbal language, they are apt to have a greater ability to express ideas and to learn to read than children who are exposed to more limited language environments. Children learn what is in their environment to be learned, and what they learn prepares them to learn more of the same.

While developmental competence may be similar across cultures, what children learn is, of course, different. If Spanish-, Black English-, or Chinese-speaking and reading children must operate in an environment where only Standard English is used, and they do not have a chance to learn it, then they are at a learning, but not developmental, disadvantage. Culture becomes a problem when children are in environments that do not recognize the way their culture has taught them to express their developmental capabilities. Our challenge, then, is to structure learning environments so that developmentally normal but culturally different children receive the support they need to learn new things.

Changes in Our Educational Expectations

The second change I want to talk about is our changed expectations for children's achievement, particularly children seen at risk for school success. Our world has changed and it is inevitable that what children need to know and need to be able to do has changed with it. As the global economy undermined the industrial focus of American industry, technology moved to the forefront, and the technological revolution is altering society as dramatically as did the industrial revolutions of the prior age. Today, the mantra of business and government is that children who are not adequately educated cannot participate in the new economy and will become a drain on society. This means that we must educate poor children as well as rich children, minority children as well as majority children, children who speak other languages and dialects as well as those who speak Standard English, and typically-developing children and those with disabilities. The challenge for our society is to educate all children.

Not only must we educate all children, they must also learn much more and learn it much faster than they used to. High standards and school reform are the hottest buttons on the social agenda of Americans today. But high educational standards have created a number of concerns, and one of the most difficult is the concern about equity. What should we do about the so-called "high risk" children who traditionally have not done well in our schools? Our challenge is to achieve high educational standards without leaving these children behind.

Changes in Family Life

Lastly, there have been enormous changes in family life. The ideal of mother-care permeated much of the 20th century, although it was not until mid-century that increases in U.S. economic well-being made this ideal realizable by the majority of Americans. The increasing ability of American fathers to earn enough to support a non-working wife and children and the willingness of the American public to subsidize non-supported women with young children lasted through almost onehalf of the century. However, the last 30 years have seen considerable change in this paradigm. Globalization eroded the industrial base of the American economic structure and the real wages of American men fell. And as they decreased, American women entered the work force, earning the difference between what men earned in the 1950s and what they earned in the 1970s. By the 1980s, as more middle- and working-class wives moved into the labor force, public support for Aid to Families with Dependent Children declined. By the 1990s, it was generally accepted that mothers, all mothers, should work if their spouses were unable to support them and their children adequately. As a consequence of these economic and social changes, more young children must spend significant periods of time each day in the care of others.

A parallel imperative is the necessity for school success. As I mentioned earlier, school achievement is no longer optional. Therefore, the early childhood enterprise has the responsibility not only for caring for children and attending to their general development, but also for making sure that they learn whatever is needed to succeed in school. Our challenge is to provide out-of-home care and education programs that attend both to children's well-being and to their later achievement.

Meeting the Challenge

The changes that I have described—in our developmental knowledge base, in school expectations for children at-risk, and in family life—have not connected as well as they should to the programs and policies we arrange for young children. Let me give you some examples of where I see the misfits, as well as some ideas about what we might do to remedy these.

It seems to me that our major challenge is to provide programs that are stimulating, interesting, and responsive to children, beginning at birth and continuing through the preschool years. What prevents us from doing this? I suggest the following: We have not sufficiently integrated new findings into the practice of early education; we have got caught up trying to decide whether a practice is developmentally appropriate rather than reflecting on the effect that practice has on children and on our goals for them; we have not devoted enough attention to the quality of programs we provide for children at risk; and we have not mobilized the American community to understand the importance of the early years.

Implementing the Knowledge Base

As a whole, what the research says is that if we want high educational standards, we must teach our children well from the moment they are born, not just from when they reach the schoolhouse door (Shonkoff & Phillips, 2001). Yet many programs fail to act on the information we have about what is good for young children in preparation for school. Let me give you just a couple of examples. I mentioned the importance of relationships in children's lives. Relationships between children and their teachers/caregivers are built on consistent and responsive interaction, yet assigned caregivers in infant programs, and looping (keeping children with the same teacher for more than one year), are not widely practiced. Indeed, a preschool teacher recently told me that she tried to not have too important a relationship with her children because she did not want to compete with their parents. Well, the research says, "don't worry," kids still prefer their parents. Our programs need to reflect what we know about children: they need discipline, information, and motivation, and underlying all of these qualities is the caring relationship.

Another of the findings is that early care and education in centers—as opposed to homes—is not harmful to children, indeed, it may be beneficial. As I noted earlier, there is a lingering belief in the United States that young children, particularly infants, should only be in the care of their mothers. (It is surprising to me that even some early childhood professionals share this belief.) This is despite 20 years of research in the United States that shows that given good-quality programs, children's development and learning in centers can be at least as good as that of similar children at home. Further, this belief lingers despite 50 years of experience in European countries that shows that systems of out-of-home childcare can provide excellent care and education for children, beginning in infancy. Yet we continue the myth that children are best off at home and that centers are poor substitutes.

Over the past 25 years, we have identified characteristics that define good-quality centers, and that result in good outcomes for children. These include small groups, low child-to-teacher ratios, and well-educated, responsive teachers who know child development and early childhood education (Howes, Phillips, & Whitebook, 1992). Yet we continue to sanction programs and arrangements where there are too many children with too few adults, and programs where adults have too little education and too little knowledge of child development and early education. Why are we so behind in providing high-quality early-childhood programs for children who need them? One of the major reasonsis lack of resources: resources to obtain buildings, resources to buy equipment and materials, resources to train teachers, and, most of all, resources to pay teachers for doing a good job. Another major reason is that some teachers and caregivers have not thought of their work as a profession—a profession that requires continuing education to be informed about new research and reflection on practice to make good judgments about curricula. I suggest that we need to do some more work in our own profession.

Developmental Appropriateness

This question has divided early childhood educators in a similar and equally unproductive way as the reading wars have divided primary grade teachers. The research in the *Eager to Learn* report (Bowman, Donovan, & Burns, 2001) indicates that children who have numerous opportunities to learn about literacy, or math, or science, or presumably any subject, can achieve higher levels of mental processing than children who have not had such opportunities. While age plays a role in what and how much children can learn, children should not be limited in their opportunities to learn simply because of their age. Further, the report says that many teaching strategies can work, and that good teachers use a range of techniques, including direct instruction.

How do these new findings fit with developmentally appropriate practices? As I am sure many of you know, the National Association for the Education of Young Children recommended that practices used in preschool/primary programs be developmentally appropriate. Unfortunately, there has been considerable confusion about what this means. Many teachers think that to be developmentally appropriate means that you should not directly teach preschoolers or focus on discipline knowledge. They think it means children choose what they want to do and that they should play a lot. Many teachers think it inappropriate for children to have to sit down and listen, to learn the alphabet and numbers, to all go to the bathroom at the same time, or to participate in a large group activity. In reality, it may be developmentally appropriate to do any or all of these things. Developmentally appropriate practices do not tell you exactly what and how to teach. They provide a set of developmental principles, or guidelines, and a number of different activities may respond to those principles. The teacher must decide what is appropriate for a particular child or group of children at a particular time and place.

So, developmental principles are not the same as recipes for practice. Principles provide a framework for thinking about practice; they do not determine the practice itself. Let me give you some examples. One principle of development is that novelty attracts the attention of infants, and that they pay attention to novel sounds, visions, and touches. We use this principle with infants when we play peek-a-boo, when we make noises with rattles, when we tickle tummies, all of which can command the baby's attention. But the principle does not tell us if, with a particular child on a particular day, we should play peek-a-boo, or shake the rattle, or tickle a tummy or do something else that is novel and perceptual.

Practice should respond to principles, but there may be a number of practices that reflect the same principle. An example from literacy learning is that young children should have an opportunity to understand uses of written language through meaningful activity. Many of our programs will respond to this principle with good books for children to look at such as *Make Way for Ducklings* (McCloskey, 1941). But it is equally valid to make books out of old magazines, to generate stories and pictures on a computer, or to use photographs to make books. A teacher who does not know a good sequence for teaching phonemic or print awareness might purchase a good computer program for children to use, for example, or if teaching children who do not have much past experience with letters and numbers, she may be more intentional in how she plans such experiences for them.

Here is another example. It is recommended that we teach the principle of measurement to young children. I was doing an in-service program for teachers recently and told them about these new standards. Some teachers have understood this to mean that children should measure with rulers and tape measures, and they thought this would be too hard for four-year-olds because they do not know their numerals. But tape measures and yardsticks are not necessary for four-year-olds to learn some of the principles of measurement. What can we do instead? Children can measure with their shoes, their fingers, pieces of string, or long blocks, and use hatch marks to indicate "how many." My point is that there are many different ways to teach in a developmentally appropriate manner, and it is the teacher's responsibility to find the most appropriate way. Developmentally appropriate has to be decided in the context of a program with particular goals for particular children.

Programs for Children at Risk

In the report, *Preventing Reading Difficulties in Young Children* (Snow, Burns, & Griffen, 1998), a committee sponsored by the National Research

Council found that preschool experiences could help lessen difficulties and improve the chances that children will learn to read well. During the preschool years, the committee recommended, among other things, that children have a literacy- rich environment with explicit opportunities to observe how literacy tools—paper, pencils, pens, and technology—are used to create signs, write narratives, make lists, get information, use computers, etc. Another recommendation was that children should receive explicit alphabetic information, including the letter-sound relationships, yet many programs still have not refocused their literacy efforts despite the fact that children without such knowledge will be disadvantaged when they get to school.

We now have a robust research base that shows that programs can successfully alter long-term educational trajectories for low-income children (Campbell & Ramey, 1995). The primary findings of this research are (a) interventions should begin as early as possible and (b) they should provide a well-planned and well-executed program for children, combined with an educational and supportive program for families.

Early intervention programs were developed to give children a leg up, to even the playing field, and they can have enormous consequence for children's later educational achievement, but only if they are planned and carried out correctly (Bowman, 1999). Head Start has a 36-year history of working with low-income children and families. And the research repeatedly has shown that children who attend Head Start do better socially and academically than their peers who have not attended—for a while. However, in order to get the robust results reported by model programs, many low-income children and families need a longer, more intense, and more carefully designed and implemented program than is currently available to them. Similarly, inclusion has been shown in model programs to have a salutary effect on children with disabilities, and to be neutral or helpful to typically developing children. But these are not the outcomes we get when children are tossed willy-nilly into inclusive classrooms with teachers who are unfamiliar with their conditions or the techniques they need to learn. To provide a high- quality classroom for children with disabilities, teachers need both information and resources.

Resources

The last challenge I want to mention is that of obtaining the resources we need to have a high-quality system for the care and education of children. I, like many of you, have been working hard in the vineyard of the state legislature to get the resources we need. But I had an eye-opening epiphany last week, when I went to two different meetings. One meeting was for the Reinvention of Center Accreditation Project for the National Association for the Education of Young Children, and the other was for the National

Board for Professional Teaching Standards. At both of these meetings, the participants noted that until we get the general public behind us, legislators are not going to do much. At both meetings, we agreed that it would take a group effort to bring young children to public attention. We need to get parents who need childcare, neurobiologists who can talk about brain development, school reform advocates who want to improve public education, business leaders who understand the importance of an educated and reliable work force, and researchers who can show the relationship between good-quality care and education and children's development, to work together. All these groups need to join early childhood educators in Head Start and childcare, in public schools and private organizations, to raise public awareness about the importance of early childhood programs and the kind of resources needed.

Too few people know what we should be doing to improve young children's development and learning. Too few know that teachers of young children are among the lowest paid professionals in America. Too few early childhood teachers have access to tax-supported higher education to get the skills and knowledge that they need. Too few parents can afford to pay the full cost of care for their children. And too few people understand the seriousness of the problem. Our challenge is to help the general public understand that teaching young children is not a no-brainer; it is rocket science, and it needs resources.

Conclusion

In conclusion, my central message is that if we are to improve children's school achievement we need to understand the importance of the years before school and ensure that all children have the kinds of preschool care and education that supports development and learning. We also need to broaden our vision about what is important for school success to include emotional-social competence, relationships, culture, and intellectual curiosity, alongside academic knowledge and skills. And finally, we need to make sure that teachers have the time and training that they need to educate themselves, to plan good curriculum, and to reflect on their own learning and on children's learning.

References

Bowman, B. (1999). Kindergarten practices with children from low-income families. In R. Pianta & M. Cox (Eds.), *The transition to kindergarten* (pp. 281–301). Baltimore, MD: Brookes.

Bowman, B., & Stott, F. (1993). Understanding development in a cultural context: The challenge for teachers. In B. Mallory & R. New (Eds.),

Diversity and developmentally appropriate practices: Challenges for early childhood education (pp. 119–134). New York, NY: Teachers College Press.

Bowman, B., Donovan, S., & Burns, M. S. (Eds.). (2001). *Eager to learn: Educating our preschoolers.* Washington, DC: National Academy Press.

Campbell, F., & Ramey, C. (1995). Cognitive and school outcomes for high-risk African–American students at middle adolescence: Positive effects of early intervention. *American Educational Research Journal, 32*(4), 743–772.

Carlson, M., & Earls, F. (1997).Psychological and neuroendocrinologicalsequelae of early social deprivation in institutionalized children in Romania. In C. Carter, I. Lederhendler, & B. Kirkpatrick (Eds.), *Integrative neurobiology of affiliation: Annals of the New York Academy of Science, 807,* 419–428.

Howes, C., Phillips, D., & Whitebook, M. (1992). Thresholds of quality: Implications for the social development of children in center-based child care. *Child Development, 63,* 449–460.

Inhelder, B., & Piaget, J. (1958). *The growth of logical thinking from childhood to adolescence.* New York: Basic Books.

McCloskey, R. (1941). *Make way for ducklings.* New York, NY: Viking Juvenile.

Piaget, J. (1952).*Origins of intelligence in children.* Madison, CT: International Universities Press.

Pianta, R., & Cox, M. (Eds.). (1999). *Transition to kindergarten.* Baltimore, MD: Brookes.

Powell, D. (1991). *Strengthening parental contributions to school readiness and early school learning.* Washington, DC: U.S. Department of Education, Office of Educational Research and Improvement.

Sameroff, A.J. (1981). Psychological needs of the mother in early mother-infant interaction. In G. Avery (Ed.), *Neonatology* (2nd ed.) (pp. 303–321). New York, NY: Lippincott.

Shonkoff, J., & Phillips, D. (2000). *From neurons to neighborhoods: The science of early childhood development.* Washington, DC: National Academy Press.

Snow, C. E., Burns, M. S., & Griffin, P. (Eds.). (1998). *Preventing reading difficulties in young children.* Washington, DC: National Academy Press.

Spitz, R. (1973).*The first year of life: A psychoanalytic study of normal and deviant development of object relations.* NewYork, NY: International Universities Press.

6. *Urban Education Challenges: Is Reform the Answer?*

SUSAN FUHRMAN
Teachers College, Columbia University
National Academy of Education

My topic for this address is Urban Education Reform. Clearly, there are challenges in urban schools, but what's important, and what I want to focus on, is that there is no shortage of reforms intended to address them. The question I want to address is: Why is reform so prevalent and so disappointing?

I think that there are three sets of reasons, some having to do with political factors, some having to do with an overemphasis on structural solutions, and some having to do with the research base that is supposed to guide us as we choose from the different ones. So, if "reform" is not the right metaphor for addressing urban challenges, as I believe it is not, what is? And, what should we do? I will try to address these questions here, and I'll refer to some things we're doing right, and maybe not so right, here at Penn's Graduate School of Education. I would like you all to help us improve as a graduate school of education that cares deeply about urban problems.

Urban Educational Challenges

To start with the background, you all know how concentrated students are in urban settings. Over 31% of all students attend school in 226 large school districts among the 15,000 or 16,000 school districts in America. That translates into 31% of all students in just 1.5% of school districts (Ladd & Hansen, 1999). So, urban education is where the challenge is, and for my money, if you are not focusing on urban education, especially for a school of education located in Philadelphia, you are not focusing on the important issues of our time.

I don't need to dwell on the litany of challenges that accompanies the concentration of students in large districts. You know that there are higher-than-average proportions of students in poverty, of students with poorly educated parents, of immigrants and other students with limited English skills, and of students from unstable family settings, and you also know that there are greater rates of student mobility. There are greater shortages of teachers, and more teachers with emergency credentials; there are also poor facilities, and low achievement—generally, significantly lower achievement than in suburban districts.

And, there are, of course, fiscal challenges. Great disparities related to wealth still exist. Districts with 25% or more of their school-age children in poverty have an average total per-pupil revenue that is only 89% of the average total per-pupil revenue elsewhere. So, poor districts spend less. And that's *total* revenue. If you adjust for the needs and the costs of educating children in urban areas with all the challenges I just outlined, and for the higher costs in urban areas where there are higher prices to be paid for labor and virtually everything else, then you will find the really significant disparities.

Just to take some figures that emerged from Standard and Poor's School Evaluation Service's recent release of Pennsylvania school district data: when you adjust for costs and needs, Philadelphia spends as much as 23% below the state average expenditure per pupil. Now this is not to say that all of Philadelphia's problems, such as extraordinarily low achievement, are related to money, but it is certainly to make a point about the disparities between the richer and poorer areas in this country. On top of that, we know that Philadelphia citizens and other urban citizens are paying high taxes for every service that they must provide, not just schooling, and are overburdened with all of these taxes.

Urban Reform

Given these challenges, it is no surprise that most urban districts are extensively engaged in reform. The following section from a book called *Building Civic Capacity* by Stone, Henig, Jones, and Pierannunzi (2001) is a description of the recent reform efforts in the District of Columbia.

> As part of the decentralization effort, every school had been required to establish a local school restructuring team. And over forty "enterprise" and "renaissance" schools had been given special discretion to shape their own policies at the school level. Many schools offer specialized programs that had developed loyal constituencies. These included an elementary school with dual language, (English and Spanish) immersion, another elementary school with an Afrocentric curriculum, and special "academies" designed to provide high school

students with career-relevant education (including a Health and Human Services Academy, a Public Service Academy and a Trans-Tech Academy). Public/private partnerships were in place in dozens of schools; many of these provided enriched career-related training, including separate programs for Culinary Arts, Interior Design, and Landscape Architecture, International Studies, Pre-Engineering, Business and Finance, and Travel and Tourism, and COMSTAT's computer and science partnership with Jefferson Junior High. In addition, during the early 1990s, an aggressive deputy superintendent spearheaded the expansion of the District's Early Learning Years program, which involves more child-friendly curriculum, and a heavy emphasis on making certain that teachers and principals receive the training and support they need to put the curriculum into place. The district is perhaps the only large urban school district to offer a full-day early childhood education program in every elementary school. And the program has been expanding to incorporate many three-year-olds. In 1995 Congress passed legislation initiating a major charter school program in D.C., but even before Congress acted, the public system had experimented with "School-within-School Charters," including a Montessori school, a Non-graded School, and a Media-Technology Social Research School. (p. 148)

That description could take place in any city in America except for the fact that Congress mandated part of it, because in the case of the District of Columbia, Congress is the big school board. So, this amount of reform is quite common. Frederick Hess (1999), the author of *Spinning Wheels: the Politics of Urban School Reform*, studied 57 large school districts and reported that the mean district proposed 11.4 reforms over a 3-year period in the 1990s (Hess, 1999). The problem is not the absence of reform. In fact, what we see is a picture of too much reform. Too many reforms, few of which are effective; too many reforms that are undertaken, and too few that are implemented. Further, the reforms are hardly coordinated; they seem to lurch in all different directions, reflecting opportunism more than any coherent improvement strategy.

Why this "policy churn," to use Hess's (1999) term? As I said before, I think that there are three sets of factors. Let me start with the political factors, and draw heavily from Hess (1999), who writes about how institutional incentives encourage a focus on proposing symbolic change, not on improving schools; on inputs, not outputs.

Political Factors

It is obvious that it is much easier to propose a reform than it is to implement it. That explains part of the "policy churn." But there are a number of other factors that are particularly characteristic of urban schools that lead to this emphasis on symbolic reform, or this posturing around change. For one thing, it is hard to hold urban schools accountable for performance, even in the current climate of accountability.

There are so many complicating factors in urban schools—high mobility, teacher turnover—that it is really hard to determine the value added by schools. Leaders can escape accountability for performance, so it does not matter much if the reform actually works because if it does not work, there are many reasons we can give for why it did not work, such as, "Well, the kids weren't here two thirds of the year when we tried to implement this new curriculum." And it is true, not a made up excuse; it is absolutely true.

Another factor is executive turnover. Urban superintendents hold office for about 3 years, which is much too short a time for reforms to really take effect. They are not around long enough to be accountable for results, so they tend to be held accountable for what they propose. And, in fact, superintendents' careers are built on advancing from district to district, to larger and larger districts with more and more prestige. Superintendents have to be active to build a reputation, and since they have a short term, they have to be active in that short term. And that means proposing and starting reforms, and calling attention to oneself for doing that, or in Hess' (1999) terms "overindulging in innovation."

This posture is reinforced by the foundation, corporate, government, and, yes, academic communities surrounding education. We get benefits when they adopt our ideas so we push our ideas on them, and these are always "new" ideas because we are not about to push somebody else's ideas on them. No one gets paid for working on old ideas, so we contribute to the problem.

The high visibility of education, particularly in urban areas, also contributes. There is much at stake. You cannot work quietly. The public thinks you're doing nothing if you're not attracting attention. You have to convince the community that you're acting, if you're an urban school leader, and proposing reforms is a way of rallying community support and resources. Also, reforms bring notoriety and prestige to a community. Unlike the quiet, much less glamorous work of improvement, school boards support reforming superintendents because it enables them to claim credit too. They can say, "We were the school board that initiated X, Y, and Z reforms."

Clarence Stone et al. (2001) saw additional reasons for urban school reform challenges such as the absence of civic capacity. Civic capacity is the ability of a community to collectively problem-solve with a supportive array of relationships across elected and district leaders. Without it, long-term support for reform is missing. Elected leaders have even more incentives than superintendents and boards to engage in eye-catching reforms; their electoral cycle drives them to short-term, catchy initiatives. Getting their cooperation for hard, long-term work requires an investment in education that has to be deeply felt and that is not present in many communities.

One of Stone's coauthors, Jeffrey Henig, and his colleagues Hula, Orr, and Pedescleaux (1999) noted in the *Color of School Reform* that in the four cities they studied—Atlanta, Baltimore, Detroit, and Washington, DC—racial factors made long-term civic collaboration on education that much more difficult (Henig et al., 1999). There was distrust and much history that was never overcome.

Structuralism

A second characteristic of urban reform that impedes its effectiveness is the emphasis on structural reforms: on centralization or decentralization, on school-based management, on charters and choice, and on altering patterns of authority within the district. The resort to structure characterizes American education reform efforts historically. We've played around with how to organize schools around grade levels with graded vs. ungraded classrooms, with large vs. small schools, and with creating large, centralized bureaucracies—in Tyack's words, the "one best system"—and then breaking them up.

Why the preoccupation with structures? Because structures are visible, manipulable, and easy, relative to the hard work of really improving teaching and learning. Structural reforms are tangible, you can see them; if you have a 3-year time frame, structural change may be something that you can do. You can see why, given the political incentives just discussed, people would gravitate to big, structural reforms.

But these reforms don't necessarily lead to meaningful improvement in teaching or learning. They focus on changing the incentives around which people work, "empowering" them, or monitoring them more closely, theoretically affecting people's will to work harder.

But sometimes, that theory of action is just wrong. For example, people don't necessarily work harder on instruction when they are "empowered" through school-based management. They may be tied up in meetings on keeping hallways clean, or determining how council representatives are elected. Even if they do work harder, motivation is just a part of effectiveness. These structural reforms don't necessarily affect the other aspects that make educators effective, i.e., their knowledge, skills, and beliefs about whether children can learn. This is the "myth of omnipotent structure," to borrow a title from public administration literature (Anne Marie Houck Walsh as cited in course material, 1973). Policy wonks and educators alike seize on structural solutions without fully elaborating the connections between the structural change and the desired results. School-based management may give teachers more authority, but what conditions would be necessary for them to use that authority to realize improvement?

Structure can, of course, be enabling, but it should not be seen as the entire solution.I find the emphasis on structuralism particularly troubling in the case of charters and choice. They are clearly today's "silver bullets," the panaceas that are going to change everything. "Break it up," one hears often with respect to large urban districts; but the next question, "and then what?" rarely gets asked.

The Research Base

This leads us naturally into the third area I will discuss: the research base underlying the reforms that cities are so busy adopting. Choice and charters are a good example of the kind of guidance, or lack thereof,that the research base gives us. With respect to those reforms, the evidence about their effects is increasingly clear: it is inclusive. There is no clear evidence of achievement gains; for example, there are gains in certain grades, certain subjects, and certain populations, and not in others.

Why don't we have better research to guide us about reform, and if we did, would it matter? Would urban educators use research to choose reforms, instead of selecting the more visible, structural reforms we just discussed?

Let me address the more sensitive topic first,which is the quality of the research. The research base is much weaker than it could be. There are many important questions about which we could use more guidance. I think education research needs to be improved in several ways. In 2000, I gave a speech at AERA about three studies that had gained a lot of policymaker attention (Fuhrman, 2000). Deborah Nelson, who worked with me on this, and I, chose three studies that policymakers were interested in and referred to in a way that they don't often do with other research. The three studies are the Perry Preschool study of early childhood education (Schweinhart et al., 1993[1]) the Tennessee STAR experiment on class size (Nye, 2000), and the NICHD (National Institute for Child Health and Human Development) studies of reading (2000). I cited four qualities of these studies that enhanced their credibility, along with a host of contextual factors, such as the presence of research brokers to help popularize their results.

First, the studies did not try to answer a question with an inappropriate design. To state that positively, the studies tried to address a question with an appropriate design. Much education research tries to get at the "what works" question, with studies that might show relationships between treatments and achievement, but cannot answer the causal question as definitively as possible. Research rigor has everything to do with matching the design to the question, something, by the way, that I don't think we as a field think enough about or pay significant attention to in the training of new researchers. I know that we at Penn GSE have excellent methods courses—both quantitative and qualitative—but I often wonder how well we prepare students with the prerequisites they need to really benefit from the methods courses. How well do we prepare them with the ability to frame a good research question and to match it with a good design that employs one or more of these methods?

I certainly don't mean to imply, by focusing on those three big studies or by the causal question, that all research should be experimental or quasi-experimental. I don't mean that at all. The "what works?" question is not the only question to be asked about reform options. We also want to know the manner in which policies exert an influence, not just whether they exert influence. We want to know how various design options play out in practice. We want to know more about the dimensions of problems, such as whether different population groups or types of schools experience issues differently. In other words, there are many things we want to know that don't require an experimental design. The important point is that research suited to the question is more likely to be considered rigorous by policymakers and by us than is research that is stretched to answer questions that it cannot.

A second point about these studies is that they were longitudinal. Either the original study, or the follow-up studies, looked at effects over a period of time, giving the results staying power and helping to sell them to policymakers. It is much easier to justify a program expense when the results of the program last, and there's no way to know that, unless some longitudinal research is conducted.

Third, these studies were replicated by other studies, confirming their findings and lending them much greater power. Replication is a way to test findings; it is through repeated studies that we learn whether original findings can be confirmed, whether they hold up. If repeated studies get different results, there's good reason to question the original findings. Lack of replicability is what did that in cold fusion, as I'm sure you all remember. But replication serves other purposes as well, purposes especially important to education reform. Repeat studies can confirm findings in different contexts, proving to policymakers that results are not just situational but have broader applicability. In other words, policymakers want to know that "this will work in my city." It is easier to make that case with studies done in a variety of settings than with evidence from just one.

And, replication creates a body of research that multiplies the importance of any one study, telling policymakers that a variety of researchers, perhaps even of different perspectives, agrees on a conclusion. This last point is very important to policymakers. Few things irk them more about research than the fact that researchers often disagree with one another and cannot provide clear guidance. It leads them to discredit and underfund research altogether.

Finally, these studies were incorporated into syntheses that helped make sense of the findings. This is what we need to do in order to create and understand the weight of the evidence. Policymakers want to know how the latest study affects what was known before, how new work fits into the total body of work, and how the research aggregates to form a conclusion.

We can do more to assure the credibility of research. We can assure that designs are suited to questions, that more studies are longitudinal, that replication takes place, and that work is synthesized to provide cumulative answers. It is true that much of this cannot be done without additional funding, and lack of adequate support for education research creates a real challenge. Elaborate designs, longitudinal studies, and replication are very expensive. And funders tend to put a premium on new work, just like reformers do, rather than on repeating existing work or doing follow-up studies. Each funder wants to claim its own unique contribution, so it is hard to get both public and private funders to support confirmatory work that's not likely to be as splashy as the original. In the case of dissertations, we can also accept some blame. We push the new and the unique no matter how narrow and arcane it can make the topic. And we rarely think about the importance of replication and confirmatory studies when encouraging students to undertake research projects.

The fact that too few large-scale, longitudinal, and replication studies are done is not all our fault, but we cannot escape the blame. We value newness over replication ourselves—in our training of future researchers and our guidance about dissertations. We argue among ourselves over paradigm rather than spending the time necessary to see how the evidence accumulates across qualitative and quantitative work and across different research approaches. We are too rarely concerned that students become adept in combining methods. Certainly, we must convince funders that we need more money to do the kind of work that they value, the kind of work that has meaning for policy and practice. But we also need to prove that we are interested in doing the sort of work that can justify a much larger investment.

There are some encouraging signs. One example that I am very proud of is the Campbell Collaboration, which is taking shape under the leadership of Bob Boruch. This collaboration, a new multi-national effort, will prepare, maintain, and promote access to systematic reviews of studies on the effects of social and educational policies and practices. The organization will provide regularly updated syntheses intended to help policymakers and other users by presenting the weight of the evidence. And it's no coincidence that by deciding what research to include in syntheses, the Collaboration can have a great deal of influence over research standards.

However, it would be naïve of us to assume that better research would automatically have stronger sway in the marketplace of ideas that surrounds urban school reform. In fact, we have reason to worry about the climate for research and the value placed on evidence by practitioners. Tom Corcoran, Cathy Belcher, and I studied the adoption and support for comprehensive school reforms in two large districts. We called them River City and Metropolis. We found that while district personnel wanted to use evidence about student learning in choosing reforms, and talked about "best practice" in a way that implied research-based decisions, they often made choices based on ideology rather than results. At the school level, there was even less pretense about the importance of research.

Our major finding was that school personnel value the opinions of other educators much more than published research. The teachers we surveyed placed strong value on the endorsements of other teachers, with between 80% and 90% agreeing that these were the "best" source of evidence on quality. On the other hand, only around 60% gave such support to published research on evidence of effects. In fact, 35% of the teachers we surveyed in these 2 cities think that the findings published by education researchers should not be trusted. Almost the same proportion is likely to distrust anything but their own eyes and own measures as evidence of effectiveness in education.

Surely there is reason to distrust educational research, as I have just discussed, but we have not built a culture of attending to evidence in education either. Of course, the relationship between a research culture that produces good evidence and a culture of use of evidence is circular. We need to work on both sides if we want to improve evidence-based decision making. It is important that we worry about the quality of the research we produce, but it is also important that we focus the education of practitioners on evaluating, and benefiting from, evidence. I know that the new mid-career leadership program we are designing at GSE takes evidence-based practice as one of its starting points. I'm encouraged by that development.

Improvement Not Reform

If "reform" is not the answer for urban schools because they already do too much of it, because they tend to rely on structural reforms, and because picking reforms that "work" is difficult to do based on existing evidence, and educators might disregard the evidence anyway—what *is* the answer?

I would like to shift the metaphor around urban school progress from "reform," to "improvement." This is not a new concept. Fifteen years ago, Richard Elmore and Milbrey McLaughlin (1988) wrote a very influential little book called *Steady Work*. Improving teaching and learning, the heart of schooling, is slow, unending, not particularly glamorous, and hard work. It is not a matter of policies coming in from the outside, swooping down. It is a matter of continued attention to the basics and to what matters in teaching and learning. It involves deep investment in teacher quality and knowledge, through recruiting, compensating, and developing teachers. It involves thoughtful, well-funded professional development. Professional development must be intensive, extensive (over a period of time), focused on the curriculum the teachers are teaching, and followed up by coaching and other on site support.

At the Consortium for Policy Research in Education, we surveyed elementary school mathematics teachers in California who had taken a variety of kinds of professional development in mathematics. Some of them took content-focused units based on the curriculum that the students were learning on fractions. Some of them took equally worthy courses that were disconnected from the curriculum: collaborative learning, diversity training, things that we think of as important but that weren't directly connected to the 4th grade mathematics curriculum. What we found was that the teachers who took the curriculum-related professional development, provided that it was intense enough and had enough follow up and support, changed their practice in ways that were envisioned by the reforms, and also had gains in student achievement that the other teachers who were engaged in other kinds of professional development did not have (Cohen & Hill, 2001). When I tell this story to a lay audience, the story that professional development focused on curriculum that students are learning has a bigger effect than professional development that is disconnected from what the students are learning, they look at me strangely, thinking, "you were paid to have that study done?" The answer is so commonsensical. In fact, that kind of intensive curriculum-related professional development is not what we do in education. We know that we do scatter-shot workshops. We teach about Lyme disease and Right-to-Know with chemicals and all things that are important for the safety of our kids, but don't influence student learning. If we want to influence student learning, if we want to improve students' knowledge of subjects and skills, then we have to think seriously about the professional development in which we engage. At Penn GSE, in programs such as the Penn Literacy Network, the Philadelphia Writing Project, and the Penn-Merck Collaborative for the Enhancement of Science in Education, we have content-focused professional development, and we need to promote that force.

Improvement over the long run and steady work involves good curriculum design. We don't make enough time for teachers to collectively develop curriculum. We also don't provide adequate choices through the web or other means if they don't want to make their own curriculum. We have this enormously romantic notion that teachers want to teach all day and come home and write curriculum all night. The teachers that we studied in our research that are implementing the various reforms that we are studying do not want to do that. They'd like to have good curricula available to them so that they can make wise choices about what to use. Improvement involves developing leaders—administrators and teachers—who know good instruction and can evaluate and support it. It means developing a collective vision for, and responsibility for, good instruction, and overcoming the norms of isolation and building communities in which teachers are accountable to one another for good instruction. This is much like what we're starting at the new Penn Assisted School, where teachers are in each others' classrooms all the time and where they talk about their practice regularly. Granted, the school has only been open for two months, but so far, it is a model; we hope that this kind of teamwork continues.

Steady improvement involves changing the culture of low expectations surrounding urban schooling. As we at CPRE have examined instruction in many settings across the nation, we see countless examples of teachers "protecting" their students by not presenting material that is more challenging. Believing that the students they teach from "disadvantaged" backgrounds need discipline, order, and basic skills, even teachers who try to teach more complex material, even those who may be better prepared than others in terms of their own knowledge and skills, even those with supportive principals and other factors in their favor, doubt that poor and under-prepared students can reach challenging and complex understandings. Encouragingly, experience—through professional development, observing experts teach their classes, seeing their own children engage in problem solving and more complex activities—can change these beliefs. In Kentucky, in 1994, only 35% of teachers agreed with the Kentucky reform principle that all children can learn, and most at high levels. By 1999, 68% agreed. How did this change occur? In the context of a stable reform environment, which Kentucky had over all these years, teachers made incremental changes in their practice, and student performance, even in the most disadvantaged settings, improved. Teachers could see that as they changed their practice, the students were learning.

Some of the efforts that I have described can be achieved by reallocating resources. Some will require new money, and while certain structural reforms might make them easier, they don't necessarily require structural change. We can see some schools and classrooms undertaking such efforts with more central direction, such as District #2 in New York City, or San Diego, or with less central direction and more flexibility from district operating procedurism, such as we see in our own Penn Assisted School.

The tough work of improvement must be separated from the glamour of reform. It requires steady work. It requires realism rather than romanticism. It requires the efforts of all of us.

Notes

1. The most recent report of this important longitudinal study was published after this lecture in 2005 by Schweinhart and colleagues. This citation is also included in the references.

References

Cohen, D., & Hill, H. (2001). *Learning policy: When state education reform works.* New Haven, CT: Yale University Press.

Corcoran, T., Fuhrman, S. H., & Belcher, C. L. (2001). The district role in instructional improvement. *The Phi Delta Kappan, 83,* 78–84.

Elmore, R., & McLaughlin, M. (1988). *Steady work: Policy, practice, and the reform of American education.* Washington, DC: Rand Corporation.

Fuhrman, S. (2000). *Education policy: What role for research?* Division L Vice Presidential address at the annual meeting of the American Educational Research Association, New Orleans, LA.

Henig, J., Hula, R., Orr, M., & Pedescleaux, D. (1999). *The color of school reform: Race, politics, and the challenge of urban education.* Princeton, NJ: Princeton University Press.

Hess, F. (1999). *Spinning wheels: The politics of urban school reform.* Washington, DC: Brookings Institution Press.

Ladd, H. F., & Hansen, J. S. (1999). *Making money matter: Financing America's schools. Committee on education finance. Commission on Behavioral and Social Sciences and Education.* Washington, DC: National Research Council, National Academies Press.

National Institute of Child Health and Human Development, NIH, DHHS, & Shriver, E. K. (2000). *Report of the National Reading Panel: Teaching Children to Read (04769).* Washington, DC: U.S. Government Printing Office.

Nye, B., Hedges, L.V., & Konstantopoulos, S. (2000). The effects of small classes on academic achievement: The results of the Tennessee Class Size Experiment. *American Educational Research Journal, 37*(1), 123–151.

Schweinhart, L. J., Barnes, H. V., & Weikart, D. P. (1993). *Significant benefits: The High/Scope Perry Preschool Study through age 27. Monographs of the High/Scope Educational Research Foundation, No. 10.* Ypsilanti, MI: High/Scope Press.

Schweinhart, L. J., Montie, J., Xiang, Z., Barnett, W. S., Belfield, C., & Nores, M. (2005). *Lifetime effects: The High/Scope Perry Preschool Study through age 40. Monographs of the High/Scope Educational Research Foundation No.13.* Ypsilanti, MI: High/Scope Press.

Stone, C., Henig, J., Jones, B., & Pierannunzi, C. (2001). *Building civic capacity: The politics of reforming urban schools.* Lawrence, KS: University of Kansas Press.

Tyack, D. (1974). *The one best system: A history of American urban education.* Cambridge, MA: Harvard University Press.

7. *Teaching For Social Justice*

Linda Darling-Hammond
Stanford University

Dr. Clayton became the superintendent of schools during the years that I spent in Philadelphia. She was a tireless worker for educational improvement and equity in this city, so, I am particularly gratified to be able to give a lecture in her honor. The current holder of the Clayton Chair, Diana Slaughter-Defoe, is another woman whose work on issues of educational equity for women and people of color I greatly admire. Of course, I could say this about so many educators in Philadelphia who I have known throughout the years since I started teaching here more than 25 years ago.

I want to frame this conversation around what is currently going on in Philadelphia because I think it is in some ways a prototype of what is going on in the country. These are momentous and difficult times in Philadelphia. A major school district has been taken over, handed out, and chopped up. The for-profit Edison schools have opened here, just as Dallas has asked them to leave for a lack of measurable improvement in their schools. We know that hundreds of teachers and administrators are leaving their positions, as they fear what will happen in this city, while those parents and children who can flee are frequently doing so. What a sad change from the years of the late 1960s and early 1970s when there was such a renaissance of innovation and hope in the Philadelphia public schools.

As a prototype of urban education, and as a sign of what may happen elsewhere, what will become of Philadelphia? What will become of her children? What will become of all of our children, and what will become of us as a society? That is what I want to talk about today.

John Dewey (1900/1968) said at the turn of the last century, what the best and wisest parent wants for his own child, that must the community want for all of its children. Any other ideal for our schools is narrow and unlovely, and acted upon; it destroys our democracy (p. 3).

Many years later, James Baldwin (1985) noted in his *Talk to Teachers*,

> The purpose of education, finally, is to create in a person the ability to look at the world for himself or herself, to make his own decisions, to say to himself

"this is black or this is white," to decide for himself whether there is a God in heaven or not, to ask questions of the universe and then to look at those questions is the way he achieves his identity—but no society is really anxious to have that kind of person around. What society really ideally wants is a citizenry that will simply obey the rules of society. If a society succeeds in this, that society is about to perish. (p. 326)

Now, I think that the question before us is: Will public education perish or will we be able to join hands and rescue probably the most important institution in our society today? Does every child have a right to learn, and how do we secure that right for every child?

The New Challenge for Education

That right has become increasingly important because our economy has changed so much since the schools that we have inherited were invented almost 100 years ago. At that time, about 5% of the jobs were so-called "knowledge work," or jobs requiring specialized training and skill. Now those are about 70% of the jobs, so that a young person who does not succeed at education has very little chance in life. And a society that does not succeed at education has a more and more difficult time competing in the world. If, in fact, the challenge in our time is to enable learning at much higher levels throughout our society, the equally important challenge is to enable teaching in ever more powerful ways so that we can support that kind of learning.

The consequences of under-education grow more severe with every year. Today, a high school dropout has a less than 50% chance of getting any job at all. If he is African American, his chance is only one in four. And, if he gets any job, it will earn less than half of what the same job earned 20 years ago. Wages are increasing only for those who have a college education. For those who have a high school education, they are declining. And for those who drop out, there is very little chance of income at all. Lack of education is ever more strongly correlated with welfare dependency, and, as welfare disappears, with incarceration. Today, we are building a two-tier society deeply divided by access to education.

A fundamental question for our society today is whether we will educate or incarcerate the children in our cities. Over the last decade, prison enrollments in the United States have tripled. For an African American male between the ages of 18 and 24, the odds of being in the criminal justice system are greater than the odds of being in higher education. Funding for the prison system went up by more than 600% over the last 15 years, while funding for schools increased by only 25% in real dollar terms. More than 50% of the growing number of inmates is functionally illiterate; they do not have the literacy skills to engage the economy. And 40% of the adjudicated juvenile justice population has learning disabilities that were never identified in school. In essence, many of these young people are in prison because our educational system did not teach them so that they could learn. We are willing to spend $30,000 a year to put a young man in prison, which is nearly equivalent to the tuition cost right now at Stanford or Harvard University. But, we will not spend even one third that much for the education of a child who needs expert teaching.

The real challenge for a society that needs to educate all of its children to high levels is to develop teachers who are able to teach every child. Teaching all children for understanding is much more complicated than merely "covering the curriculum" or getting through the book. This kind of teaching is not just standing up and telling students what you know. It requires understanding what kids are thinking, where they come from, and what it will take to connect to their experiences, their understandings, their language backgrounds, and create a bridge to the curriculum.

The challenge is, that what our schools are now asked to do is something they have never before been asked to do, and something for which they are not currently designed and organized. In recent years, we have heard a lot of talk about the failures of education. There is a view that public education has got worse. But in fact, in 1950, the so-called "good old days," more than 50% of all students dropped out of high school; students with exceptional needs did not have a right to education and most were not in school; and students of color were in segregated, underfunded schools, and frequently were denied access to high school altogether. It was the "good old days" only for a narrow slice of the population who had access to reasonably good schools and who managed to learn in the ways that schools taught.

In those days, high levels of education were less essential than they are today. For example, when I grew up in Cleveland, Ohio, people with less than a high school education could get a good job in a factory, make a good union wage, buy a house, and raise a family. Those jobs are nearly all gone in cities such as Cleveland and elsewhere. Today, only 10% of jobs are low-skilled jobs like the ones that dominated our economy then. To meet the demands of the current labor market, we have to educate nearly all students to the levels we have typically reserved for the 20% to 25% who were streamed off into gifted and talented programs or "honors" courses. This new challenge is to educate a more diverse group of students to higher levels than we have ever before attempted.

The Persistence of Unequal Educational Opportunity

The ongoing problem of educational inequality is suggested by the persistent gap in achievement for majority and "minority" students (a term that is increasingly a misnomer, as students of color are the majority in urban districts, and they are the majority in the state of California, and will be within a couple of decades in the country as a whole). Over the last decade, the achievement gap has widened, and graduation rates have also begun to decline for the first time in this century. There are a lot of explanations for why we have such an achievement gap: We hear about the "bell curve," Herrnstein and Murray's (1996) argument that achievement differentials are race-linked and hereditary; we hear arguments that low achievement is due to a lack of effort, a "culture of poverty," deficient homes and communities, or inadequate school "accountability" (what most proponents generally mean by that is that there is not enough testing in the schools or enough sanctions associated with test scores).

What are the actual sources of inequality? I think there is a big disjuncture between the popular conversation about what is going on and what the reality is in our schools. There are lawsuits now in New York, California, South Carolina, Massachusetts, Nebraska, Montana, and other states, protesting the fact that some students get many fewer resources for their education than others. Here in the United States of America, where presumably all men are created equal—and maybe some women too—we have the most inequitable funding system for education of any country that we think of as a peer or competitor. In fact, the data show that nationwide, schools that serve students of color and low-income students have lower resource levels than schools that serve the most affluent students. Expenditure levels in the top-spending 10% of districts in this country are 10 times higher per pupil than in the bottom 10%. Within any given state there is about a three-to-one ratio between the highestspending districts and the lowest spending districts. Districts serving large numbers of low-income and "minority" students tend to have: larger class sizes and larger school sizes; less well-qualified teachers; fewer computers, books, and supplies; less access to information technology; and fewer college preparatory or AP courses. In fact, in many schools it is not possible to take college preparatory courses, because they are not offered.

When I was in Philadelphia in 1975, I did a study as a research assistant for a nonprofit education law center that was looking at the distribution of resources to students in Philadelphia. At that time, the schools were extremely segregated. They are still well segregated, but it was even more pronounced then. We found that in schools that primarily or exclusively served Black students, the instructional funding levels were lower, the access to qualified teachers was much lower (whether you count that by content degrees, higher degrees, credentials, or other measures), and the courses were much different. There were many fewer academic courses, many fewer advanced courses, many more vocational courses, and many more general education courses. The lawyers were considering whether to litigate that issue in 1975. I will never forget one of the consultants to the strategy session who argued against that line of litigation, saying, "Well, 'those' kids don't need those courses anyway." I was stunned at that response and distressed that the decision was not to litigate that issue in 1975. Two years ago, the Public Education Network of Philadelphia collected data that looked almost exactly like the data I had collected in 1975—showing the differential access to resources found in schools that serve different populations of students in Philadelphia.

Not much has changed in all these years. The inequalities students experience are made easier to inflict by the fact that our schools continue to be deeply segregated. In fact, over the last decade, our schools have become more highly segregated, according to Gary Orfield's (1996, 1997) research out of the Civil Rights Project at Harvard. Two-thirds of Black and Latino students attend primarily "minority" schools, and these are typically schools with lower levels of instructional resources. One of the more important arguments for integration is not that a student might learn better sitting next to someone with a different skin color, but that by having those with more power in the schools with those who have less, it may be harder to maintain the inequalities that are otherwise inflicted on those with little voice and clout. However, there are also inequalities within integrated schools, where most "minority" students are concentrated in low-track classes, which have less well-qualified teachers, lower quality and less well-taught curriculum, and fewer and lower quality materials.

We know much more about how to achieve greater equality in educational outcomes than we can implement. As Yogi Berra once said, "In theory, theory and practice are the same, but in practice, they're not." I think that really holds true. We know, for example, from a number of studies, that students who are placed in higher-track courses achieve more than those with comparable initial achievement who are placed in lower-track classes; that ultimately, what kids achieve is determined more by the curriculum they get and the resources brought to bear on their education than it is by their initial test scores. Jeannie Oakes (1993) did a recent study of a city not far from where I live, in which she showed that at every band of achievement, for students who had the same test score levels, Latino students were much less likely than White and Asian students to be placed into the higher tracks, and these track placements strongly predicted later achievement.

Other researchers have also shown that students of different races who have the same grades and test scores are generally sorted into different tracks offering different curriculum opportunities. I saw it with my own children's education in Montgomery County, Maryland and New Rochelle, New York.

They ended up, quite often, being the only, or one of the only, African American students in the upper track as they watched their equally bright friends tracked down in middle school. Gloria Ladson-Billings describes the same thing occurring in Wisconsin that I watched happening in New York. This racially based tracking system is a nationwide phenomenon that is played out as one of the "regularities of schooling," as Seymour Sarason calls them; curriculum access creates educational opportunity. When you hold socioeconomic status constant, White and "minority" students who have equally well-qualified teachers and comparable curriculum perform comparably in reading and mathematics. But rarely do they have equally well-qualified teachers and comparable curricula. Curriculum opportunity is to a great extent allocated by race and class both within and across schools.

Achieving Genuine Accountability

I want to give you a sense of how these inequalities play out for real children in real schools. And while we consider this, I want you to hold the question in your mind, "What is accountability, really?"

Video Transcript From "The Teacher Shortage: False Alarm?" by John Merrow

Narrator: What this does tell us is that many school systems have low standards, and some operate under the misguided assumption that any teacher can teach any subject. But, there are classrooms without qualified math and science teachers. School systems say they just cannot find instructors. For example, inside this portable classroom at Brett Park Middle School in California is an eighth-grade math class that has been without a regular math teacher for most of the year.

Interviewer: How many math teachers have you had?

The students: Let's see, there is Mr. Barry, Miss Gaines, Mr. Lee, Mr. Dijon, Mr. Franklin, Coach Brown, plus one of our other teachers. . . . There is another man named, uh . . .

Interviewer: So you've had so many teachers you can't remember all their names.

Student: Yeah.

Narrator: Fifty miles away at Oakland High School, this eighth-grade science class has had nothing but substitutes all year long—the entire year without a certified science teacher.

Interviewer: What has that been like, having 16 teachers or seven or nine during the year?

Student: It's just weird, it's like you have to get used to a new teacher every couple of weeks or something.

Another student: I feel betrayed, because this is the third year, ever since I've gotten to junior high school, I haven't had a science teacher.

Interviewer: So you've had substitutes?

Student: All three years.

Another student: All it is . . . is like the same thing over again, when a new teacher comes, sometimes we've got to skip the chapters and start all over again. It's difficult.

Interviewer: Have you learned much science this year?

Students: Nope . . . haven't had a chance to . . .

Teacher: It breaks my heart . . .

Narrator: Nancy Coruso teaches science at Irvine High School.

Nancy Coruso: People are not getting the classes here . . . they come down and they beg me, can I get into your class, please, I want to learn, I really need a science class. And they're not getting them. (1999)

The video goes on to highlight three certified science teachers who applied to teach in Oakland and were not called in for job interviews. The real story is that unqualified teachers and substitutes have been hired in this and other districts to save money because they cost less. This school district happens to be Oakland, but there are schools in Philadelphia that have the same kind of situation. There are schools in Newark, in Jersey City, and all up and down this coast as well as the West coast that have children deprived of an education in this way.

So what are we accountable for—to these children? Some say, "Let them eat tests. Accountability is all about testing, so we will give them more tests." But we have to ask, will that make our system more accountable to students for providing them with the basic services that they deserve and need? What do we mean by accountability today? And what are the obligations of the state, the obligations of the district, and the obligations of every school to every child within it? When most people talk about accountability, they talk mostly about what the kids are accountable for, such as what test score they have to achieve before we hold them back or take away their diploma. We rarely talk about the accountability of the adults in the system—those with the power to change policy—and what they are accountable for on *behalf* of the children.

Well, what matters most for student learning? We know some things about what factors influence achievement, and I would argue that this is what states, districts, and schools should be held accountable for. Parents are compelled by compulsory education laws to send their children to school. What is the obligation of those in power to ensure that these children are treated appropriately when they get there?

We know, for example, that one of the most important determinants of how students achieve is the quality of their teachers: What teachers know and can do makes a big difference to what students learn. This includes not just what teachers know about the content that they teach, but also what they know about *how* to teach so that it can be understood. This encompasses what teachers know about how to appreciate the backgrounds, cultures, and experiences of their students; what they know about how to teach such things as reading and writing; what they know about how to teach second language learners; and more. We also know that students tend to learn more in smaller classes and smaller schools. In fact, we have been accruing research for about 40 years that shows that, when all else is equal, students do better in schools that have between approximately 300 to 800 students, depending on which studies you read. Students, especially those who have the greatest needs, tend to do much more poorly in schools of 2,000 or 3,000 students where they are anonymous, where no one knows them well, and where their teachers cannot work together well.

When I was teaching in a comprehensive high school, seeing more than 150 kids a day, I had a little tenth-grade English niche in a big bureaucracy; I did not know my kids' math teachers or their science teachers or their social studies teachers. Within each class, all of my students had different teachers who had no knowledge of each others' curricula or students and no time to plan together. I became aware of how little I could be truly accountable for my students beyond my classroom when one of my students, whom I had finally managed to get to begin writing and to engage, stopped showing up for class. After two or three days I called and could not get anyone at the home, so I called the office and found out that he had been expelled for using drugs. Nobody had bothered to tell me. There was no sense that teachers should be involved in decisions affecting their students, that educators should work as a team, or that there was an obligation to get to know each student and be accountable for his or her overall welfare and progress.

Organizing Schools That Work

We know from both research and practice that schools that organize themselves so that the kids are well known, and so that teachers can take care of their students, have better outcomes. We also know that students achieve at higher levels when the curriculum is coherent and when it is aimed at understanding and performance. In the kinds of bureaucratic schools that we inherited, there is little collaboration: Each teacher typically does his or her own thing. The standards movement is trying to change that, trying to encourage a more coherent curriculum so that it adds up from one year to the other, so that what goes on in one class is similar to what goes on in others.

But most kids have to make sense of a fragmented school experience themselves. They go from one teacher to another, each with different standards and expectations. One says, "I want you to put your name in the right hand corner," another says, "Put your name in the left hand corner." This one says, "Write in pen," and another one says, "Write in pencil." This one says, "Tell me what the book says," and another one says, "I want you to be creative and think for yourselves." And you are 11 years old, going into middle school and wandering from one side of the big building to the other, with a lot of adults telling you different things about what they expect and what they care about, and you are supposed to make sense of that for yourself.

Imagine if you went to your job everyday, and after about 45 minutes sitting at the desk somebody rang a bell and said, "Now you've got to run to another desk and work for another boss at the other end of the building, one with different rules and different activities. And we are not going to tell you all the rules or expectations; you've got to figure it out for yourself. Please don't talk to your co-workers; that would be cheating." After 45 minutes of trying to work there, somebody blows a whistle and you have got to run to another part of the building and get another boss with another set of rules. And 45 minutes later you go to another end of the building and do the same thing all over again. How much productive work do you think that you would get done? And then, after a few months, somebody says, "Well, that's enough of that; we're giving you a whole new batch of jobs with new bosses." Some students can handle this complexity, but others become overwhelmed and have few anchors to hold on to. That is why we start losing kids in middle school.

Another key factor in achievement is instruction that focuses on understanding. Accomplishing this on a wide scale is a challenge in this country. When students come to this country from other systems, they tend to say that the work here is much more rote-oriented and memorization-dependent, and less is expected in terms of thinking, writing, and performing. These differences are related to the very different kinds of performances we cultivate on examinations. The U.S. is almost alone in the world in our reliance on multiple-choice standardized tests. Students who go to school in most other countries, including most parts of Europe, the Caribbean, Asia, Canada, and parts of Africa, take essays and oral examinations, and create work that is evaluated by teachers and moderated in scoring sessions by teachers. Learning is enhanced when students receive the kind of instruction that reflects the knowledge and skills that they are going to use when they get out of school.

The Importance of Teacher Quality

Teachers are central to all of this, and evidence suggests that qualified teachers are one of the most important elements (for a review, see Darling-Hammond, 2000). In an analysis of nearly 900 Texas school districts, Ronald Ferguson (1991) found that teachers' expertise—measured by scores on a licensing examination, master's degrees, and experience—accounted for more of the inter-district variation in students' reading and mathematics achievement in grades 1 through 11 than student socioeconomic status. An additional, smaller contribution to student achievement was made by lower pupil-teacher ratios and smaller schools in the elementary grades. The moral of the story is that student achievement relies on teachers who know what they are doing, in settings where they know the kids well.

We can create all kinds of special programs, but if we do not have teachers who know what they are doing in settings where they know the kids well, all the peripheral programs—compensatory education, dropout prevention, pregnancy prevention, and so on—are not going to get kids where they need to go. The other finding of Ferguson's (1991) study was that, holding socioeconomic status constant, almost the entire Black/White achievement gap would be eliminated if the students had equally well-qualified teachers. Yet qualified teachers are the most inequitably distributed school resource.

Another study (Strauss & Sawyer, 1986) found that North Carolina teachers' average scores on the National Teacher Examination (a licensing test which measures subject matter and teaching knowledge) had a strong influence on average school district test performance. Taking into account per-capita income, student race, district capital assets, student plans to attend college, and pupil/teacher ratios, teachers' test scores had a strikingly large effect on students' failure rates on the state competency examinations: A 1% increase in teacher quality (as measured by NTE scores) was associated with a 3% to 5% decline in the percentage of students failing the exam. The authors' conclusion is similar to Ferguson's:

> Of the inputs which are potentially policy-controllable (teacher quality, teacher numbers via the pupil-teacher ratio and capital stock), our analysis indicates quite clearly that improving the quality of teachers in the classroom will do more for students who are most educationally at risk, those prone to fail, than reducing the class size or improving the capital stock by any reasonable margin which would be available to policy makers. (Strauss & Sawyer, 1986, p. 47)

The effects on achievement are large. Another study that looked at matched samples of teachers who were certified in mathematics and teachers who were not, found that the students of those who *were* certified made significantly greater gains in achievement in general mathematics, and even larger gains in algebra (Hawk, Coble, & Swanson, 1985). Yet in schools that serve the largest proportions of students of color, there is only a 50% chance of getting a mathematics or science teacher who has a license and a degree in the field in which they teach (Oakes, 1990).

Poor and minority students all across the country get the least qualified teachers. In California, the proportions of unqualified teachers are almost 10 times greater in high-minority schools than in low-minority schools, and these trends are very similar in a number of other states and cities. The teaching gap is, in fact, what causes much of the achievement gap; because of the recent "shortages" of teachers and the hiring of less and less qualified teachers in many cities over the last five years, there are now lots of places where lots and lots of kids are taught by teachers who do not have a background in their content area, who do not have knowledge about teaching, and who are unable to help students learn.

The Enforcement of Sanctions for Students

Despite these inequalities, states increasingly hold students to the same standards. And studies in California, Texas, and New York have shown that, after controlling for student background, students whose schools have less qualified teachers score significantly lower on the state reading and math tests, which now have very high stakes attached to them. That was always the case, but now the stakes are higher and the punishments are stronger. The punishment falls on the child, for the most part. In some states with high-stakes testing and exit examinations, there are now as many as 50% of students of color not receiving diplomas, and sometimes as many as 30% or more of all students failing to graduate.

The problem is severe. Graduation rates in Texas for a cohort of ninth graders four years later are now less than 70% for Whites and less than 50% for African American and Latino students. The same process is happening in a number of other states, especially where testing is not accompanied by investments in the quality of schools and teaching. Where incentives to increase average school test scores are strong, the easiest way to achieve this is often to push out the lowest scoring kids. (see, for example, Vasquez Heilig & Darling-Hammond, 2008.)

Some recent studies have documented several effects of such incentives. One is that kids are pushed out to special education where the scores do not count in school averages. Another is that students are held back so that their scores look better in the short run because they are being tested at a lower level. And yet another is that they are transferred out to GED programs or encouraged to leave. Studies have found, over and over again, that in districts using tests mostly for grade retention, retained students do not do better. In fact, they achieve at lower levels than similar students who are promoted, and they drop out in higher rates. Now, this does not mean that we ought to socially promote students. However, the answer for students who struggle is not to punish them, but to teach them more effectively.

Holding them back and doing the same thing all over again is not a solution, particularly if they are in a school where the quality of education that they are getting is poor anyway, and the quality of teaching that they are getting is also poor.

Under these circumstances, kids get discouraged. They try and try to pass the test and finally give up. In Texas, new reports are documenting how students disappear. Although many high schools have a senior class one-third or one-fourth the size of the freshman class, dropout rates do not include the missing students. They cannot find them. They are not in the data system. They do not know where they are. As low-scoring students disappear, average scores go up, but education is not necessarily improving. We have to start asking questions: What really is going on here? Who is getting educated? How are they getting educated? And what are we doing to ensure that education actually improves for all students?

What will we do, in a society where increasing numbers of jobs require higher levels of education, if we have more and more young people leaving school earlier and earlier? That is one of the unintended outcomes of retaining kids in eighth or ninth grade so that they will do better on the test in the 10th grade. In addition to Texas, data from Massachusetts, New York, and other states with high-stakes tests, show that dropout rates are going up; students are leaving school earlier and are less likely to return. Kids are leaving school with an eighth- or ninth-grade education in an economy that has almost no work that pays a living wage for that level of education.

Can we afford a set of policies that essentially fail our children once by offering them an inadequate education, and once again when they cannot achieve standards they were never prepared to meet? And then when they have been failed, put them out on the street without the wherewithal to be a productive member of society? What will happen to us as our prisons become nearly as populated as our higher education institutions?

Alternatives That Work

The situation I have described is, fortunately, not universal and not inevitable. There are redesigned schools in urban areas that support powerful teaching and learning for all students (Darling-Hammond, 1997, 2010). These are small schools where teams of teachers stay with the same students for a couple of years, where resources are allocated so that more teachers can be hired, where classes and pupil loads are smaller so that students are well known. In New York City, there is a set of schools with these features— schools such as the Urban Academy, International High School, Landmark High School, and others—that have had more than 90% of their students graduating, and more than 90% going on to college, in communities where the graduation rate is typically 30%. To achieve these kinds of outcomes more widely, we will need to redesign the schools that we inherited from Franklin Bobbitt and Frederick Taylor and the scientific managers of the 1920s—who had a very different idea of what they were trying to accomplish—in order to create places where all kids can be well taken care of and can learn.

As one of the students in one of these schools said to a researcher who was studying the school, "School should not be mass production. It needs to be loving and close. That is what kids need. You need love to learn" (Darling-Hammond, Ancess, & Ort, 2002). We have to remember that. We cannot teach kids well if we do not know them, particularly if they come to school not having had the kind of support, day to day, that can compensate for poor schools.

The differences in such schools are obvious when you spend time in them. This clip is from Vanguard High School, one of several schools designed in the way I have just described (Darling-Hammond, Ancess, & Ort, 2002).

Video transcript from the School Redesign Network, *The Julia Richmond Education Complex: The JREC Story*. Stanford, CA: Stanford University, 2004.

> **Narrator:** Students play together on interscholastic teams. They share the gymnasium, a library and an art gallery. The graduation and college attendance rates are over 90%. It is a very safe school. There is no graffiti. The community is involved in that school. It is a wonderful success story.
>
> Vanguard [is] one of four high schools in the Julia Richmond Education Complex. There is also an elementary and middle school in the building. Students remain in the same schools with the same teachers for four years. At Vanguard, 340 students are taught by 26 full-time teachers. That is a student to teacher ratio of 14:1.
>
> **Principal:** I put all of my resources into teachers. I don't have assistant principals. I don't have a social worker.
>
> **Narrator:** Vanguard aims to help students become intellectually resourceful and to develop lifelong learning skills. You will not find as many tests given here as in most public schools. Vanguard relies on portfolio assessments. Francesca Smith is a senior at Vanguard. She says that portfolios are like multifaceted term papers. A student has two to 12 weeks to research a subject, write a paper, and then defend its thesis in an oral presentation before a committee consisting of students and teachers. The idea is to get students away from formulated learning. (Merrow, 1999)

There are features that Vanguard and similarly successful schools have in common. First of all, there are teams of teachers, each of whom see no more than 80 students, rather than 150 or more. This is accomplished by having longer class periods and by having more of the staff committed to full-time teaching. In the United States, only 43% of education employees are classroom teachers. In Japan and Belgium, it is 80%. In most European countries, it is about 70%. So we have a lot of people who are involved in schooling around the edges, but not nearly as many of our resources are invested in the classroom, where the most important work has to happen. In these schools, most staff *are* classroom teachers.

Each team of teachers works with a group of students whom they share. The social studies, English, math, and science teachers stay with the same group of kids for two years; they get to know them well. They have time in their schedule to plan as a team around the kids and time to plan with other teachers in their discipline around content. Every adult is an advisor who is responsible for about 10 or 12 students, as a guide and advocate. The advisor calls students' parents, goes to the home, and connects with other teachers on behalf of the student. The parents come in for parent conferences. The bond is there.

The assessments are portfolios in which students have to conduct a number of projects and meet standards within each discipline. For example, they must conduct a science experiment—design it, meet certain criteria, control the variables, write it up and then defend it against standards to a committee, like a dissertation committee. They have to do the same thing with a social science research project, a literary critique and analysis, a mathematical model, and so on. They graduate with a portfolio of ambitious work that most people think kids like this cannot do. If they had gone to a traditional high school most of the students would be doing worksheets and questions at the end of the chapter most of the day.

I have been to defenses of such portfolios—we have started a school modeled after this approach in a community where I am working—and it is thrilling to see students' pride at the exhibition and their sense of accomplishment that they have met a standard they understand and respect. There is a culture now that says if we teach it and you do not learn it, too bad, we go on to the next unit and the next course. At these schools, in contrast, there is a culture of revision and redemption. You work on the task. We give you feedback. You revise it. We give you more guidance. You revise it until you meet the standard. At every juncture, there is greater and greater competence, and we point out your growing competence to you, and we make sure that you get the coaching you need to improve.

Anybody who achieves anything great in life in a performance area goes at it over and over again until they get it right. If you are an Olympic skater, it is not like you do a couple of turns and fall on your butt and your coach says, "Well, that was too bad, now let's move onto the next thing." No, you get up. You learn what you need to do to get it right and you keep at it. Similarly, what we see in schools that have this kind of performance standard, with a culture of revision and redemption, is that performance increases and the gap begins to narrow. At the end of the process, the result is a very narrow gap and a steep improvement between where people started and where they finished, because it is not about, "Did you get it right the first time?" It is not about teaching by assignment—I give you the assignment and your parents teach it to you at home—whereby the parents that are at home and know how to do it have kids who get better grades than the kids who do not have parents who are at home and know how to do it. It is about teaching with lots of scaffolding. It is about teaching with lots of skill. It is about performance that is continually rewarded and challenged to the next level. Under these circumstances, we see that all kids can learn.

Policy for Successful Schools

How can we, as a nation, create a system of schools within which all students have the opportunity to learn? We have tried lots of kinds of accountability strategies over the last decades. There is political accountability, enforced by voting for school boards and other elected officials; bureaucratic accountability, enforced through rules and regulations; market accountability, reflected in schools of choice. We have seen all of these in Philadelphia and other urban districts over periods of time. Professional accountability is a newer idea: it is based on the notion that we need to develop teachers' skills. Policymakers are currently pursuing standards-based reform. It is critical to realize that high standards have to be for the adults as well, not just for the students.

Accountability is not achieved through a system that says, "We have high standards and we know they are high because so many students cannot meet them." You hear that in many schools: "Our standards are so high, few students can meet them." If that happens, I believe standards are too low for adults in the system. The adults have to improve their teaching and their ability to design and run schools, so that kids can learn.

What we see across the country are many different approaches to standards-based reform. Some states have used tests to drive reform, attaching incentives to test scores for students (for example, promotion and graduation); for teachers (for example, merit pay or poor evaluations); and for schools (for example, extra funding if they see an increase, or "D" or "F" if they don't). Other states have engaged in a more systemic reform, in which they have developed standards for teachers as well as students, used learning and teaching standards to guide professional development and curriculum reform, and used tests for information, rather than for punishment. And they have also begun to redesign schools and to equalize resources.

In districts that have pursued this kind of approach—San Diego being one that was recently studied—they recruited the most able teachers.

They invested in a well-qualified teaching force. They raised the salaries to recruit fully certified teachers. They did more outreach. They created mentoring programs for new teachers. They put in place intensive professional development around student literacy. And, when a student is not meeting a standard, they are assigned to the best teacher for the next year, the most expert teacher, rather than the least. Achievement has been increasing and the gap is narrowing in San Diego, because the focus has been on improving the quality of education, not just on testing.

At the state level, Connecticut provides another example. During the 1990s, Connecticut raised its reading scores to the highest level in the country. The public school population is about 35% African American, Latino, and recent immigrant students. There are a growing number of English language learners who are second-language speakers, as well as a growing number of low-income students, and yet, achievement is going up along with graduation rates.

What did Connecticut do? They invested in higher salaries for teachers and they also increased the standards for entering teaching so that the knowledge base for practice increased. Teachers were expected to know their subject matter more deeply and to learn how to teach students with special education needs, students whose first language is not English, and students who need a variety of types of instruction. They invested more money in the schools that were doing the least well, instead of taking money away from those schools. And they used assessment data to guide improvements rather than to punish students or schools. What we see when those kinds of investments are made is that the picture changes dramatically. All students learn to higher levels. The question is: Do we have the will?

Do we have the will? Do we have the courage? I know all of you who are out there in the school system are working hard, day in and day out, often unappreciated by the people who stand on the sidelines and point fingers and criticize. God bless the people working in our public school systems. We need to join hands among those who are in higher education, those who are in school systems, those who are in political roles where they can change policy, those who are working in the legal system, those who are working in the health and community systems. We need to join hands. This is probably our last opportunity as a society to take the steps needed to reclaim our democracy. When Frederick Douglass talked about the process of change, he said,

> Power concedes nothing without a demand. It never has. It never will. If there is no struggle, there is no progress. Those who profess to favor freedom and yet deprecate agitation are men who want crops without plowing the ground. They want rain without thunder and lightning. They want the ocean without the awful roar of its waters.

Well, we can make a difference together. I want to leave you with the words of my favorite democrat (with a small "d"), Langston Hughes (1943), whom I think described what it is we need to do. In his poem *Freedom's Plow*, he says,

> When a man starts out with nothing
> When a man starts out with his hands empty but clean
> When a man starts out to build a world
> He starts first with himself
> And the faith that is in his heart
> The strength there, the will there
> To build.

> First in the heart is a dream
> Then the mind starts seeking a way . . .
> His eyes look out on the world
> On the great wooded world
> And the rich soil of the world
> On the rivers of the world.
> The eyes see the materials for building,
> See the difficulties too,
> And the obstacles.

> The hand seeks tools to cut the wood
> To till the soil and harvest the powerful water
> And then the hand seeks other hands to help
> A community of hands to help
> Thus, the dream becomes not one man's dream alone
> But a community of dreams
> Not my dream alone but our dream
> Not my world alone but your world and my world
> Belonging to all the hands that build.
> America is a dream
> The poet said it was promises
> The people say it is promises
> That will come true.

> The people do not always say things out loud
> Or write them down on paper
> The people often hold great thoughts

In their deepest hearts
And sometimes when blunderingly express them
Haltingly and stumbling say them
And faultily put them into practice.
The people do not always understand each other,
But there is somewhere there
Always the trying to understand
And the trying to say,
"You are a man, you are a woman,
Together we are building our land."
America
Land created in common
Dream nourished in common,
Keep your hand on the plow, hold on.
If the house is not yet finished
Don't be discouraged builder,
If the fight is not yet won
Don't be weary, soldier.

The plan and the pattern are there.
Built into the warp and woof of America.
All men are created equal.
No man is good enough to govern another man
Without that other's consent.
Better die free than live slave.
Who owns those words?
America.

Freedom, brotherhood, democracy.
A long time ago an enslaved people
Heading toward freedom made up a song
"Keep your hand on the plow.
Hold on!"
That plow ploughed a new furrow
Across the field of history
Into that furrow, the freedom seed was dropped
From that seed, a tree grew
Is growing, will ever grow

That tree is for everybody
For all America
For all the world
May its branches spread
And its shelter grow
Until all races and all peoples
Know its shade
Keep your hand on the plow.
Hold on.

References

Baldwin, J. (1985). *The price of the ticket: Collected nonfiction* (p. 326), *1948–1985*. New York, NY: St. Martin's Press.

Berra, Y. Quotes. Retrieved from http://www.brainyquote.com/quotes/quotes/y/yogiberra141506.html

Darling-Hammond, L. (1997). *The right to learn: A blueprint for creating schools that work.* San Francisco, CA: Jossey-Bass.

Darling-Hammond, L. (2002). Teacher quality and student achievement. *Educational Policy Analysis Archives, 8*(1). Retrieved from http://epaa.asu.edu/epaa/v8n1

Darling-Hammond, L. (2010). *The flat world and education: How America's commitment to equity will determine our future.* New York: Teachers College Press.

Darling-Hammond, L., Ancess, J., & Ort, S. (2002). Reinventing high school: Outcomes of the Coalition Campus Schools Project. *American Educational Research Journal, 39*(3), 639–673.

Dewey, J. (1900/1968). *The school and society.* Chicago, IL: University of Chicago Press.

Douglass, F. (1857, August 3). "West India Emancipation." Speech at Canandaigua, New York. In *Frederick Douglass, Two Speeches by Frederick Douglass.* (Rochester, NY, 1857). Retrieved from http://www.blackpast.org/?q=1857-frederick-douglass-if-there-no-struggle-there-no-progress.

Ferguson, R.F. (1991). Paying for public education: New evidence on how and why money matters. *Harvard Journal on Legislation, 28*(2), 465–498.

Hawk, P., Coble, C., & Swanson, M. (1985). Certification: It does matter. *Journal of Teacher Education, 36*(3), 13–15.

Herrnstein, R., & Murray, C. (1996). *The bell curve: Intelligence and class structure in American life.* New York, NY: Simon & Schuster.

Hughes, L. (1943). *Freedom's plow*. New York, NY: Musette.

Ladson-Billings, G. Personal communication with the author.

Merrow, J. (Writer) (1999). The teacher shortage: False alarm? [Television series episode]. *Merrow Report*. Arlington, VA: PBS.

Oakes, J. (1990). *Multiplying inequalities: The effects of race, social class, and tracking on opportunities to learn mathematics and science*. Santa Monica, CA: The RAND Corporation.

Oakes, J. (1993). *Ability grouping, tracking, and within-school segregation in the San Jose Unified School District*. Los Angeles, CA: UCLA.

Orfield, G., Bachmeier, M. D., James, D. R., & Eitle, T. (1997). Deepening segregation in American public schools: A special report from the Harvard Project on School Desegregation. *Equity and Excellence in Education, 30*(2), 5–24.

Orfield, G., & Eaton, S. E. (1996). *Dismantling desegregation: The quiet reversal of Brown v. Board of Education*. New York: W.W. Norton & Company.

Sarason, S. (1971). *The culture of the school and the problem of change*. New York: Wiley & Sons.

Strauss, R. P., &. Sawyer, E. A. (1986). Some new evidence on teacher and student competencies. *Economics of Education Review, 5*(1), 41–48.

Vasquez Heilig, J., & Darling-Hammond, L. (2008). Accountability Texas style: The progress and learning of urban minority students in a high-stakes testing context. *Educational Evaluation and Policy Analysis, 30*, 75–110. http://epa.sagepub.com/cgi/reprint/30/2/75.

8. What Shall I Tell My Children Who Are Black?[1] An Overview of Parent Education Research During the Civil Rights Era and Beyond

Diana T. Slaughter-Defoe
University of Pennsylvania

I begin by noting that from the perspective of this nation as a whole, at least one author reminds us that,

> Common themes in ideas about rearing infants and young children in the United States can be traced from the nation's beginnings to the present day. These themes include a strong concern about child rearing; belief that human beings are perfectible through better child rearing; an eagerness by parents to listen to the advice of "experts"; a belief that infants and young children should be educated in schools or day-care centers by experts, competing with the belief that infants belong at home with their mothers; and a commitment to social reform, competing with the conviction that families should be autonomous. These themes provide a background for contemporary research, political controversy, and future discussion concerning how children should be reared. (Clarke-Stewart, 1998, pp. 101–102)

This orientation applies to the larger American culture and is *not* the subject of this paper. Rather, in this paper I argue that during the Civil Rights era, during that time of great concern regarding Black American voting and citizenship rights, ideas about rearing young Black children in the United States were explicitly introduced to guide parent education programs. Early emphases on deficits linked to educability shifted to themes associated with parental empowerment, ecological and cultural sensitivity, social supports for family strengths, and, most recently, parental involvement and empowerment, particularly vis-à-vis urban school reform. The themes, also inevitably political in nature, provide background to parent education research focusing on Black children. Given political and social conditions in Black communities, expert opinion on parental behavior and "parents as teachers" of children competes strongly with the conviction that outsiders have little understanding of the realities confronted by Black families. I conclude by discussing what I believe is the continuing challenge to educability, voting, and citizenship, which parents of Black children must confront in the near future, notably, parental empowerment.

The Moynihan Report

I was just a graduate student in the Committee on Human Development at the University of Chicago when the Moynihan Report was issued in 1965 (Patterson, 2001). I had just completed a master's degree in the aging area, during which time I was part of a research team that investigated the effects of institutionalization on an aged Jewish population in Chicago. I decided, after completing the study, that I wanted to research a different population for my doctoral dissertation, specifically, Black children and their parents. In truth, at the point of that decision, after two and a half years in graduate school, I was revisiting an interest area that I had initially abandoned upon entry in 1962. I had dropped my initial interest when a staff member on an earlier research project had indicated, in what seemed to me at the time to be the same breath, that the project was seeking "lower class Negroes" to participate in the study while asking how my great-grandmother (who raised me, and whom she did not know) was doing. Whatever the inquirer's true intentions, from that conversation I believed her to be a person I could not trust, and so I decided against joining the earlier project funded through the research of my mentor, Robert D. Hess. I think discussions about the Moynihan Report with fellow students brought me back to my initial interest area, and thanks to new funding support received from the U.S. Office of Economic Opportunity by Hess at his University of Chicago-based Urban Child Study Center, I could become engaged in research with one of the founding Head Start programs without associating with the particular staff member who had personally offended me (Slaughter, 1969; Slaughter-Defoe & Rubin, 2001).

Entitled *The Negro Family: The Case for National Action*, the Moynihan Report was issued while Daniel P. Moynihan was on leave from Harvard University and serving in the U.S. Department of Labor. Using census track data from the years 1920–1960, the report documented a trend over time towards increasing numbers of single-parent families in both Black and White communities. However, within Black communities, the incidence of single-parent families (21%) was nearly three times that of White families (8%). Moynihan, building upon a thesis originally developed by Black sociologist E. Franklin Frazier, argued that children being reared in single-parent families were, by definition, at greater risk for poor school adjustment and achievement. Being at risk for educability led in turn to a poorly prepared labor-force pool, and therefore, reasoned the author, the situation provided a clear impetus for government intervention to provide supports for improved family life, specifically, improved parenting. In this framework, the emphasis is on compensating for cumulative deficits by getting children ready for school, when they are from communities in which there are high numbers of single-parent families (McLoyd, 1998; Patterson, 2001).

What a different time that was! Almost without exception, the nation had undisputed faith in the quality of urban schools, inclusive of their ability to educate all children, and the utility and potential of quality research. Few disagreed with the "facts" of the Moynihan report. Rather, disagreements emerged from interpretations of the "facts." Moynihan was perceived by Blacks and many Whites as having targeted and blamed the victims of racial, economic, and social injustice for their own conditions. Middle-class (and aspiring middle class) Black family members, the group that was then spearheading the civil rights movement for equity and social justice for all Black families, were especially enraged. The framework regarding Black educability provided a context for academics to engage the discussions and debates, pro and con, of Black achievement in the United States. It also provided a socially acceptable rationale for early intervention programs with young Black children and their parents, of which Head Start is undoubtedly the best known today, originating as it did in 1965 as a comprehensive early childhood intervention program designed to compensate for potential cumulative deficits experienced by lower-income children prior to school entry.

Intervention for Educability

My involvement and research with the nation's first eight-week summer Head Start program in 1965 fueled some enduring research-related questions in my career and solidified my belief that empirical social research can never be sufficiently "objective" to extricate itself from contemporary social and political policies. My generation learned that selection of the problem, and identification of the conceptual frameworks and methodologies, inevitably reflects intended or unintended biases that are not merely scientific problems linked to concepts and methods of inquiry. They are problems with social and political ramifications that the ethical researcher is duty-bound to respect. Nonetheless, I continued to believe that, given appreciation of its limitations, scientific research could be a valuable tool for learning about the world in which we live.

The major question I posed was in the domain of the contribution of social class or social status to children's educability (Davis, 1948; Hess, 1970).

Given average social status differences in children's achievement, what could be made of individual child adjustment/achievement differences within lower-income (social status) families at children's kindergarten entry? The Head Start population entering kindergarten in Evanston, Illinois, seemed an ideal sample to study this issue since the school system enjoyed an especially good reputation, and the Evanston Black community met lower-income criteria. (In fact, in 1965, middle-class Blacks could not find suitable housing in Evanston, due to *de facto* segregation; most lived in the city of Chicago, commuting to work in Evanston as teachers, social workers, etc.) For the record, I found individual differences in reported maternal behaviors within the 90-subject Head Start sample that were positively correlated with children's achievement/adjustments during their first kindergarten year (Slaughter, 1969). Based on existing child development literature, I had theorized that differences in maternal behaviors within lower-income Black communities, based upon perceived sensitivity to the child's unique qualities, closeness to the child, and structuring of the child's home environment, would favorably impact children's early school achievement, inclusive of IQ performance scores, teacher ratings, and Metropolitan readiness tests. I was right of course, and therefore I completed my doctoral thesis five and a half years after I entered the program at the University of Chicago, inclusive of a double major in human development and clinical psychology.

The tradition in Head Start research has continued until the present; improved sampling and methods exist, but the basic approach is the same. For example, I recently stated in a Senate briefing (Slaughter-Defoe, 2003) on the subject, that D'Elio, O'Brien, and Vaden-Kierman (2003) reported research on the relationship of family and parental characteristics to children's cognitive and social development in Head Start. In a non-random sample of 2,573 Head Start children, both risk (maternal depression; exposure to violence, including domestic violence; involvement with criminal justice system) and protective factors (family activities; family support in Head Start) presumed associated with children's development were studied. Results of this important study indicate that the degree of parental involvement in Head Start, parental experience at Head Start, and parental satisfaction with Head Start can serve as moderator variables to attenuate the otherwise predictable adverse effects of family risk variables on early childhood cognitive and social-behavioral outcomes. These variables made a contribution to more favorable child outcomes even when parent education, income and employment, child gender, age, ethnicity, and frequency of parental reading to the child were controlled. The researchers concluded that Head Start is best viewed as a protective factor, and that it is important to understand the social and mental health challenges facing families in poverty when considering how best to prepare their children for school.

Importantly, the ongoing study supports the view that school readiness is enhanced when early intervention programs work with families as well as children (Slaughter-Defoe, 2003).

Interventions as Vehicles for Parental Empowerment: Head Start as Example

It is important to point out that early intervention programs such as Head Start were not conceived by all designers and participants as simply compensatory educational programs for children. Early on, Head Start was also perceived as a vehicle for empowering parents, another tradition that endures today. In 1987, with a former student colleague, I described Valentine and Stark's characterization (cf. Zigler & Valentine, 1979) as follows, emphasizing the importance of the concept of "maximum feasible participation" as an integral aspect of President Johnson's Great Society programs:

> for many low-income parents, Head Start has served as a basis for excellent "grass-roots" training in political participation . . . the best early example of this latter role was located in Mississippi. The Child Development Group of Mississippi (CDGM) at one time served more than 6,000 children in 84 centers throughout the state. Indigenous poor were responsible for all decision-making, including preschool curriculum and the hiring of staff at the centers. In such a climate, Head Start parent Fannie Lou Hammer emerged as an important political figure. Valentine and Stark conclude that at least two quite distinct conceptual underpinnings of parent involvement in Head Start have existed since the beginning of the program, the emphasis on social and political empowerment of parents and the emphasis on parent education. Over time, greater emphasis has been given to the latter perspective. Without the emphasis on empowerment, however, they believe that the essence of Head Start, as a program designed to help eradicate poverty would be significantly compromised . . . the parent and overall community's need for control and self-determination are compromised. (Slaughter & Kuehne, 1987, pp. 61–62)

Parenthetically, I think it is precisely the confluence and merger of different traditions that contributes to Head Start's status in the minds of many as a "national treasure."

While the concept of parental empowerment yielded to the concept of "parent as child's earliest teacher," it is important to observe that its initial frontal attack was not in the early childhood arena, but occurred when lower-income and Black parents attempted to effect change in New York City's urban schools. I am referring to the reasonably well-known Ocean Hill-Brownsville conflict that occurred between1967 and 1971 (Gordon, 2001).This conflict was preceded by Kenneth Clark's publication of first, the *Haryou Report*, and second, the sustained discussion of the meaning of its contents in the book, *Dark Ghetto*, in 1965. Parental and advocate efforts to exercise community control and to change urban schools were thwarted and resolutely defeated by New York's United Federation of Teachers. Despite this eventuality, some studies, even today, emphasize the role of parents as educational change agents (Edgecombe, 1999). In emphasizing the need for scaffolding parent support in an urban school, one researcher recently reported that "[parent] participation skills should be modeled for parents by peers who engage them in horizontal relations that allow them to learn without fear of being silenced, alienated, or embarrassed" (Friedlaender, 1999). With respect to parental empowerment issues in Head Start, however, even today I have a student at the University of Pennsylvania who is finishing a doctoral thesis that is an ethnographic case study of these issues in a selected Michigan program (Slaughter-Defoe, 2003).

One other feature of Head Start that has not changed is, notably, the primacy of socioeconomic status, specifically poverty, as the focus of this intervention program. However, we know much more about the conditions under which poverty can have the most deleterious effects, and the factors that can be erected to buffer against those factors (Johnson et al., 2003; McLoyd, 1998; Slaughter-Defoe & Brown, 1998). For example, single parenting is frequently associated with poverty because of reduced family income—thus, it is poverty that places children at risk and not single-parenting per se. Further, being truly a single parent, as contrasted with simply being a never-married, separated, or divorced parent, is more risky because the former parent may have no reliable extended family members (e.g., maternal grandparents or aunts) to share child care, or no resources to secure and purchase quality extra-familial care (Johnson et al., 2003; McLoyd, 1998).

Engaging and Sustaining Parent Involvement in Parent Education Programs

From the beginning in 1965, Head Start programs recruited staff, inclusive of teachers and even directors, from neighboring communities. And from the beginning, given their focus on parental education and empowerment, Head Start programs had less difficulty recruiting and retaining parent involvement in comparison to other parent education programs. Other approaches to research that favored naturalistic field studies instead of laboratory research, engaged pediatric clinics rather than schools. Nonetheless, despite a penchant for conducting the research in natural or field settings, in that time, the standard child "outcome" or indicator of program success was IQ score. Other criteria for success de-emphasized child socio-emotional and parent outcomes. I think a study reported in 1977 by Morris and Glick is illustrative and typical. The authors described a short-term (12 bimonthly sessions) intervention study in which Hispanic and Black parents of children aged 20 to 39 months were introduced to play with educational toys. The sample initially consisted of 518 children matched on age, sex, and ethnicity, and randomly assigned to an early or late treatment group in two New York City child health clinics. All children were pre-tested. However, at the end of the study, only 147 children remained to be given the post-test IQ measure. Favorable outcomes for early, and subsequently, late-treated, groups were obviously overshadowed by the 72% attrition rate. Even though this intervention study was conducted in a clinical setting that participants were presumed to be familiar with, other factors severely affected parent participation and involvement with the educational program. Then and now, programs that sustain parent participation receive the attention of prospective program developers and of child development researchers (Auerbach, 1968; Badger, 1971; Blumenthal, 1985; Levenstein, 1970; Smith, Perou, & Lesesne, 2002).

Another impetus for the parent education programs of the 1970s that I believe is important to mention is the focus on provision of social supports that would minimize the combined threat of Black parental child abuse and neglect (Fantuzzo, Wray, Hall, Goins, & Azar, 1986; Stevens, 1981; Unger, 1987). As one example, in 1979, Wesley published an article that concluded that programs should be developed to teach Black parents how to parent and how to find alternative ways of expressing anger. As another example, a working paper by Gray (1983) for the National Committee for Prevention of Child Abuse discussed the results from an evaluation of 11demonstrations programs of three types: perinatal programs; "culturally relevant" parent education efforts; and community-wide education, information, and referral. One of the three programs that combined both a community and parent-education focus served impoverished Blacks in Atlanta, and is described as having sought to provide parent and family education along with courses on childrearing skills; to strengthen informal helping networks; and to use the media to educate the public about family support resources. For various reasons associated with premature births and the like, similar early-intervention research persisted into the 1990s and beyond (Lee & Alfonso, 2003; Swick, 1992). I am keenly aware of this focus, because I contacted the federal government to request that my ongoing intervention study be removed from the list of resources available to assist in the prevention of child abuse and neglect. Regardless of how others perceived my research, I perceived myself as primarily conducting an educational intervention study, a study that would promote and enhance cognitive/intellectual development, not a study that would remedy, or circumvent the need to remedy, socio-emotional deficits.

Given these comments, this is my opportunity to discuss the background and rationale to the educational intervention study that I conducted and published 20 years ago (Slaughter, 1983, 1996). When I completed the correlation study for my thesis described earlier, the chance remark of a peer impressed me. She commented that the next step should probably be an experimental study, to determine if I really understood the "individuating" process I had attempted to describe. I resolved that if I had the opportunity, I would conduct an experimental intervention. I found the rationale and support for that in two longitudinal naturalistic and home-based observation studies that were just concluding, one by the late Jean Carew (1980; Carew, Chan, & Halfar, 1976) and the other by a colleague at the University of Chicago, K. Alison Clarke-Stewart (1973). Both researchers found in their studies of mother-toddler dyads that a mother who was judged warm, contingently responsive, stimulating, and enriching, from both visual and verbal perspectives, appeared to produce an intellectually competent, secure child as observed from behaviors, whether at home or outside the home. Further, the best single predictor of the child's overall competence score was the amount of maternal verbal stimulation, whether or not indirect response to children's vocalizations. In the Clark-Stewart study, whereas maternal behaviors appeared to determine childhood cognitive competencies, childhood social behaviors appeared to determine whether mothers and children at these ages (nine to 18 months) engaged in reciprocal interactions. Carew's focus on the contribution of human relationships to the elaboration of adaptive intelligence was compatible with the Clarke-Stewart study, though the latter reported similar-based findings on the results of factor analyses of discrete behaviors, rather than on predetermined behavioral categories as identified in the Carew study. Though African American herself, Carew did not involve African Americans in her first path-breaking research; however, Clarke-Stewart had Black and White mother-child dyads in her research sample.

To summarize to the present day, in the developmental field, descriptions of effective parenting have portrayed mothers as being active and participatory in their exchanges with their young, preschool children. Effective mothers set standards of excellence, structure learning experiences, are verbally stimulating, and are firm and consistent in their disciplinary practices. They appear to use reasoning and persuasion and their knowledge of the personal interests of their children in order to motivate them. Knowing the child's personal needs and being contingently responsive is my definition of an "individuating" mother. Such parents are neither extremely permissive nor severely punishing, but instead are contingently responsive to their children's needs in accordance with the child's perceived developmental status.

Missing from studies in the genre of Carew and Clarke-Stewart, I thought, was a serious consideration of the parent's social context, a tradition in which I had been steeped at the University of Chicago (Davis, 1948; Slaughter-Defoe & Brown, 1998). For example, my mentor Robert D. Hess, in his best-known research, had stressed average differences in mother-child interactions and child performance outcomes between social status groups (Hess, 1970). He believed patterns of parental authority and interactive styles between children and parents at home derived from experienced work roles, and therefore he argued that parents who reacted passively to authority demands at work were more likely to parent similarly at home where they were "the authorities." Conversely, parents who engaged in more entrepreneurial work styles were more likely, for example, to encourage assertive and negotiating behaviors in parenting relationships with children. My view, and my self-imposed problem, was different; I had to use the socio-cultural context to account for diversity *within* the lower-income African American community. At the start of my intervention study, I argued that the element of traditionalism associated with earlier, more rural patterns of childrearing had been sustained and perpetuated in urban Chicago, much to the academic disadvantage of many children. If true, then changes in maternal and child behaviors in the direction of more "modern" approaches to childrearing as encouraged by intervention programs such as Head Start should be most pronounced in the African American mother-child dyads judged least "traditional" in child rearing beliefs and attitudes.

In defining "traditionalism," I sought support from the writings of cultural anthropologists (e.g., Clyde Kluckhohn) and sociologists (e.g., Alex Inkeles). In summarizing some of this literature, I later stated (Slaughter-Defoe, 1996):

> Two lines of research have addressed cultural values and social mobility as reflected through the expressed value orientations of members of the culture. The first line was developed by Kluckhohn and Strodtbeck, the second by Inkeles. Since each . . . had serious conceptual and methodological problems, the two traditions were reformulated and integrated to meet present needs. . . . Ethnic cultures which possess similar values and traits are more likely to function effectively in American society, and therefore, experience more rapid assimilation and advancement. . . . The modernization position, developed by Inkeles . . . [emphasized] . . . The concept of psychological modernity [that] . . . psychological adjustments and competencies required because of rapid modernization or industrialization of cultures. . . . Neither focused on intra-societal urban contrasts . . . [and both] failed to include women in their researches and they rarely specifically addressed the role of prejudice and racial discrimination. . . . Therefore, I [Slaughter] chose to develop a new measure of expressed values. The measure would incorporate: (a) an emphasis on the more familiar and traditionally adaptive styles within lower status Black communities, as contrasted with styles which might be more characteristic of middle or upper-status communities; (b) an expansion of the original Kluckhohn (1961) dimension categories to include Personal Control—the perceptions of desired control and influence over social others; and, (c) a greater opportunity for each respondent to locate her own personal position relative to her perceptions of the position of African Americans and Other Americans. . . . Review of the historical and sociological literature, as well as discussions with our predominantly Black research

team, led me [Slaughter] to posit that some value preferences would be more characteristic of the respondent who was currently actively pursuing educational mobility than others. The "modern" and "traditional" ends of the value continuum for each [presented] situation were thus defined. (pp. 146–147)

This lengthy quote indicates how I struggled with ways to bring the prevailing insights of sociology and cultural anthropology to the developmental psychology paradigm embraced by colleagues such as Carew and Clarke-Stewart. Mothers, I reasoned, were not just practitioner-parents, they also had beliefs and values that resulted from the socializing influences of their own interpersonal environments and significant others (i.e., their subculture). Further, as women and persons, some were more committed and competent at using education as a vehicle for social mobility for themselves and their children. Knowledge of these beliefs and values would help to identify those families likely to be most responsive to early interventions, particularly early interventions designed to support school readiness.

Support for this view was obtained from my study of early intervention with 83 Black mother-child dyads who resided in Chicago's housing authority complex. Two parent education models of intervention were introduced to the stratified random sample of dyads: the Levenstein Toy Demonstration (TD) model (Levenstein, 1970), and the Auerbach/Badger Mothers Discussion (MD) group model (Auerbach, 1968; Badger, 1971). In a productive collaborative arrangement, United Charities of Chicago, a social service agency, introduced both models, using experienced social workers as parent education interveners. In the TD format, mothers observed as the social worker modeled how to use a new toy in participatory, interactive play with the demonstrator. Afterwards, they tried the method themselves and the toys were left as a gift. Controls received only the toys and no special services in parent education. Discussion group mothers (MD) had their own relationships facilitated by a participating social worker, also available to mothers for special case services. Children in the three dyads ranged between 18 to 24 months at the start of the two-year study.

Mothers' discussion (MD) group participants were favored over the TD dyads and the no-treatment controls on all study outcome measures (Slaughter, 1983). Generally, mother-child dyads who were most participatory and interactive during a structured 20-minute play session in an experimental setting were also more likely to be "less traditional" with respect to maternal child rearing beliefs and values. Children in these dyads tended to continue to perform better as measured by scores on traditional IQ tests, with advancing age over the two-year time period of the study in comparison to children in other treatment conditions.

Despite elaborate praise of the scientific merit of this study by both monograph commentators, Bettye Caldwell and Felton Earls, I felt as if only a small group of informed devotees really appreciated the study and its utility. By that time, I had come to believe that social policy appeared to be made not by research findings, as had been hoped (and taught by Hess and colleagues), but at best by collaborative relations between researchers and persons in the practice and policy arenas. It seemed that the ultimate goals of my research were noble but naive. The larger society did not care about the origins of the beliefs and values of a group of Black women, and their impact, favorable and unfavorable, on their children. This interest in the importance of cultural context seemed to be a peculiar "affliction" of myself, born and raised on Chicago's Southside, in a predominantly working-class African American community in the 1940s and 1950s, to four generations of "mothers," which extended from great-great maternal grandmother to mother, who were available to me at birth.

In contrast, the larger society seemed to care most about accounting for dysfunctional parents and families, those with multiple problems, who were also prone to child abuse and neglect. Some argued that the parents' childrearing practices had absolutely nothing to do with their children's school failures. In focusing on parent-child relations, one was essentially "blaming the victim" instead of the sorry state of her child's school and its failure to educate children. Others pointed to the importance of the larger cultural context in shaping parental goals, subsistence goals that included emphasis not on formal schooling, but rather, on survival skills. And still, others stressed that other relationships, such as those with fathers, peers, and siblings were being neglected by narrowly focusing on mother-child relations. Importantly, I felt the dominant culture was not interested in a socio-cultural defense of the women who were being challenged for not rearing children who could advance themselves through the public education system.

Parent Education and Cultural Sensitivity

Nonetheless, I would like to think that the publication of my monograph and other related papers (Slaughter-Defoe, 1996; Slaughter-Defoe & Rubin, 2001) helped to push parent education research in the direction of increased cultural sensitivity. In truth, it is likely that my professional support for the research and theorizing of the late anthropological scholar, John Ogbu (2003), was just as important. By the 1980s, research scholars were ready to take seriously his argument that understanding the contribution of families and parents to children's learning and development required an understanding of the larger social and cultural context in which they subsist. Ogbu's (2003) last book, published just this year, continued in that same tradition when he analyzed the academic achievement gap between Black and White families in an affluent Ohio suburb by referencing the importance of removing Black parental barriers to participation and involvement in children's schooling that have long-standing socio-cultural reference.

Black theorists such as Andrew Billingsley (1980) and scholar-researchers such as Harriette McAdoo (McAdoo & Crawford, 1998) also had significant roles in broadening the paradigm associated with parent education research. For example, in 1988, McAdoo and Crawford reported the evaluative findings of Project SPIRIT, a study of an initiative of the Congress of National Black Churches that began in 1986. Project SPIRIT sought to nurture a variety of child virtues through program elements that included after-school tutoring, parent education, and pastoral counseling in the overall program. The evaluators indicated that assessments of 253 five- to seven-year-old children in three cities (Indianapolis, Atlanta, and Oakland) had been made, and pilot data had been collected from parents in Oakland. Parents reported that the components of the program that children liked most concerned Black history and the positive contributions of the Black race. Parents (mostly Baptist) were not regular church attendees. Though most had gone no further than high school, the parents expressed a high value for educational attainment on the part of their children. In this Black community initiative, children, but not parents, received explicit attention to Black history and the contributions of Black people, though it seems that in this ecological and community context (i.e., the Black church), parents favorably supported the program's efforts to support children's emergent awareness of Black history and culture.

Furthermore, in the 1980s, a number of papers addressing parent education programs and research emphasized cultural differences in relation to Black parents and families, in addition to the importance of viewing parents and parent educators as adult learners with contributions to make to their shared educational process (Alvy, 1985; American University ALPI, 1980; Memphis State University Symposium, 1980; Moore, 1986; Slaughter et al., 1989; Strom, 1990). Here I think it important to point out that I experienced the Reagan era, the 1980s, as a time that was highly supportive of the concept of culture and race differences, but also a time that undervalued the importance of socio-economic status differences, particularly in relation to child and family poverty. It was in the 1980s, for example, that I was funded by the National Institute of Education to study the arrival of Black students—in significant numbers—in elite private elementary schools in the Chicago area. We labeled the study "Newcomers: Blacks in Private Schools." As another example, around the nation during the 1980s, African American museums, art, and culture—more specifically cultural artifacts—received support.

Such institutions, of course, heralded the availability of new and expanded cultural resources for both teachers and parents of Black children (Boykin & Allen, 1988).

Pluralistic Perspectives on Black Parent Education –1990s and Beyond

I believe that since the earlier studies of parent education were published in the 1970s and early 1980s, our nation's desire for sustained global and international competitiveness emerged and became strongly connected to getting a healthy start in the early years. Further, the arrival of newer immigrant, frequently impoverished, populations, and the annexation of the concerns of childcare advocates since Welfare Reforms were enacted (Johnson et al., 2003) also served to keep the parent education field active. Advances in biology and scientific technology renewed faith in the significant contribution of early intervention to learning and development. Finally, the nation's concern for literacy and for educating all the children occasioned a revisit to issues associated with child and family poverty by the late 1980s and early 1990s (McLoyd, 1998; Slaughter et al., 1989; Slaughter et al., 1988).

The metaphor for parent education and intervention in the 1990s is that of a thousand flowers blooming in the same garden, with only a few bound to be dominant, none of which have emerged as yet. In concluding this lecture, I have time to identify and describe examples of only a few flowers that I believe to be leading contenders for the limited space in the garden.

Parent Education in Child Literacy as Parental Empowerment

No one should think that the processes of Black parental empowerment are simple, as is evidenced in the description of what happened when Dr. Patricia Edwards, currently on faculty at Michigan State University, attempted to encourage lower-income African American mothers to read regularly to their children. Edwards (1989, 1994, 1995a, 1995b) engaged in literacy training of parents of young African American Head Start children in rural Louisiana in the late 1980s. She decided to find out what parents understood when kindergarten and first grade teachers told them to "read to their child." She found that parents had many and varied reactions that ranged from being concerned that they could not read themselves, and worrying about that; to opening a book and helping children sound out words; to having little idea what should come first, second, or third in such a "reading" process; to just "opening the book and reading to the end, just to get the job done" (1995a, p. 57).

Edwards' (1989) experiences during this early training subsequently led her to develop the Parents as Partners in Reading Program, a three-phase, 21-week program in which parents first receive demonstrations or coaching as to how they might read to their children, later engage in shared peer modeling experiences, and finally are observed in specific parent-child interactions around storybook reading. In reporting her observations, Edwards stated that parents (usually mothers) indicated they were pleased to finally understand what the school expected of them, and that her work with the primary grade teachers has been designed to help them to understand that parents need help in interpreting teacher directives. Importantly, these mothers did not initially feel empowered to actively participate in the early education of their own children. I think the above experience should be contrasted with similarly situated families in many Asian cultures, where it is culturally normative to expect the mother to teach the child to read print before the child enters kindergarten.

Parent Education as Black Self-Help Genre

Primarily because of the era in which I began work in this field, a time in which African American communities resisted parent education programs, a resistance, I might add, that continues today, particularly in the form of resisting "White scripts for Black parenting" (Luschen, 1998; Stevenson, Davis, & Abdul-Kabir, 2001), I find this development especially interesting. Fortunately, the occasion of this lecture provided me with an opportunity to read some of the books in the Black self-help genre, in which I found many creative ideas. Some reports simply annotate available resource materials or provide criteria for appraising those materials for purposes of Black parent education (Family Resource Coalition, 1994; Goetz, 1995–1996; Wingo & Mertensmeyer, 1994). Other books originate from professional observation and practice (Boyd-Franklin & Franklin, 2000; Comer & Poussaint, 1992; Stevens, 1981). These books and materials seem directed toward middle-class Blacks, many of whom are rearing children in desegregated communities, or toward Black and White professionals working in lower-income communities. Still other "self-help" books emphasize the vulnerability of the Black male population to the hegemony of dominant White privilege, or White racism (Bush, 1999; Madhubuti, 1991). Generally, these latter reports are not researchbased, save for the conducted dissertation research of relevance to Black parent education conducted by Bush.

For this research project, in an attempt to address the question "Can Black mothers raise our sons?" Bush interviewed a cross-section of 27 Black mothers, and at least one of the sons of the 23 women who did not have infants at the time of the study. The investigation was inspired by those who predict dire consequences for Black males, particularly those being reared in single-parent homes with limited positive male role models (Madhubuti, 1991; Rolle, 1990). Bush (1999) stated that all mothers had at least one son and were selected from middle- and lower-class backgrounds by him from "churches, a homeless shelter, schools, and other locations. . . ." The sons ranged in age from six to 19, 24, and even older. Commenting on the importance of his study, Bush argued,

> Little work has focused on how Black women conceptualize, construct, and act upon their paradigm of manhood. This is an important question in the discourse of human development. As a majority of Black males are now being raised by single mothers, and because Black mothers, single or married, play a significant role in raising their sons, it is necessary . . . to understand how Black mothers define manhood. (pp. 82–83)

Bush found the following traits included on the mothers' list of positive masculine qualities: love of people; believes that there is a God; Christian; compassion for everyone; concern for the human race; financially independent; good morals; honest; honorable . . . responsible. The findings that stress moral and spiritual support are consistent with another case study of five African American women (Mullins, 1992).

Bush concluded:

> When comparing the list . . . with Eurocentric concepts of masculinity (e.g., aggression, ambition) and femininity (e.g., passive, illogical) . . . I realize that these Black mothers have constructed a masculine model that is not Eurocentric. *The qualities are balanced between the European and African models.* (italics added) (pp. 82–86)

Whatever we think of the sampling methods, this study is original and important, especially because it has been conceptualized within the sociocultural context of how significant numbers of Black children are being reared and socialized today. Bush's report of his interviews with the sons clearly indicates that the messages are being received. Importantly, he observed that Black mothers' strong emphasis on spirituality, and the strength of character needed by them to induce these qualities in their sons, argues well for alternative perspectives on female parenting strategies and, I might add, of the role of parent education as a buffer and support of that very challenging process (Murry, 2003).

Parent Education as an Exploration of Black Community Values, Inclusive of Concepts of Race

The final area I have time to mention explicitly addresses the role of parent education as a protective, supportive factor in western societies where race and racism are omnipresent. This is not a new concern. For example, Hill and Peltzer (1982) reported a study of parent education for White adoptive parents of Black children. Recent focus has included racial socialization of Black parents relative to parental teaching and development of racial coping strategies in children. Coard (2003) reported that in an open pilot study, lower-income parents of children aged five to six stated that they engaged in socialization activities perceptibly associated with children's racial preparation, pride, equality, and achievement. She is presently designing a parent training program based on these four principles for African American parents of diverse socioeconomic strata; the design is inclusive of an evaluation strategy. Acknowledging the complexity of this line of inquiry, Coard is aware that she has crafted a program of study that could last a lifetime. She described her preliminary research on the Black Parenting Strengths and Strategies Program (BPSS) as follows:

> The present study of children growing up in the inner-city found that despite the young age of the children, more than 70 percent of the parents engaged in racial socialization practices that focused on racism preparation. . . . While all African American parents do not parent in the same way, the reality is that today's African American children are burdened with the facts of their lives. . . . Therefore, parenting interventions must be designed with the consideration of the societal realities in which we live, and the formidable task African American parents have of helping their children interpret information related to such matters from an early age (e.g., how to talk to young children about race). The methods used . . . are consistent with basic behavior techniques emphasized in standard interventions with parents of young children. (pp. 15–16)

Taylor (1994) and colleagues at the Center for Family Excellence at the University of Pittsburgh have devoted many years to the study of the Values-For-Life curriculum (VLC). The curriculum was partly developed to help teachers implement instructional routines that support preschool children's learning and socio-emotional development, following an earlier study in the 1970s of Black and White parental perceptions of their children's futures. According to Taylor and colleagues, the comments of the parents of preschoolers when asked the question "How would you like your child to be 15 years from now?" were instructive; they report,

> Quite aside from parents' responses to the question, we were struck with their evaluation of the question: "No one ever asked us to do this before." Most seemed amazed that we should ask, and some were moved to tears as they reflected on their children's futures. It seemed we had tapped an underdeveloped subject of ego-involving significance to parents. Subsequently, we used a more differentiated strategy of inquiry . . . extended this line of inquiry to clinical and nonclinical samples of Black and White mothers and fathers of low and middle income. For these parents of children between one and 54 months of age, we found that between 80% and 99% of what parents said could be coded into one of six categories . . . 1. Love and Respect . . . 2. Learning Orientation . . . 3. Self-Confidence . . . 4. Self Persistence . . . 5. Self-Esteem . . . (and) 6. Self-Reliance. (pp. 211–212)

Taylor and colleagues discussed many implications of their program of intervention and research evaluation, concluding that the curriculum they have developed with parents and grandparents for children could also have implications for the parents themselves, in that changes in the children could indeed effect changes in the parents. In a later paper, Taylor (2003) stated that:

> In moving from identification of values to design of interventions that achieve these values, we confronted two major challenges—each reflecting the nettlesome possibility that values could be implemented in ways harmful to individual and communal viability. The first challenge we characterize as spiritual, the second as cultural. . . . To avoid . . . implications of this kind . . . we have normalized our values set to promote . . . integrative ways of being . . . we chose to normalize each value in a manner that prevents or corrects identification with culturally disintegrative ways of being . . . we believe our normalizing standard of spiritual and cultural integration may have deep theoretical implications for the human sciences and broad practical implications for the design of prevention and intervention activities in minority, poor, or majority communities. (pp. 2–3)

The Illusive Pursuit of Black Parental Empowerment

In 1965, the same year that the first Head Start program was initiated, President Lyndon Baines Johnson signed the Voting Rights Act into law. The Voting Rights Act suspended literacy and other racially discriminatory tests, including grandfather clauses, which had been used by states and local communities to prohibit Blacks from voting. It required that election ballots be in two languages in areas where many persons do not speak English as a primary language. It authorized federal examiners to replace local registrars, and allowed federal observers at polling places. Finally, it required federal approval for changes in election laws and voting procedures. The 15th and 19th Amendments to the U.S. Constitution conferred voting rights on Black men and women, respectively, but despite this and the Civil Rights Acts of 1957, 1960, and 1964, public consensus seems to be that the 1965 Voting Rights Act gave earlier amendments their "teeth" and thus provided the absolutely necessary supports to reverse the historic disenfranchisement of the Black electorate, which had characterized southern politics since the end of the Reconstruction. Reauthorization of the Voting Rights Act in 2007 requires a majority vote in both houses of Congress and the President's signature (Salzman, Smith, & West, 1996).

The achievement of the 1965 Voting Rights Act resulted from the collaboration of many community organizations and civil rights groups and activists over an extended period of time (Morris, 1984; Patterson, 2001).

For example, consider the Southern Regional Council. Founded in 1919 in Atlanta, the Southern Regional Council, initially identified as the Commission on Interracial Cooperation, provided seed money and other resources to develop the Voter Education Project. Throughout its history, this non-partisan southern organization opposed racial segregation and lynching and campaigned for rural economic development. It has focused on access to the polls and the political process as a means of achieving these goals. Therefore, in 1962, the Council founded the Voter Education Project to collect statistical data on voter registration in the South, assigning this group the task of conducting the registration drive among Black Southerners. This project subsequently became freestanding in 1965, and successfully registered more than two million Southern Black voters in the 1960s. Later, the organization's educational campaigns helped lead to the extension and strengthening of the Voting Rights Act in 1970, 1975, and 1982, and it expects to play an active role in the 2007 reauthorization of this Act.

In 1997, the Southern Regional Council (SRC) published an audiotape history (*Will the Circle Be Unbroken*) of the Civil Rights Movement, with special focus on five southern communities. The transcripts quote historian Vincent Harding as characterizing the Civil Rights Movement as being "An epic, life-affirming, non-violent struggle for the expansion of democracy." The struggle used lawsuits, sit-ins, marches, and boycotts to successfully overturn and eliminate, in my lifetime, *de jure* racial apartheid in the United States of America. According to Patterson (2001), the Civil Rights movement peaked between the occasion of the Brown decision in 1954, and 1965, losing force almost immediately after passage of the 1965 Voting Rights Act, and the passage of the Elementary and Secondary Education Act, also in 1965, which authorized cutoffs of federal aid to school systems practicing *de jure* racial segregation. The transcript of SRC Episode 26 (1997) quotes Myles Horton's discussion of the Movement's accomplishments:

> Something very important happened. We had legally enforced racism and segregation. There were all kinds of regulations and laws that prevented Black people from voting. Now in terms of this, the dignity of a person to be able to get rid of those laws, in fact reverse them, so that it's illegal now to discriminate where it used to be illegal if you didn't discriminate. Those are steps forward.

Another interviewee, Charlie Cobb, stated that:

> At bottom, it seemed to me that the movement was not so much about getting a cup of coffee at a restaurant or something like that. It was about people gaining more say so over the decisions that affected their lives; and politics is obviously a part of that.

By the end of 1967, two years after the conventional agreement that the Civil Rights Movement had peaked, the Moynihan Report had been issued, and Lee Rainwater and William Yancy had published both the Report and rejoinders in a book entitled *The Moynihan Report and the Politics of Controversy* (Patterson, 2001). By now, this audience understands that I believe this report definitively catapulted issues of Black family functioning and education for parenting to the forefront of social science and educational research.

Concluding Remarks

The astute listener will also have noted that I have not personally studied parent education and intervention since the late 1980s. Actually, in the 1990s I participated in a school-based intervention study of the implementation of the Comer model in Chicago and I did not research parental involvement in that process due to funding limitations. I am looking forward to my upcoming sabbatical semester in part to summarize my observations and findings in reference to that study. However, one of my motivations for updating the status of this line of inquiry is because I think I may embark on another look at parent education research. Any such research would be both highly personal and political; though I am quite sure it will be "objective." It would be personal because large numbers of African American youth are being reared today in extended family contexts, with both maternal and paternal kinfolks, similar to my own early socialization years ago. Many other children reside with foster care parents or "fictive" kinfolk, also in extended family contexts. It would be political because disparate American policy groups have widely different ideological positions about this phenomenon, although the fact that it is the socio-cultural context encountered by the majority of African American youth today is not disputed. Although I no longer firmly believe that particular research findings will significantly inform or influence either policy or practice, I do believe that empirical research and theorizing can serve the function of highlighting important problems and issues that, despite a few precious exceptions (Brooks-Gunn, Berlin, & Fuligni, 2000; Levine, & Schnell, 2001; Slaughter-Defoe, Addae, & Bell, 2002; Strom & Griswold, 1994; Watson, 1997), are being virtually ignored in everyday professional discourse.

Ironically, some of the most celebrated research in parent education today did not surface online when, in preparation for this lecture, I required explicit attention to Blacks or African Americans in reference to parent education. On occasion, authors made specific reference to race and gender, using a sample from one of these studies in a sub-study report. For example, I believe Fuerst and Fuerst's (1993) report of gender differences in followup research of the Child Parent Centers in Chicago to be a sub-study of the research of Dr. Arthur Reynolds (Brooks-Gunn, Berlin, & Fuligni, 2000; Smith, Perou, & Lesesne, 2002) The good news is that the paucity of research with this focus rendered the topic manageable for this lecture; the bad news is that apparently even in 2003 many of the most respected researchers still write as if they can study and evaluate efforts to change the life course of Black children and their parents without attention to socio-cultural context. Happily, several recent reviews have been critical of this perspective (Garcia-Coll et al., 1996; Gorman & Balter, 1997; Lee & Alfonso, 2003; Lewis, 1992).

In any case, we know little about intergenerational transfer of strategies for coping with racism and the potential role of parent education in buffering and supporting that process in diverse settings like the urban school. Therefore, and in conclusion, though I have not completely abandoned the power of science to push us past the conventional ways of approaching issues of practice and of policy, I am clear that doing scientific research is simply a tool that can be placed in the service of evil as well as for good, and that this is no less true in reference to parent educational research. However, I am quite positive, all myth-making aside (Mattingly et al., 2002; Rogoff, Matusov, & White, 1998; Slaughter, 1991; Slaughter-Defoe, 2003; Slaughter-Defoe & Rubin, 2001; White, Taylor, & Moss, 1992) that parental teaching in the earliest years, and parental empowerment, as revealed in parental choice of schools and involvement in the educational process, are critical and necessary components of the effective schooling of urban African American children.

Note

1. This lecture is named for the poem written by African American artist and Chicagoan, Dr. Margaret Burroughs (2002). The Museum of African American History that she and her late husband, Charles, founded in their home in 1961 had reached its zenith by the mid-1980s, and is now in its permanent home in Washington Park on Chicago's Southside where Dr. Slaughter-Defoe was born and raised. In fall, 2010, Margaret Burroughs made her transition. Today, the Du Sable Museum of African American History continues to thrive and prosper.

References

Alvy, K. (1985). *Parenting programs for Black parents.* Retrieved from ERIC database. (ED274414)

American University Adult Learning Potential Institute (1980). *Guide to parent involvement: Parents as adult learners. Overview of parent involvement programs and practices.* Retrieved from ERIC database. (ED198370)

Auerbach, A. (1968). *Parents learn through discussion; Principles and practices of parent group discussion.* New York, NY: Wiley.

Badger, E. (1971). A mothers' training program—the road to a purposeful existence. *Children, 18,* 168–173.

Billingsley, A. (1980). *The educational needs of Black children: Working papers on meeting the educational needs of cultural minorities.* Retrieved from ERIC database. (ED198219)

Blumenthal, J. (1985). *Mother-child interaction and child cognitive development in low-income Black children: A longitudinal study.* Retrieved from ERIC database. (ED262892)

Boyd-Franklin, N., & Franklin, A.J. (2000). *Boys into men: Raising our African American teenage sons.* New York, NY: Penguin Putnam.

Boykin, A.W., & Allen, B. (1988). Rhythmic-movement facilitation of learning in working-class Afro-American children. *The Journal of Genetic Psychology: Research and Theory on Human Development, 149*(3), 335–348.

Brooks-Gunn, J., Berlin, L., & Fuligni, A.S. (2000). Early childhood intervention programs: What about the family? In J. P. Shonkoff & S.J. Meisels (Eds.), *Handbook of early childhood intervention* (2nd ed.) (pp. 549–588). New York, NY: Cambridge University Press.

Burroughs, M.T.G. (2002)(Original work published 1963). *What shall I tell my children who are Black?* Available from the Du Sable Museum of African American History, 740 E. 56th Pl., Chicago, IL 60637.

Bush, L. (1999). *Can Black mothers raise our sons?* Chicago, IL: African American Images. Retrieved from http://AfricanAmericanImages.com

Carew, J. V. (1980). Experience and the development of intelligence in young children at home and in day care. *Monographs of the Society for Research in Child Development, 45*(6–7), 1–115.

Carew, J. V., Chan, I., & Halfar, C. (1976). *Observing intelligence in young children: Eight case studies.* Englewood Cliffs, NJ: Prentice-Hall.

Clark, K. B. (1965). *Dark ghetto.* New York, NY: Harper & Row.

Clarke-Stewart, K. A. (1973). Interactions between mothers and their young children: Characteristics and consequences. *Monographs of the Society for Research in Child Development, 38*(6–7), 1–109.

Clarke-Stewart, K. A. (1998). Historical shifts and underlying themes in ideas about rearing young children in the United States: Where have we been? Where are we going? *Early Development and Parenting, 7*(2), 101–117.

Coard, S. I. (2003, April). Towards culturally relevant preventive interventions: The consideration of racial socialization in parent training with African American families. In N.E. Hill (Chair), *African American parenting in context.* Symposium conducted at the Black Caucus Pre-Conference of the 70th Biennial Meeting of the Society for Research in Child Development, Tampa, FL.

Coard, S., Wallace, S., Stevenson, H., & Brotman, L. (2004). Towards culturally relevant preventive interventions: The consideration of racial socialization in parenttraining with African American families. *Journal of Child and Family Studies, 13*(3), 277–293.

Comer, J., & Poussaint, A. (1992). *Raising Black children.* New York, NY: Penguin Putnam.

Davis, A. (1948). *Social-class influences on learning.* Cambridge, MA: Harvard University Press.

D'Elio, M., O'Brien, R., & Vaden-Kiernan, M. (2003, April). Relationship of family and parental characteristics to children's cognitive and social development in Head Start. In L.B. Tarullo & R. H. McKey (Chairs), *A whole-child perspective on Head Start reform: Findings on children's cognitive and socio-emotional development from FACES 2000.* Symposium conducted at the biennial meeting of the Society for Research in Child Development, Tampa, FL. Retrieved from http://www.acf.hhs.gov/programs/opre/hs/faces/pres_papers/whole_child_perspective/whole_title.html

Edgecombe, N. (1999).*Redefining parents as change agents: An ethnographic analysis of the Alliance Organizing Project for Educational Reform* (Unpublished master's thesis). University of Pennsylvania, Philadelphia, PA.

Edwards, P.A. (1989). Supporting lower SES mothers' attempts to provide scaffolding for book reading. In J. Allen & J. Mason (Eds.), *Risk makers, risk takers, risk breakers: Reducingthe risks for young literacy learners* (pp. 225–250). Portsmouth, NH: Heinemann.

Edwards, P.A. (1994). Responses of teachers and African-American mothers to a book reading intervention program. In D. Dickinson (Ed.), *Bridges of literacy: Children, families, and schools* (pp. 175–208). Cambridge, MA: Blackwell.

Edwards, P.A. (1995a). Combining parents' and teachers' thoughts about storybook reading at home and school. In L.M. Morrow (Ed.), *Family literacy: Multiple perspectives to enhance literacy development* (pp. 54–60). Newark, DE: International Reading Association.

Edwards, P.A. (1995b). Empowering low-income mothers and fathers to share books with young children. *The Reading Teacher, 48*(7), 558–564.

Family Resource Coalition (1994).*Working with African American families: A guide to resources.* Retrieved from ERIC database. (ED371837)

Fantuzzo, J. W., Wray, L., Hall, R., Goins, C., & Azar, S. T. (1986). Parent and social-skills training for mentally retarded mothers identified as child maltreaters. *American Journal of Mental Deficiency, 91*(2), 135–140.

Friedlaender, D. (1999). *The need for scaffolding parent support in an urban school.* Retrieved from ERIC database. (ED432654)

Fuerst, J., & Fuerst, D. (1993). Chicago experience with an early childhood program: The special case of the Child Parent Center Program. *Urban Education, 28*(1), 69–96.

Garcia-Coll, C., Lamberty, G., Jenkins, R., McAdoo, H., Crnic, K., Wasik, B., & Vazquez-Garcia, H. (1996). An integrative model for the study of developmental competencies in minority children. *Child Development, 67*(5), 1891–1914.

Goetz, K. (Ed.). (1995–96). *Culture and family-centered practice. FRC Report, 1995–1996.* Retrieved from ERIC database. (ED393594)

Gordon, J.A. (2001). *Why they couldn't wait: A critique of the Black-Jewish conflict over community control in Ocean Hill-Brownsville (1967–1971).* New York, NY: Routledge.

Gorman, J.C., & Balter, L. (1997). Culturally sensitive parent education: A critical review of quantitative research. *Review of Educational Research, 67*(3), 339–369.

Gray, E. (1983). *What have we learned about preventing child abuse? An overview of the "Community and Minority Group Action to Prevent Child Abuse and Neglect" Program. Prevention Focus Working Paper No. 009.* Retrieved from ERIC database. (ED231548)

Gross, D., Fogg, L., Webster-Stratton, C., & Grady, J. (1999). *Parent training with low-income multi-ethnic parents of toddlers.* Retrieved from ERIC database. (ED436280)

Hess, R.D. (1970). Social class and ethnic influences upon socialization. In P. Mussen (Ed.), *Carmichael's manual of child psychology. Vol. 2.* New York, NY: Wiley.

Hill, M., & Peltzer, J. (1982). A report of thirteen groups for White parents of Black children. *Family Relations, 31*(4), 557–565.

Hoover-Dempsey, K., & Sandler, H. (1997). Why do parents become involved in their children's education? *Review of Educational Research, 67*(1), 3–42.

Johnson, D. J., Jaeger, E., Randolph, S., Cauce, A.M., Ward, J., & NICHD Early Child Care Research Network (2003). Studying the effects of early childcare experiences on the development of children of color in the United States: Toward a more inclusive research agenda. *Child Development, 74*(5), 1227–1244.

King, G., Bond, J., Suitts, S., & Dent, T. (with V. Grosvenor). (1997). Episode 26: Prologue. On *Will the Circle Be Unbroken? An audio history of the Civil Rights Movement in five. Southern communities and the music of those times* [CD and Cassette Recording]. Available from Southern Regional Council, 133 Carnegie Way, N.W., Suite 1030, Atlanta, GA 30303–1054.

Lee, J.M., & Alfonso, V. (2003). The effectiveness of early intervention with young children "at risk": A decade in review. *The School Psychologist,*

57(2), 42–49. Retrieved from http://www.apadivisions.org/division-16/publications/newsletters/2003/04/issue.pdf

Levenstein, P. (1970). Cognitive growth in preschoolers through verbal interaction with mothers. *American Journal of Orthopsychiatry, 40*(3), 426–432.

LeVine, R.A., LeVine, S., & Schnell, B. (2001). "Improve the Women": Mass schooling, female literacy and worldwide social change. *Harvard Educational Review, 71*(1), 1–50.

Lewis, A. (1992). *Helping young urban parents educate themselves and their children.* Retrieved from ERIC database. (ED355314)

Luschen, K. (1998). Contested scripts: The education of student-mothers in childcare schools. *Educational Studies: A Journal in the Foundations of Education, 29*(4), 392–410.

Madhubuti, H. (1991). *Black men: Obsolete, single, dangerous? The African American family in transition.* Chicago, IL: Third World Press.

Mattingly, D.J., Prislin, R.A., McKenzie, T.L., Rodriguez, J.L., & Kayzar, B. (2002). Evaluating evaluations: The case of parent involvement programs. *Review of Educational Research, 72*(4), 549–576.

McAdoo, H., & Crawford, V. (1988). *Project SPIRIT Evaluation Report: 1987–1988.* Retrieved from ERIC database. (ED318538)

McLoyd, V. (1998). Children in poverty, development, public policy, and practice. In W. Damon (Series Ed.) & I. Sigel & K. Ann Renninger (Vol. Eds.), *Handbook of child psychology: Vol. 4: Child psychology in practice* (5th ed.) (pp. 135–208). New York, NY: Wiley.

Memphis State University Symposium (1980, December). *Parenthood in a changing society. Papers from a symposium at Memphis State University.* Retrieved from ERIC database. (ED196553)

Moore, C. (Ed.). (1986). *Reaching out: Proceedings from a special education symposium on cultural differences and parent programs (Phoenix, Arizona, May 2–3, 1986).* Retrieved from ERIC database. (ED284408)

Morris, A.D. (1984). *The origins of the Civil Rights movement: Black communities organizing for change.* New York, NY: Free Press.

Morris, A.G., & Glick, J. (1977). *A description and evaluation of an educational intervention program in a pediatric clinic.* Retrieved from ERIC database. (ED160190)

Mullins, B.K. (1992). *Makin' a life: Parenting in families of color.* Retrieved from ERIC database. (ED368870)

Murry, V.M. (2003, April). Rural African American youth development and adjustment: Buffering effects of parental and community protective processes. In N.E. Hill (Chair), *African American parenting in context.* Symposium conducted at the Black Caucus Pre-Conference of the 70th Biennial Meeting of the Society for Research in Child Development, Tampa, FL.

Ogbu, J. (2003). *Black American students in an affluent suburb: A study of disengagement.* Hillsdale, NJ: Erlbaum & Associates.

Patterson, J. (2001). *Brown v. Board of Education: A civil rights milestone and its troubled legacy.* Oxford, England; New York, NY: Oxford University Press.

Rogoff, B., Matusov, E., & White, C. (1998). Models of teaching and learning: Participation in a community of learners. In D. Olson & N. Torrance (Eds.), *The handbook of education and human development: New models of learning, teaching and schooling* (pp. 388–414). Malden, MA: Blackwell.

Rolle, S. (1990).*Raising the level of self-concept, attitudes, and academic achievement of Black male students, ages 8–12, through art and cultural heritage materials.* Retrieved from ERIC database. (ED328364)

Salzman, J., Smith, D., & West, C. (Eds.). (1996). *Encyclopedia of African-American culture and history.* New York, NY: Simon & Schuster Macmillan.

Slaughter, D. T. (1969). Maternal antecedents of the academic achievement behaviors of Afro-American Head Start children. *Educational Horizons, 48*(1), 24–28.

Slaughter, D.T. (1983). Early intervention and its effects on maternal and child development. *Monographs of the Society for Research in Child Development, 48*(4, Serial No. 202).

Slaughter, D.T. (1991). Parental educational choice: Some African American dilemmas. *Journal of Negro Education, 60*(3), 354–360.

Slaughter, D.T., & Johnson, D. J. (Eds.). (1988).*Visible now: Blacks in private schools.* Westport, CT: Greenwood Press.

Slaughter, D.T., & Kuehne, V.S. (1987–88). Improving Black education: Perspectives on parent involvement. *Urban League Review, 11*(1–2), 59–75.

Slaughter, D.T., Washington, V., Oyemade, U.J., & Lindsay, R.W. (1988). Head Start: A backward and forward look. *Social Policy Report, 3*(2), 1–19. Available from Washington Liaison Office, Society for Research in Child Development.

Slaughter, D.T., Lindsey, R.W., Nakagawa, K., & Kuehne, V.S. (1989). Who gets involved? Head Start mothers as persons. *Journal of Negro Education, 38*(1), 16–29.

Slaughter-Defoe, D.T., Addae, W.A., & Bell, C. (2002). Toward the future schooling of girls: Global status, issues, and prospects. *Human Development, 45*(1), 34–53.

Slaughter-Defoe, D.T., & Brown, E. (1998). Educational intervention and the family: The Chicago tradition in policy and practice. *National Head Start Research Quarterly, 1*(4), 39–111.

Slaughter-Defoe, D. T. (1996). The Expressed Values Scale: Assessing Traditionalism in lowersocioeconomic status African American women. In R. Jones (Ed.), *Handbook of tests and measurements for Black populations* (Vol. 2) (pp. 145–167). Hampton, VA: Cobb & Henry.

Slaughter-Defoe, D. T. (2003, June 6). Head Start parental involvement. In L. Aber (Chair), *Congressional Briefing on the Head Start Advantage.* Symposium conducted in Washington, DC.

Slaughter-Defoe, D.T., Nakagawa, K., Takanishi, R., & Johnson, D. (1990). Toward cultural-ecological perspectives on schooling and achievement in African and Asian-American children. *Child Development, 61*(2), 363–383.

Slaughter-Defoe, D. T., & Rubin, H. (2001). A longitudinal case study of Head Start eligible children: Implications for urban education. *Educational Psychologist, 36*(1), 31–44.

Smith, C., Perou, R., & Lesesne, C. (2002). Parent education. In M. H. Bornstein (Ed.), *Handbook of parenting. Vol. 4 Social conditions and applied parenting* (2nd ed.) (pp. 389f). Mahwah, NJ: Erlbaum.

Stevens, J.H. (1981). Support systems for Black families.*Childhood Education, 57*(4), 200–204.

Stevenson, H.C., Davis, G., & Abdul-Kabir, S. (2001). *Stickin' to, watchin' over, and gettin' with: An African American parent's guide to discipline.* San Francisco, CA: Jossey-Bass.

Strom, R. (1990). Perceptions of parenting success by Black mothers and their preadolescent children. *Journal of Negro Education, 59*(4), 611–622.

Strom, R., & Griswold, D. (1994). *Strengths and needs of Black grandparents as perceived by grandchildren, parents, and grandparents.* Retrieved from ERIC database. (ED371877)

Swick, K (1992). *A descriptive assessment of Project Focus' Home Visit Program.* Retrieved from ERIC database. (ED346962)

Taylor, J. (2003, September). *Values for Life Early Childhood Initiative.* Available from the Center for Family Excellence, Inc., 409 Dinwiddle, Pittsburgh, PA 15219.

Taylor, J., Turner, S., Underwood, C., Franklin, A., Jackson, E., & Stagg, V. (1994). Values for Life: Preliminary evaluation of the educational component. *The Journal of Black Psychology, 20*(2), 210–233.

Unger, D. (1987). *Differences in participation in a support program for adolescent mothers.* Retrieved from ERIC database. (ED294083)

Watson, J. (1997). Factors associated with African American grandparents' interest in grandparent education. *The Journal of Negro Education, 66*(1), 73–82.

Wesley, R. (1979). Understanding the child abuser. *Journal of Non-White Concerns in Personnel and Guidance, 7*(4), 159–169.

White, K.R., Taylor, M.J., & Moss, V.T. (1992). Does research support claims about the benefits of involving parents in early intervention programs? *Review of Educational Research, 62*(1), 91–125.

Wingo, R., & Mertensmeyer, C. (1994). *The guide for choosing African American parenting curricula.* Retrieved from ERIC database. (ED433107)

Zigler, E., & Valentine, J. (Eds.). (1979). *Project Head Start: A legacy of the War on Poverty.* New York, NY: Free Press.

Response to "What Shall I Tell My Children Who Are Black?" A Focus on Research

Mary Beth Gasman
University of Pennsylvania

I was asked to comment on today's lecture from the perspective of someone doing research in the field of higher education. In listening to Dr. Slaughter-Defoe, I am reminded of the power of research. Her understanding and interpretation of past research, especially the Moynihan Report, are very telling and should make us stop and think about what we as researchers (including student researchers) do and how we interpret and use the research of others. We must ask ourselves about the background and purpose of the research: "Who is putting it forth?"; "What is their background and experience?"; "Who is publishing it?"; and "How is it being used to inform policy and policy makers?" In the case of Daniel P. Moynihan, a report that might have been well meaning was dangerous to the African American community and served to undermine the structure of the African American family (Moynihan, 1965; Rainwater & Yancy, 1967). Not only did Moynihan's work blame the victim rather than the oppressor for the Black families in situations of poverty, it also vilified Black women and pitted them against Black men. If Moynihan had consulted members of African American families and been familiar with African American history and culture, he might have crafted a richer study that was less susceptible to misinterpretation and misuse. In addition, his research might have been not only more accurate but also more useful to the very community he claimed to want to help.

I'd like to talk about a parallel incident of the dangerous consequences of research in the realm of higher education. In 1967, two esteemed Harvard sociologists, Christopher Jencks and David Riesman, published an article in the *Harvard Educational Review* entitled "The American Negro College" (Jencks & Riesman, 1967). Because of the prestige of the journal and the institutional affiliation of the authors, their work received much attention in both the academic community and in the popular press, including *Time, Newsweek, The New York Times,* and *The Washington Post.* Jencks and Riesman's article severely criticized Black colleges, describing them as "academic disaster areas" and labeling their presidents as "cowardly and tyrannical." Among Black Americans there was a sense of shock, dismay, and betrayal. Although the Black college community came together to formally respond to the Jencks and Riesman article— critiquing its method and tone of racial superiority—they could not erase the national stigma that the article placed on these post-Bellum, once legally segregated, institutions (Wright, Mays, Gloster, Dent, Jencks, & Riesman, 1967). Although there are those who would say that the Black community would not have been accepting of any kind of critique, it was the particular approach of Jencks and Riesman's research that was most objectionable. The Harvard sociologists visited only a few Black colleges and relied primarily on the work of others and on hearsay to generate their conclusions. Their lack of knowledge of Black culture and history, in particular the history of Black education, led to certain mistaken assumptions. For example, rather than comparing Black colleges to the whole spectrum of higher education, and in particular to predominantly White institutions belonging to the same category, they measured all of these colleges against the standard of the elite northeastern institutions—such as the colleges of the Ivy League. In fact there were many White institutions that were failing according to the measures used by Jencks and Riesman—but this was not mentioned in their research. The *Brown v. Board* decision, combined with the Jencks and Riesman article, created a tendency by policy makers, media, and the government to lump all Black colleges together—to view race as their defining characteristic and to ignore the diversity among them. Closer attention to African American research on Black colleges, and consultation with those working within the Black college community, would have shown the varied missions, student populations, and leadership of these institutions. The Jencks and Riesman article caused the media to denigrate every aspect of Black colleges' performance; it was the reason several funding agencies and foundations decided to support predominantly White institutions trying to attract Black students, instead of Black colleges, and it provided the impetus for several decades of continued government scrutiny of these institutions (Gasman, 2003).

Significantly, Columbia University professor Earl J. McGrath (1965) conducted a study one year prior to that of Jencks and Riesman's which, although critical in its portrayal of Black colleges, was a collaborative effort with Black college presidents. The findings of McGrath's study were more nuanced and its comparisons considered more valid by the Black community. Had McGrath's findings received as much media attention as Jencks and Riesman's, they would have had a more helpful impact on policy formulation. Moreover, McGrath's research might have opened people's eyes to the complexity of issues surrounding Black colleges, rather than inviting them to see the Black college question as simply "Should Black colleges continue to exist?" However, McGrath did not have the national name recognition of sociologist David Riesman, nor were his findings what policymakers wanted to hear. In thinking of this study by McGrath, I am reminded of the Bush study mentioned by Dr. Slaughter-Defoe. As you will recall, Bush, when trying to answer the question, "Can Black mothers raise our sons?" went to the source—interviewing Black mothers to gain their perspectives. The results were surprising, and didn't fit into any predictable discourse about what Black mothers are or are not. Again, I wonder if policymakers really want to hear this perspective.

Looking at a broad cross-section of studies on African American education gives us reason to ponder both the positive and negative potential of research. Although some positive results came out of both the Moynihan and the Jencks and Riesman studies—for example, African Americans created their own body of research to refute both Jencks and Riesman and Moynihan—these uninformed examinations of African Americans emphasize the need to have an understanding of the history and culture of those we study. In the case of Black colleges, Harvard professor Charles V. Willie provided scholars and policy makers with a comprehensive and historically rooted study (co-authored with Ronald Edmonds) of Black colleges in 1978—in his words, "This study was an overt response to the poor scholarship of Jencks and Riesman." (C. Willie, personal communication, September 2, 2003). In the case of African American children and families, scholars such as Asa G. Hilliard and Dr. Slaughter-Defoe herself have shown us how scholarship that begins with the perspective of the African Americans involved is most effective and long lasting in its transformation to meaningful policy.

Recently, I read a newspaper article by Black conservative scholar Thomas Sowell (2003) of Stanford's Hoover Institute. He pointed to the Moynihan Report and the work of Jencks and Riesman as "the last honest assessments of African Americans"—suggesting that work that has been done in more collaborative ways is less than candid about the situation for Blacks in the United States (Sowell, 2003). I want to be clear that I am not calling for covering up or softening research results that pertain to "sensitive" topics. Instead, I am saying that the problem lies in the research method. By planning our studies with knowledge of history and culture and by structuring them with an opportunity for collaboration and input from those who would be affected by the study, we are, in the words of Dr. Slaughter-Defoe, "considering the social and political ramifications that the ethical researcher is duty-bound to respect."

References

Gasman, M. (2006). Salvaging "Academic Disaster Areas": The Black college response to Christopher Jencks and David Riesman's 1967 Harvard Educational Review article. *Journal of Higher Education, 77*(2), 317–352.

Jencks, C., & Riesman, D., (1967). The American Negro college. *Harvard Educational Review, 37*(2), 3–60.

McGrath, E. J., (1965). *The predominantly negro colleges and universities in transition.* New York, NY: Institute of Higher Education, Teachers College, Columbia University.

Moynihan, D. P. (1965). *The negro family: The case for national action.* Washington, DC: Office of Policy Planning and Research, United States Department of Labor.

Rainwater, L., & Yancey, W. L. (1967). *The Moynihan Report and the politics of controversy.* Boston, MA: MIT Press.

Sowell, T. (2003, October 3). On racial censorship and Rush Limbaugh. *Jewish World Review.* Retrieved from http://www.jewishworldreview.com/cols/sowell.asp

Willie, C., & Edmonds, R. (1978). *Black colleges in America: Challenge, development, survival.* New York: Teachers College Press.

Wright, S. J., Mays, B. E., Gloster, H. M., Dent, A.W., Jencks, C., & Riesman, D. (1967, Spring). The American Negro college: Four responses and a reply. *Harvard Educational Review, 37*(3).

Response: Parent Education and the Role of Young Fathers

ALTON C. STRANGE
School District of Philadelphia

My remarks this evening will briefly focus on parent education and the role of young fathers. The research on parent education has focused primarily on the dynamic between mother and child. The needs of young fathers have been ignored and their importance has been downplayed, except when discussing dysfunction, as Dr. Slaughter-Defoe alluded to in her presentation.

Young fathers have also been largely ignored when it comes to social service programs. According to Mazza (2002), despite the great number of adolescent maternity and mother-baby programs available in the U.S., few of them focused on young fathers. Of the programs that were available to young fathers, the programs concentrated on pregnancy prevention (p. 681). The absence of parent education programs for young fathers has allowed these young fathers to shun their parental responsibilities while experiencing few consequences. It could also be argued the lack of parent education for young fathers could be attributed to many of these young fathers having multiple children with other adolescent girls.

It is time to examine ways to provide parent education for young fathers and to hold them responsible for the welfare of their children. This past summer (2003) I was asked, along with Probation Officer Bennie Price, to develop a Fatherhood Initiative program for the Family Court and the School District of Philadelphia. This program, which we call Teaching and Uplifting Responsible Fatherhood (TURF) will serve adjudicated, delinquent youth of ages 12–17 who are on probation and are fathers. Since neither of us were experts in this area, we met with representatives from city and private organizations that specialized in facilitating fatherhood initiative programs. From our meeting we found that there was only one fatherhood initiative program that served the young adult (ages 18–24) population. All the other programs catered to adults.

The MARS (Males Achieving Responsibility Successfully) program is run by the organization Communities in Schools, and is located in 15 of the 22 comprehensive high schools. MARS' focus includes parenting skill workshops, lectures, academic and personal enrichment, and counseling. However, not all young fathers take advantage of MARS to develop the skills associated with these initiatives, because the program is voluntary.

The program that my colleague and I have developed would expand MARS by mandating that participation be apart of the adjudicated delinquent youth probation. This would ensure that the young fathers attended school regularly and were learning valuable parenting, academic, social, and personal development skills. Our program would also add an after-care program where participants would learn valuable job readiness skills, learn how to become self-efficient, be provided with social services to assist them with psychological and personal needs, and learn how to navigate the Family Court system as it pertains to child custody and monetary support. We also wanted to focus on them developing a relationship with the mothers of their children that would lead to shared responsibility for the welfare of the children. The uniqueness of this program is its objective, which is to affect the young father holistically by combining education (academic and parental), social and psychological services, job readiness, mentorship, and parental responsibility. Lastly, this program has brought together two systems that do not have a history of collaboration.

Dr. Slaughter-Defoe's presentation has provided us with the opportunity to challenge traditional views of parent education. By expanding the boundaries though research, we could shape a whole new agenda that would take parent education in a direction that is empowering, and therefore, even more beneficial to the populations we serve.

References

Mazza, C. (2002). Young dads: The effects of a parenting program on urban African-American adolescent fathers. *Adolescence, 37*(148), 681–693.

9. From Racial Inequality to Social Justice: The Legacy of Brown v. Board and Lessons from the New South Africa[1]

JAMES M. JONES
The University of Delaware

I am a social psychologist, trained in experimental social psychology. When I began my career, I was interested in macro-level phenomena of racism. I was contracted, however, in 1970 to write a book about prejudice. That was the label we gave to problems of inter-group relations, and it is the title of the classic book, as most of you know, *The Nature of Prejudice*. I was interested in phenomenology of experience as a Black person as well as a social psychologist, and I am about to explain what really mattered in the terms that I understood. Racism is the problem, not prejudice. Labeling the problem as racism took me in a different direction. I renamed the book *Prejudice and Racism*. The individual unit of analysis undertaken by prejudice and favored in psychology required a more macro-level account of institutions and, actually, the entire culture. So, the individual, the institutions, and the culture are interwoven in a mosaic of top-down influences as well as bottom-up modifications and changes. In the 1997 2nd edition, I provided a more detailed account of this interplay by exploring—separately and in combination—individual, institutional, and cultural racism. The dynamic interplay of these elements over time is central to issues of race and social justice.

Today, it is my goal to share with you my observations regarding the relationships of micro-level processes in social psychology and macro-level forces for and against social justice, and to compare and contrast the large-scale cultural dynamics of South Africa and the United States, in an attempt to understand why we seem, as a society, to have such a difficult time committing to processes, policies, and programs that attack social injustice directly. South Africa has made policies and programs a core component of their constitutional democracy. I'm a social psychologist. I don't do urban education. As such, I hope my comments will be useful to you.

These are several major sections of my presentation. First, I will talk about the legacy of *Brown* and certain aspects of that legacy. Then I will talk, briefly, about social justice as a point of view. We often think about social justice as something that exists, but it is really a point of view. Then we will talk about racial inequality, the fact that it persists substantially, and some reasons why I think racial inequality persists in the United States. My analyses will be primarily social psychological, although there are always more macro-level forces out there. I am going to talk about South Africa, but I will also talk a bit about the nature of South African society, in the way in which I experienced it, and how those observations caused me to reflect a great deal about my own experience here in this country and how we might think about life in America differently. And finally, I'll talk about a cultural framework for achieving social justice by trying to extrapolate some principles from South Africa to what I think are some of the issues that we face in the United States.

The Legacy of **Brown v. Board of Education**

I thought it would be appropriate to begin the legacy by talking about the decision, or the major parts of the decision. This is the *Brown v. Board of Education,* won in 1954. That is the trial that we normally talk about, and this is the quote that established the essential interpretations of that [ruling].

> To separate colored school children from others of similar age and qualifications, solelybecause of their race, generates feelings of inferiority as to their status in the community thatmay affect their hearts and minds in ways unlikely ever to be undone. Whatever may havebeen the extent of the social psychological knowledge in the trial of *Plessy v. Ferguson*, this finding is amply supported by modern authority. (p. 494)

This quote from the decision establishes two important principles. The first one is the principle of psychological inferiority, which was determined to not only occur as a result of that status, but also to endure virtually indefinitely. And the other one is the relevance of the social science researchers establishing the authority on the fact that that occurred. Another outcome of *Brown I* is the conclusion that separate educational facilities are inherently unequal, which follows from the conclusion that those scars of enforced segregation persist for a very long period of time and that there is no way you can avoid it. That is the consequence of enforced racial segregation.

> Therefore, we hold that the plaintiffs and others similarly situated, for whom the actions have been brought, are by reason of the segregation complained of, deprived of the equal protection of the law as guaranteed by court referendum. (*Brown*, 1954)

So now the referendum enters the justification for racial desegregation. The question that was posed by the community was very clear about what was at stake at *Brown*. The question posed by the court was, "Does segregation of children, solely on the basis of race, even though the physical facilities and other tangible factors may be equal, deprive the child of equal educational opportunities?" And when you think about that, I think it is significant, because the court assumes that those tangible other factors were equal, and they ruled solely on the basis of race—that race itself produced an inequality, an unfairness that was inherent to the fact that the races were separated by law. And I think one of the consequences of that is that the *Brown* decision deflected attention from the content of education, the processes of education; the fact that the so-called tangible assets were given as equal meant that the growing inequality in those very tangible assets was not the focus of attention. The focus of attention was on race and the desegregation that was prescribed. I think that is one of the legacies that we need to acknowledge.

Then we have *Brown v. Board of Education II,* and this was issued in 1955. *Brown II* established "all deliberate speed" as a standard for desegregation, and this mandated, or led to, a substantial White resistance, and a substantial amount of violence ensued. Blacks took matters into their own hands and mounted a moral crusade for their rights and their humanity. I should note that boycotts, protests, and non-violent resistance to racial apartheid were occurring in South Africa in the early '50s, even before *Brown*. So, we think of ourselves as leading, but the South African resistance started very early on in the apartheid regime.

Brown I invalidated *Plessy* and racial segregation and staked out the constitutional rights of African Americans under the Fourteenth Amendment, but it also asserted the inherent inequality and the negative psychological consequences of that status. *Brown II* rolled back the impetus created by *Brown I* and fueled a reaction to it. I will quote here three views, three ideas, proposed by Michelle Fine (2004), who used to be one of the faculty here at the University of Pennsylvania. In a recent *American Psychologist* article, she writes about the failure to sustain the impetus of *Brown*. She argues three points. One is that the understanding of *Brown* failed to appreciate the sacrifices that Blacks made, and those were a number of different sacrifices. I don't have the time to really describe them, but at the very least they included missing a whole year of school in some cases because the schools were closed in defiance of the court ruling; the underestimated White resistance—which was substantial—that fueled the Civil Rights Movement in many respects; and the narrowing of the focus, or the vision, from dismantling White supremacy. *Brown* never really addressed White supremacy, but I think that you can interpret enforced segregation as a manifestation of White supremacy. The vision of dismantling White supremacy was replaced by the technical processes of busing for desegregation. And that became a lightning rod in the battle.

Another legacy of *Brown* is Civil Rights—the Movement and the Act. The Movement, as a legacy of *Brown*, created an action agenda of collective self-determination and transformation. And I think it is a legacy of *Brown II*, because the failure of White America, generally, and southern White society, in particular, to be responsive, helped to make the Civil Rights Movement a necessity. I have argued on a number of occasions that it is the Civil Rights Movement that empowered people to take control of their lives, and that negated the idea that the negative composition of our psychological inferiority that was the result of enforced segregation. I cannot overstate my belief that it was the Civil Rights Movement that created a generation of strong, assertive Black students and others who made their livesbetter through concerted action (cf. Gurin, Gurin, Lao, & Beattie, 1969). I will further argue that the Civil Rights Movement brought to the world's attention the disadvantages and discrimination against Black folks, but also created a vision—a vision of America as a society that was better if it included people who were different, people who were diverse. That vision, I think, has a strong moral argument and moral force that was very, very important. And I would include that as one of the legacies of *Brown*.

The Act, the Civil Rights Act (1964) is interesting. Let me mention by the way, Gary Orfield (2004), who has probably written as effectively and importantly about school desegregation as anyone ever has, quotes in a recent article that "absent of the Civil Rights Movement, *Brown* would have been remembered as a failure." I think that's just how important that movement was. The Act itself diminished the significance of race and failed to address the continued problem of racism. So we have people selectively remembering and arguing for the importance of disregarding race while, in fact, leaving people exposed to the continued pernicious effects of racism in our society. And the conclusion that I think is important about the Civil Rights Act and its aftermath is that it introduced a certain degree of ambiguity because it negated race as a relevant consideration and failed to address, specifically, the problems of continuing discrimination and racism. So now we have the conditions where it is unclear to what extent disadvantage continues as a result of racial discrimination, as a result of lack of preparation, or lack of capacity, or what have you. The tendency, of course, has been to blame the people who fall behind and not to examine the systems that may be responsible.

So, these are different ways of construing the legacy of *Brown*. There have been many different people writing and talking about it, and there are a number of different versions. One version acknowledges the fact that society is forever changed as a result of *Brown*, that opportunities are substantially and manifestly greater, and that children have access to schooling in ways that they never did before. A second version is that the fundamental problem of White supremacy, racial disadvantage, and racial discrimination was not directly affected by *Brown*, and therefore we continue to struggle with that. I think the other thing that I mentioned earlier is that the focus on race failed to deal with the quality of education and the nature of educational procedures, programs, and policies that are needed to provide quality education, and that simply putting kids together by race is not necessarily the final answer to that.

Social Justice as a Point of View

And now, social justice. Meritocracy is based on an equity analysis. I know we talk about educational equity and I do not want to discount that at all, but equity in social psychology has a very specific meaning. It means that the inputs—the qualities, the attributes that we bring to a situation—should be proportional to, and precisely predict, the outcomes that we receive. A situation is equitable if those are in a proper proportional relationship, and it is inequitable if they are not. Inputs include such conditions and causes that are subject to inequality, and further, inputs are determined by, and evaluated by, those who are in positions of authority and control, to determine what is a valuable input and what that value is to be placed on. So if you think about very simple things, such as GPA and SAT scores and so on, someone has decided those criteria are valid inputs, and people do make arguments that if your SAT score is not proportional to your admission rate, then there is inequity in the system. And people who oppose affirmative action make a similar argument as to why attempts at producing social justice are unfair.

Social justice, on the other hand, is commonly referenced by outcomes. Lyndon Johnson talks specifically about the need to have equality of outcomes. If we want to have equality in concept, we have to have it in fact. We have to do something about it. And what we have to do about it is equal employment opportunity and, ultimately, affirmative action. In this view, inequality rises when outcomes are disparate. So when outcomes are different, we've got inequality regardless of the inputs. That's the way the story goes.

Social justice, I would argue, depends on your point of view and not necessarily whether you are for or against it. It isn't a matter of if someone opposes a policy that you think promotes social justice then they are therefore against social justice. It is very much a point of view and a calculation. Equity analysis, thus, is based on inequality. Merit, by definition, requires inequality. If inputs are different, outputs should be different. If outputs are different, inputs should be different. Inequality is part of the calculation. Social justice, as defined by merit analysis, and social inequality are not in opposition. So, when we talk about social justice, we have to recognize that we have to, either way, have a conversation, a discourse that allows us to talk about what people need to be fully human and to be fully participatory in society.

The Persistence of Racial Inequality

Now, racial inequality persists. I could spend a whole talk discussing ways in which racial inequality persists but I am not going to do that. Frank Raines is the CEO of Fannie May. If parity existed between Blacks and Whites, he argues, in education, there would be 6 million more African Americans who have high school/ college degrees and are in managerial positions and earning $200 billion more in income. In housing, there would be more than 2 million African Americans who own their own homes. In wealth, there would be over a trillion more dollars in equity value in the stock market, retirement funds, and in the bank. If there were complete racial equity. Recent statistics show that between 1996 and 2002, wealth increased by 17% for Whites, 16% for Hispanics, and *decreased* by 16% for African Americans (cf. Stewart, 2004). So we are not moving forward on the equality dimension. And I am sure that you are familiar with statistics on education, health, criminal justice, you name it, that face continuing racial inequalities. Pettigrew (2004) has done an analysis,which shows that in almost every arena where there are gains for Blacks, the gain *relative* to Whites has been actually very small, and in some cases, reversed. So when you talk about social justice, unless you believe thatby definition that the ethnic and racial minority groups are less of an input, then you have to come up with a way to explain the continuing inequality that we see.

The United Nations Development Programme (UNDP, 1993) looked at countries around the world in terms of their overall well-being, by accounting for GDP, health, and literacy. The United States, as a country, ranked 6th in this statistic in the world. If you count Blacks as a country, we were 32nd, and Hispanics as a country, we were 34th. If you remove Hispanics and Blacks from the United States population, the United States was number 1! The United States as a society suffers by the kind of perpetual and consistent inequality that members of ethnic and racial minority groups are experiencing. Inequality is costly to us all.

So why does racial inequality persist? I have several points that I could make, so I will just mention a couple of them and spend more time on the last three. Racial inequality is punitive and built into our society. And this is something we really have a hard time figuring out. The fact is, that you cannot eliminate the historical discrimination as the factor in continuing inequality. Dinesh D'Souza has writtena book provocatively titled *The End of Racism* (D'Souza, 1995). I always want to ask him, "Do you have a date on that?"; "Was it July 2, 1963?"; "When was it?" The fact is, that it's written into the fabric of our society, and it's punitive, so it's very difficult to disentangle historical forces in inequality and contemporary forces. I think that's powerful. And one of the reasons inequality persists is because we don't quite know how to make the calculations, and we don't know what to do about it.

The second point is that constitutional rights and racism intersect. Constitutional rights, as our conservative friends often say, belong to individuals. Individuals have rights; groups do not have rights. But racism is clearly a group-based pattern of discrimination and bias. So you have a pattern of bias that is directed specifically at groups, but you have no recourse to remedy, unless it is only directed at individuals. So how do you address a problem that is group-based if you only have rights as individuals? Furthermore, people who argue the constitutional validity and importance of individual rights take arguments for group-based programs as a violation of fundamental values, and the reverse is true. If you argue against group-based remedies on the basis of individual rights you're considered to be a racist. So these positions are not only contradictory, they lead to oppositional thinking and oppositional relationships, so that it becomes very difficult to come up with social policy that can work because they go in opposite directions. In addition, the situational influences are confounded. They statistically show that if you ask people to explain socioeconomic outcomes, Blacks and women will frequently see them as being caused by situational or structural factors, and men and Whites will see them as being individual-based. So when you talk about people seeing different sources of the problem, it's not surprising to me that the Welfare Reform Act is titled the Personal Responsibility Act. That is completely and wholly consistent with the view that socioeconomic outcomes are directly attributable to personal qualities and attributes, and our policies reflect that.

The next point is persistence of conservative thought. Persistence of conservative thought and arguing is one of the reasons for persistence in inequality, and I will talk a little bit about that. The automaticity of race affects—this is what we really know in social psychology. We know about how automatically race affects everyday life—in interpersonal relationships, in psychological processes, in perception, cognition, and even in the neural networks by which our brains work.

So, let's talk about the persistence of conservative thought. This is not meant as an attack on conservatives or on any Presidential candidates or anybody else. This is simply an analytical exercise to try to explain how something could happen. The basic idea comes from a *Psychological Bulletin* article by John Jost and colleagues (Jost et al., 2003), who did a meta-analysis of published studies that assess psychological attributes and qualities as a function of liberal or conservative dimensions of personality. And they defined conservatism as resistance to change, acceptance of inequality, and positions on certain issues such as supporting the death penalty, believing in harsher treatment for criminals, and opposition to affirmative action.

They found that persistence of conservative thought was positively related to death anxiety, fear of threat and loss, system instability, intolerance of ambiguity, and need for order, structure, and closure. It was negatively associated with tolerance of uncertainty, cognitive complexity, and self-esteem. So it's not surprising that a conservative perspective would be nullified to support a status quo, and would be more fearful and intolerant of change, specifically changes that were not clear or understood. A conservative thinker would rather not look for complex analyses of issues but would prefer, more quickly, to find more direct ways of explaining events. It seems reasonable then, that if you are talking about a society that, in the last 50 years, has attempted to transform itself along racial lines, or class lines, or the ways that we have— changes that are dramatic, powerful, difficult, and complex—these will not be the kind of thing that will be easily managed by a person who has the kind of psychological impatience that this analysis suggests that persons who are conservative may have. I would submit that persons of conservative thought have risen to leadership in public policy arenas, and as a result, that way of thinking has been relatively stronger in our society of the last 50 years than it was, particularly strategically, in the years preceding and immediately following *Brown*. I further postulate, and this is just a postulate, not a fact, that a cultural ideology is more likely to be endorsed by conservatively oriented people. And one of the things we have found is that if you introduce a person into a colorblind argument for ethnic relations, we can demonstrate empirically that they are more likely to show bias, both in their explicit and their implicit attitudes, toward members of ethnic groups, than people who have been specifically, experimentally mandated to endorse or embrace a multicultural perspective. So the colorblind perspective, which is often used as a rational way of dealing with a complex issue, actually has built into it in some way—I don't know what the mechanism is—a tendency to seed discrimination, to be less tolerant of differences, and to lead to more bias on cultural attitudes.

Implicit racial attitudes show consistent pro-White and anti-Black bias. Implicit attitudes are those that are automatically extracted from society and from our everyday life. The associations are often made between racial groups and evaluative information. The IAT, Implicit Attitudes Test (Greenwald & Banaji, 1995),which you may be familiar with and which you can take online, shows a strong White bias in thousands and thousands of people that have taken it online. It seems that research consistently shows that people with negative racial attitudes as measured by the Implicit Test, show discrimination in relations with others. There are a number of different ways of measuring it, and all have basically the same effect. The observation is that when *good* and *White* are associated and *bad* and *Black* are associated, discrimination follows. There is a substantial amount of information to support that.

Another finding that is interesting is that if you assess the person's explicit attitudes—what they say they believe—and their implicit attitudes—what they seem to have associated in their minds—what predicts their perception of their interaction with another race person is their explicit attitude.

If I think I like Black people, then when I interact with them, I think I am doing a good job. But, if you ask Black people how this person is interacting, or if this person has a negatively interested attitude, they do not think this person is doing so well. And the implicit and explicit attitudes are correlated with each other. So, I am living in one world and you're living in another, and I believe my world is correct, but the person I'm interacting with is experiencing a different world. That is a real source of complication and contradiction in society. And as I said before, one of the consequences of the way in which we are interpreting the 1964 Civil Rights Act is that there is ambiguity about how to take race into account. So if you are introducing ambiguity here, into a climate where ambiguity is anathema, you really have a problem.

Another interesting little study shows—this is in education relating to Carol Dweck's theory of entity-based thinking—that entity theorists believe that the racism is inside them, but they also believe that racism is inside of other people. People with the entity orientation are more inclined to be conscious of race, and respond to race cues, to a greater extent than people who have the incremental theory perspective. People with incremental theory perspective are more likely to see diversity in the ways in which people could possibly be. That is the kind of finding that has been replicated many times, but even finding it is pretty astounding to me and suggests that this is going very deep.

Social information influences attitudes, perceptions, and brain activity. There are a number of studies here, and I am just going to describe a few of them. The general proposition is, and we have found it in many cases, that first of all, the amygdala is associated with fear in the brain. And we have social neuroscience studies that show that people's amygdalae are activated when they perceive faces of people from different groups. That is true of Blacks who see White faces and Whites who see Black faces. So, the amygdala is saying that there's some sort of fairly natural, hard-wired brain response to difference. And it happens at a very automatic level. Related to that, we have a brain connection between the constructed social information that we have about our society and our perceptional mechanisms. Jennifer Eberhardt (2004) at Stanford has shown that the fusiform portion of the cortex is active in perceiving faces. In order to perceive faces accurately, that is the part of the brain that activates. And it turns out that that part of the brain is also very active in perceiving faces that vary by race; face recognition is also implicated in race recognition.

Further research finds that stereotypical social association of objects with racial groups is connected in the brain as well (Eberhardt, Goff, Purdie, & Davies, 2004). This particular study looked at crime-related objects as a function of whether or not race was salient. The idea is, if Black is salient to you, then you become more perceptually attuned to information that is consistent with a racial stereotype about Blacks. Crime is one of the stereotypes that is associated with Blacks (Devine & Baker, 1991). Participants viewed a sequence of up to 41 frames in which an object transformed from a completely fuzzy, unrecognizable image to increasingly reveal its features. The question is, at what point did that fuzzy object reveal itself as a gun? And did it matter whether race was salient or not? Participants were subliminally primed with Black or White faces as a means of making the Black racial stereotype salient. The objects they had to identify were crime related (e.g., a gun) or not crime related (e.g., a house). When they had White on their minds, it took until frame 27 to recognize it as a gun. When they had Black on their minds, they recognized it at frame 18. Was this due to sensitivity, perceptual acuity, or race-relevant information? For the non-race relevant information, there was no difference in their perception as stated. This effect was initially found in college students, but Eberhardt (2004) replicated the same effect in police officers. The implications of that, I think, are pretty clear.

These dynamic processes on racial recognition and perception are very fundamental in a society where race has the kind of meanings it has here. And it is not surprising that people who rise to positions in institutions, whether it's police officers, or teachers, or politicians, or whomever, are subject to the same basic processes demonstrated here. If you want to talk about how you extrapolate and magnify these kinds of basic psychological effects into a broad social policy problem, we argue that people are seeing things very differently and responding very differently. The point is that you can go the other direction. If I give you a gun, you are going to think Black. If you see an object that is linked to social stereotypes then you are more sensitive to people who have that stereotype. If you are witness to a crime and crime related information is available, then you will be more sensitized to a Black face if that is associated with the kind of activity that you're trying to evaluate.

There is a very interesting study of information from the state of Pennsylvania about convicted murderers, which was obtained with photographs. Participants rated the racial proto-typicality (dark skin, short hair, broad nose, large lips) of the features in photographs of Black males who had been convicted of murder in Pennsylvania between 1955 and 1985. Looking at these photographs, participants were asked "How many of them got the death sentence?" We find that 57% of the dark-skinned stereotypical Blacks got the death sentence, and 24% of the lighter-skinned, less-stereotypical Blacks got the death sentence. More than a 2:1 death sentence rate as a function of how they looked. They were matched on the nature of the crime and things like that. And remember, this is only for White victims. If you look at Black victims, there is a Black-White dynamic in a murder situation, and the more Black you look, the more likely you are to be sentenced to death. These are empirical observations from Pennsylvania. It is pretty chilling to think that how you look could have such profound effects on something as fundamental as someone's life. Well, that is another story.

Finally, threats to social identity undermine performance. You all know stereotype threat. I am not going to talk about it except to say that it does provide a fairly compelling argument for persistent underperformance that is unrelated to the ability of the performer. I think that is what makes stereotype threat such an interesting idea.

In Claude Steele's (1995) analysis, another part of the response to stereotype threat is dis-identification. If you anticipate the possibility is probable that you will verify some negative stereotype of your group, one way to avoid that is to dis-identify with that in some way. To reject it for your own self esteem. So dis-identification, which is not talked about as much, is also a stereotype threat response. Osborne (1995) evaluated data on academic performance and self-esteem from the National Center for Educational Statistics for 24,599 8th grade students from over 1,000 different schools in the United States. He looked at correlations between GPA and self-esteem for Black and White males and females in the 8th and 10th grade. In the 8th grade, the correlations are fairly high and fairly equal across gender and race categories (WM = .23; WF = .27; BM = .20; BF = .25). By the 10th grade, the correlation is almost the same for White females (.26) and White males (.24). It drops a fair amount for Black females (.20), but for Black males the drop is precipitous (.08). So, what happens between the 8th and 10th grade? By the 10th grade, it becomes very clear that Black males do not link their self-esteem to academic performance. I'm sure that you have all sorts of theories and ideas about why that might be, but here is an example of a 25,000-student sample followed in schools around the country. We are talking about a pretty robust finding here. You can label it however you want, and we can theorize however you want, but the fact is that this is the kind of disengagement that certainly shows up as a statistic in studies of inequality . . . you can see there is a fundamental problem with lack of education and the nature of jobs, particularly in urban environments. That is a death sentence if you do not have those kinds of attributes and experiences.

All of these psychological processes and structural patterns, in different levels and different ways, I submit, contribute to a continuing infrastructure of racial inequality, an infrastructure that manifests itself in strong and silent ways. And policy makers are operating at a level that will protect those mechanisms and further adopt and embrace perspectives, values, and beliefs that make the inequality that arises accepted as perfectly normal.

The New South Africa: Observations and Reflections

The new South Africa was one of the themes we came across when we were in South Africa. I have four points to summarize my experience in South Africa. The first is that South Africa reinvented itself as a multiracial democracy in part to trigger reconciliation. And I do believe that they have obviously reinvented themselves as a multiracial democracy because they were not a democracy, and although there are many races, they were not a multiracial society, but maybe I got that wrong. But true reconciliation was a very important part of that, and I will say more about that in a minute. It also became clear to me that Nelson Mandela put his personal charismatic humanitarian mark on the evolution of South Africa, and it was powerful enough for me to believe that no other person that I knew about could have had that profound of an influence on that society. Again, I might be wrong. I also found it important that the relevant historical experience of Apartheid informed South African development as a society, and I contrast that with the fact that we want to just forget about slavery, forget about Jim Crow, forget about everything that is in the past. But in South Africa, that past is more recent, which makes it more salient and accessible, but it is also formulated directly into the statutes and policies that have been adopted as a way of creating a new South Africa. Finally, the cultural principle of *Ubuntu* created the possibility of forgiveness. I think this transformation of South Africa includes a controversial but very important general principle of forgiveness. How can people who have been oppressed so violently for so long adopt a multicultural, multiracial society that includes and encompasses all people? That is an extremely important question.

An association of some 45–50 social behavioral scientists, myself included, traveled around South Africa and learned about social reconciliation and its problems, health (and mental health) issues, etc. It was a wonderful and profound experience for all of us and we learned a lot. As I said, it kept me thinking about the contrast with our (American) society. A billboard outside our hotel room in Johannesburg, with a picture of a Black woman with a Black child and White man with a White child said, "There's more pulling us together than keeping us apart." I was impressed, because it captured this conclusion that it is a society in which everyone is included and is taking part, and you see it in so many different and subtle ways. We saw it in other billboards around South Africa; there is a very strong message that is being given to people in South Africa.

We visited the Apartheid museum, and as I said before, remembering Apartheid is important, and the museum is a very powerful representation of a very recent history, a painful history, a violent history, and a history, I would guess, that South Africans would feel as powerfully about as we feel about the Civil Rights movement and what we learned from that. Before I went to Cape Town, people told me it was like the Riviera, and when we got there, it was an incredibly beautiful place. But in the process of going around South Africa, you learn about the way they used to treat the people who lived there and created conditions that were ripe for social pathology and the self-fulfilling prophecy of Apartheid. The idea that Cape Town should belong to the people it belongs to is a continuing issue in that society.

We visited the townships. I grew up in Ohio, and for a while I lived in the projects, and the Ohio projects are different from the high-rise projects. There were one- or two-story houses that were built after the Second World War. We had little neighborhood streets with lawns, and it was actually kind of cool. And the striking thing to me was that what I got a sense of, being in these townships, was that it was like the projects, that people liked being there, they liked the community, and it was important to them to have those relationships, but they did not appreciate the kind of discrimination that they continued to experience. So if they could just have the other assets and the ability to control their lives, living in the townships would not necessarily be as bad as one might think. Of course, they have photographs of Puff Daddy and Will Smith, so the influence of the West is pretty evident. The evidence of religious influences is very clear as well.

We also went to the shantytowns. The shantytowns are not like the townships. They are really poor with minimally viable houses. And the people who live there are often people who have come to look for work, and they have no money. They usually just put up a tin roof, they have no running water, and the housing is a major problem. There are things that the government wants to do on behalf of the people, but you really wonder how they will be able to get it done.

We went to Robben Island, and I think anyone who goes there has the feeling of being in the presence of Nelson Mandela and experiencing the kind of sentiment and humanity that he must have felt for the 18 years he was imprisoned on Robben Island. It was a powerful experience. There is a story, and a very important story, about how a guard came to have respect for Mandela, and one day, Mandela got a visit from his grandchild and they were told they were not allowed, when in fact the guard decided he would arrange a way for them to see Mandela. So he brought the baby around the back so that Nelson could see her, and after he accomplished that, he had to disguise the fact that he had done it. The point is, that even the guard was a victim of Apartheid himself, but there was humanity there. He found a way to let that humanity become part of his relationship with Nelson Mandela, and with Nelson Mandela's family. So even in the most draconian circumstance, there is opportunity for humanity to rise up, and that was one of the important lessons.

In South Africa, the Proof of Reconciliation Commission [PRC] was conceived as a way to adjudicate the end of Apartheid and the creation of a new democratic society. And they considered a number of options. One was a Nuremberg trial option in which they would essentially search out perpetrators and try them. The other was like amnesty. These are extremes and they rejected both of them and created the Proof of Reconciliation Commission.

The principle of the Proof of Reconciliation Commission was that people who confessed to what they had done were given amnesty, and people who could prove that they had been hurt were eligible for compensation and reparation. And so that process played out over two years and the result of it was the instillation of a view that says that everyone should have an equal place in society. You had to allow for that animosity and anger to be deadened. The PRC was mostly successful in doing that. There are a lot of critiques of it, since a lot of people think that Whites got more out of it than Blacks did, which is probably true, but it did establish a cultural approach that is powerful.

Ubuntu is a cultural concept of forgiveness. Bishop Desmond Tutu (1999) asked, what would motivate a person to forgive rather than seek retribution, and he said it's the spirit of *Ubuntu*. What is this *Ubuntu*? It is the spirit of humanity and can be characterized by the expression, "My humanity is inextricably bound up in yours, I am human because I belong, I participate, I share." The whole idea is the idea of connectedness and relations among people, and humanity is dependent upon that concept. So a cultural approach that separates people, and we do this all the time, is very un-*Ubuntu*-like. I want to foreshadow the idea that some *Ubuntu*-like principle is important for us to try to achieve a socially just society. Forgiveness is a consequence of, and a characteristic of, this kind of sentiment, and it is not just altruistic, but also life affirming and self interested. Forgiveness is not letting people get away with stuff. It is a way to protect your own humanity, and to avoid dehumanizing others, because that dehumanizes you, and to recognize that your goals to survive depend upon your humanity. Forgiveness is a very positive attribute. And it is very hard for people to imagine forgiveness as a principle for adjudicating race relations in America.

I will briefly go through a couple of characteristics of the Constitution, which was written with clear consciousness of the abuses of Apartheid and with the desire to undo the negative consequences of it. The Preamble to the Constitution of South Africa establishes very clearly that South Africa belongs to all the people who live in it, united in our diversity (diversity is a core value of the South African constitution). And it is important to recognize the past and get beyond it. It lays the foundation for a democratic and open society, and a new united democratic South Africa is the goal. Among the final provisions are the core values of human dignity and non-racialism and non-sexism. I could tell you Nelson Mandela's opening lines from his inauguration speech as the first president of the New South Africa in 1994, in which he specifically mentions the non-racial and non-sexist provisos. Other provisions include languages. There are 11 official languages in South Africa and all official languages must be treated equitably. I can only contrast this with "English only" in America and with the opposition to bilingual education. It is just striking that we would have a society that values languages to this degree compared to one that is so intent on protecting just one. Not only are their official languages valued, but all languages used are valued. So, in South Africa, any language used in the course of everyday life is to be respected.

In the Bill of Rights, through the Constitution, a person in South Africa enjoys the right to make decisions in regards to reproduction. The Constitution guarantees it so they do not have to be sorry about *Roe v. Wade* or any legal matters. A person in South Africa enjoys the right to security and control of their body and the right not to be subjected to medical or psychological experiments without their informed consent. (Now they had to have got that from the Tuskegee incident!) Regarding education, everyone has the right to education, but further, everyone has the right to receive education in the official language or languages of their choice in public educational institutions. I want to go back to Ebonics here, and the idea that when you think about language as an instrument of culture, we are saying that everyone has a right to be instructed in the culture of their origin. How do you accomplish that? It is pretty challenging! Regardless, the sentiment is a powerful one and I believe that school reform in this country can learn a little bit about trying to find ways to educate people so that they can learn in the environment that is most conducive to their race. Language is a contract or a relationship between many different people in the learning environment.

From the South Africa website, the Labor Act of 1997 establishes Affirmative Action as a legitimate approach to including equity and diversity in the workplace. Further, preferential treatment in appointments and promotions, as well as accelerated development and advancement, are commonly referred to as affirmative action. So preferential treatment is part of affirmative action in South Africa. In our country, a majority opposes affirmative action except in very special cases, and particularly if it mentions preferential treatment at all. Preferences are almost the defining quality of the program in South Africa. I am not arguing that we should have preferences here because South Africa does, but there is a contrast that you cannot help but notice.

A Cultural Framework for Achieving Social Justice: Extrapolating Principles From South Africa

A cultural framework for achieving social justice. I believe that *Ubuntu* as a way of protecting diversity, as a fundamentally human way to relate to people in a broad way, is a framework for achieving social justice in America. Compassion, caring, humanity, belonging, and participation are all instruments of a strong, positive cultural identity and cultural matter. And I believe that there is evidence already in the work we do with inter-group relations, school reform, teaching, and instruction that already embraces this element of *Ubuntu*. I picked three that I thought were particularly useful.

First is a common group identity model, which shows that you can create in-group synergy by bringing people from different groups into the same group, and utilize the positive values of the group culture to break down the boundaries between groups. One particular study using the Green Circle, which is a program for creating this kind of sentiment in 2nd- and 3rd-grade children, was able to use this technique to produce very positive effects including altering the tendency of children to choose as their best friends, other children who had no different qualities than they did. After intervention, they were more likely to choose friends that were different from them. I think that is a very positive consequence.

My colleagues developed a teacher-development program called Talent Quest (Boykin, 2002), by investigating integrity, complexity, coherence, texture, lived experience, and context. Methods emphasize collaboration, communal techniques, and democratic principles in the multiple levels of interaction between teachers, parents, administrators, and children that are culture-specific and culture-relevant.

And finally, we have an Intergroup Relations Program (Gurin, Nagda, Ratnesh, & Lopez, 2004), at the University of Michigan, which shows that diversity in school enhances civil leadership and civil participation, which is so fundamental to any society's ability to function. Gurin finds that as people become more interested in other people, they are more likely to do civic things, they are more likely to live in integrated environments, they have friends of different races, they do not worry about other groups, they believe that diversity is a good thing, and so on. Many very positive consequences accrue from simply having these experiences during your undergraduate years, and then following though after you graduate. Thus, there is evidence of the real benefit of taking the kind of caring and sharing involvement perspective that I found to be so important in the transformation of old South Africa to the new South Africa. I want to bring that lesson back as a guide when we think about what we have to do. The principles employed there are the ones that we need to look at, to think about, and figure out how to apply to our current situation.

Next, the cultural framework of reconciliation. I think that reconciliation will go forward if we find a way to acknowledge the past's influence in the present. The past does influence, and modern inequality is historically derived. You cannot get away with saying "I wasn't there so it doesn't affect me." We need to create new superordinate multicultural identities. South Africa has new identities and they work hard at it in everything they do. I think we have to recognize that the identity of the founding fathers is not adequate to be the identity of contemporary America. So we have to find some new identities and create a meaning out of that coming together that has coherence to it. Cultural transformation is the application and the broad proof of the *Ubuntu* in our society. And if you do have that kind of principle as a transforming idea, relations in the community become automatic and obvious, and it reduces the opposition to those problems and their solutions.

Concluding Comment

I close with a quote that I continue to find particularly apt, and I use it because it comes from Xerox Corporation and it says,

> I am convinced that diversity is the key to success, experience tells us that the most diverse companies, companies ruled by a hierarchy of imagination and filled with all ages races and backgrounds are the most successful. Some how diversity breeds creativity. Maybe it's because people of different backgrounds challenge each others underlying assumptions bringing everyone from conventional orthodoxies. We at Xerox provide the shining proof that diversity and all it's wonderful manifestations is good for business, good for our country, and good for people.

Note

1. This Clayton lecture, given in 2004, preceded a more expanded lecture given on the same topic in 2006 during Professor Jones' Presidential Address to the Biennial Convention of the Society for the Psychological Study of Social Issues (SPSSI). The SPSSI paper was subsequently published and is included in the Reference section of this chapter. It is highly recommended for further reading.

References

Bakke v. California Board of Regents, 438 U.S. 265 (1978).

Bargh, J. A. (1994). The four horsemen of automaticity: Awareness, intention, efficiency, and controlin social cognition. In R. S. Wyer & T. K. Srull (Eds.), *Handbook of social cognition, Vol. 1: Basic processes* (2nd ed.) (pp. 1–40). Hillsdale, NJ: Erlbaum.

Bell, D. (2004). The potential value of losing *Brown v. Board*. In J. Anderson & D. N. Byrne (Eds.), *The unfinished agenda of* Brown v. Board of Education (pp. 63–76). New York, NY: Wiley.

Berkowitz, L., & Walster, E. (Eds.). (1976). *Advances in experimental social psychology. Vol. 9, Equity theory: Toward a general theory of social interaction*. San Diego, CA: Academic Press.

Boykin, A. W. (2002). Talent development, cultural deep structure, and school reform: Implications for African immersion initiatives. In S. J. Denbo & L. M. Beaulieu (Eds.), *Improving schools for African American students: A reader for educational leaders* (pp. 81–94). Springfield, IL: Charles C. Thomas.

Boykin, A.W., & Jones, J. M. (2004). The psychological evolution of Black children's education since *Brown*. In J. Anderson & D. N. Byrne (Eds.), *The unfinished agenda of* Brown v. Board of Education (pp. 138–150). New York, NY: Wiley.

Brown v. Board of Education of Topeka, 347 U.S. 483 (1954).

Correll, J., Park, B., Judd, C. M., & Wittenbrink, B. (2002). The police officer's dilemma: Using ethnicity to disambiguate potentially threatening individuals. *Journal of Personality and Social Psychology, 83*, 1314–1329.

D'Souza, D. (1995). *The end of racism: Principles for a multiracial society.* New York, NY: The FreePress.

De Tocqueville, A. (1945). *Democracy in America.* New York, NY: Vintage Books.

Devine, P. G., & Baker, S. M. (1991). Measurement of racial stereotype subtyping. *Personality and Social Psychology Bulletin, 17*(1), 44–50.

Devos, T., & Banaji, M. R. (2005). American = White? *Journal of Personality and Social Psychology, 88*, 447–466.

Dovidio, J. F., Kawakami, K., & Gaertner, S. L. (2002). Implicit and explicit prejudice and interracialinteraction. *Journal of Personality and Social Psychology, 82*, 62–68.

Dweck, C. S., & Leggett, E. (1988). A social-cognitive approach to motivation and personality. *Psychological Review, 95*(2), 256–273.

Eastland, T., & Bennett, W. J. (1979). *Counting by race: Equality from the founding fathers to Bakkeand Weber.* New York, NY: Basic Books.

Eberhardt, J. L. (2005). Imaging race. *American Psychologist, 60*(2), 181–190.

Eberhardt, J. L., Dasgupta, N., & Banaszynski, T. L. (2003). Believing is seeing: The effects of racial labels and implicit beliefs on face perception. *Personality and Social Psychology Bulletin, 29*(3), 360–370.

Eberhardt, J. L., Goff, P. A., Purdie, V. J., & Davies, P. G. (2004). Seeing Black: Race, crime, and visualprocessing. *Journal of Personality and Social Psychology, 87*(6), 876–893.

Fine, M. (2004). The power of the *Brown v. Board of Education* decision: Theorizing threats to sustainability. *American Psychologist, 59*, 502–510.

Franklin, J. H., & Starr, I. (Eds.), (1967). *The Negro in twentieth century America.* New York, NY: Vintage Books.

Futrell, M. H. (2004).The impact of the *Brown* decision on African American educators. In J. Anderson & D. N. Byrne (Eds.), *The unfinished agenda of* Brown v. Board of Education (pp. 79–96). New York, NY: John Wiley.

Gaertner, S. L., & Dovidio, J. F. (2000). *Reducing intergroup bias: The common ingroup identity model.* Philadelphia, PA: Psychology Press.

Gobodo-Madikizela, P. (2003). *A human being died that night: A South African story of forgiveness*. Boston, MA: Houghton-Mifflin.

Greenwald, A. G., & Banaji, M. R. (1995). Implicit social cognition: Attitudes, self-esteem, and stereotypes. *Psychological Review, 102*(1), 4–27.

Greenwald, A. G., McGhee, D. E., & Schwartz, J. L. K. (1998). Measuring individual differences inimplicit cognition: The implicit association test. *Journal of Personality and Social psychology, 74*(6), 1464–1480.

Gurin, P., Gurin, G., Lao, R. C., & Beattie, M. (1969). Internal-external control in the motivational dynamics of Negro youth.*Journal of Social Issues, 25*(3), 29–53.

Gurin, P., Nagda, B., Ratnesh, A., & Lopez, G. E. (2004). The benefits of diversity in education fordemocratic citizenship. *Journal of Social Issues, 60*(1), 17–34.

Henderson, C. B. (2004). Reaffirming the legacy. In J. Anderson & D. N. Byrne (Eds.), *The unfinished agenda of* Brown v. Board of Education (pp. 165–170). New York, NY: Wiley.

Houlette, M. A., Gaertner, S. L., Johnson, K. M., Banker, B. S., Riek, B. M., & Dovidio, J. F. (2004). Developing a more inclusive social identity: An elementary school intervention. *Journal of Social Issues, 60*(1), 35–55.

Jones, J. M. (1997). *Prejudice and racism* (2nd ed.). New York, NY: McGraw Hill.

Jones, J. M. (2006). From racial inequality to social justice: The legacy of *Brown v. Board* and lessons from South Africa. *Journal of Social Issues, 62*(4), 885–909.

Jost, J. T., & Banaji, M. R. (1994). The role of stereotyping in system-justification and the production of false consciousness. *British Journal of Social Psychology. Special Issue: Stereotypes: Structure, function and process, 33*(1), 1–27.

Jost, J. T., Glaser, J., Kruglanski, A. W., & Sulloway, F. J. (2003). Political conservatism as motivated social cognition. *Psychological Bulletin, 129*(3), 339–375.

Major, B., Gramzow, R. H., McCoy, S. K., Levin, S., Schmader, T., & Sidanius, J. (2002). Perceiving personal discrimination: The role of group status and legitimizing ideology. *Journal of Personality and Social Psychology, 82*(3), 269–282.

McCullough, M. E. (2001). Forgiveness: Who does it and how do they do it? *Current Directions in Psychological Science, 10*(6), 194–197.

Myrdal, G. (1944). *An American dilemma: The Negro problem and modern democracy*. New York, NY: Harper & Row.

Nosek, B. A., Greenwald, A. G., & Banaji, M. R. (2005). Understanding and using the Implicit Association Test: II. Method variables and construct validity. *Personality and Social Psychology Bulletin, 31*(2), 166–180.

Orfield, G. (2004). *Brown* misunderstood. In J. Anderson & D. N. Byrne (Eds.), *The unfinished agenda of* Brown v. Board of Education (pp. 153–163). New York, NY: Wiley.

Osborne, J. W. (1995). Academics, self-esteem, and race: A look at the underlying assumptions of the disidentification hypothesis. *Personality and Social Psychology Bulletin, 21*(5), 449–455.

Pennebaker, J. W., Barger, S. D., & Tiebout, J. (1989). Disclosure of traumas and health among Holocaust survivors. *Psychosomatic Medicine, 51*(5), 577–589.

Pettigrew, T. F. (2004, June). *Still a long way to go: American Black-White relations today.* Invited address, fourth biennial conference of the Society for the Psychological Study of Social Issues, Washington, DC.

Prentice, D. A., & Miller, D. T. (1999). The psychology of cultural contact. In D. A. Prentice & D.T. Miller (Eds.), *Cultural divides: Understanding and overcoming group conflict* (pp. 1–19). New York, NY: Russell Sage Foundation.

Richeson, J. A., & Nussbaum, R. J. (2003). The impact of multiculturalism versus color-blindness on racial bias. *Journal of Experimental Social Psychology, 40*(3), 417–423.

Ross, L., Amabile, T. M., & Steinmetz, J. L. (1977). Social roles, social control, and biases in social-perception processes. *Journal of Personality and Social Psychology, 35*(7), 485–494.

Shelton, J. N., & Richeson, J. A. (2005). Intergroup contact and pluralistic ignorance. *Journal of Personality and Social Psychology, 88*(1), 91–107.

Sidanius, J., & Pratto, F. (1999). Social dominance: An intergroup theory of social hierarchy and oppression. New York, NY: Cambridge University Press.

Steele, C. M. (1992). Minds wasted, minds saved: Crisis and hope in the schooling of Black Americans. *The Atlantic Monthly, 269*, 68–78.

Steele, C. M., & Aronson, J. (1995). Stereotype threat and the intellectual test performance of Black Americans. *Journal of Personality and Social Psychology, 69*(5), 797–811.

Stewart, S. D. (2004). *Remarks.* Retrieved August 16, 2006, from http://www.fanniemaefoundation.org/news/Speeches/CBC04.pdf.

Tatum, B. D. (1998). *Why are all the Black kids sitting together in the cafeteria? And other conversations about race.* New York, NY: Harper-Collins.

Tutu, D. M. (1999). *No future without forgiveness.* New York, NY: Doubleday.

United Nations Development Programme (1993). *Human development report.* New York, NY: OxfordUniversity Press. Retrieved from http://hdr.undp.org/en/reports/

Witvliet, C.V., Ludwig, T. E., & Vander Laan, K. L. (2001). Granting forgiveness or harboring grudges:Implications for emotion, physiology and health. *Psychological Science, 12*(2), 117–123.

Response to 2004 Clayton Lecture by Dr. James Jones

AUDREY MBEJE
University of Pennsylvania

Professor Jones addresses an important issue of racial/social inequalities and offers an interesting vision of how we can actually address the problem. Your discussion of how South Africa in its current reformation process is handling the problems of racial inequalities of the former apartheid era, and how the United States can learn from South Africa's approach, suggests to me that we need to go beyond our boundaries in our efforts to finding solutions to the challenges of racial/social inequalities. That, to me, is crucial, and it can yield more productive research results that can enhance the process of social change, if we can consider what we are learning from research across the borders in our ongoing process of reforming our societies—reformation is actually an ongoing process.

I do also want to mention that the history of this country has also informed most of South Africa's decisions and plans for the country's post-apartheid reformation. So, you can be sure that South Africa has also learned from the United States. It has definitely been a two-way learning process, and I think that such a sharing of ideas can be further reinforced through collaborative research of this nature with specialists in South Africa; that way we might be able to identify some commonalities, and even avoid re-inventing the wheel in this particular area of research. I think there should be more dialogue between experts in this field here and in South Africa. You clearly point out that the problem of racial inequality has become so much embedded in the culture, and I was wondering whether there are efforts in the education system to address this issue at the level of education planning. I was wondering whether you have taken any measures to inform education policy makers by sharing with them the results of such research as this. I was also wondering if there have been any efforts to address the issue through the curriculum in schools, and also how the communities may be involved to actively participate in the process of social change?

A Response to 2004 Clayton Lecture by Dr. James Jones

DAVIDO DUPREE
University of Pennsylvania

Being trained in the study of cognition and development, I couldn't help but get excited about some of the research that Dr. Jones puts forward on the cognitive representations indicating racial bias or stereotypes.

But I (also) want to cue in on something about the legacy of *Brown vs. the Board of Education*. Oftentimes we fail to effectively translate culture into school settings. It's not just the physical integration of culture into school curricula and activities. We need to start thinking about how to integrate culture in meaningful ways. Sometimes we make things so that, conceptually, culture is so romantic that it is difficult to integrate meaningfully into curriculum. We often focus on things such as food and dress, and it goes so much deeper than that. Often it's about the meaning that we give to our culture beyond our experiences. Dr. Jones explained this point in his presentation when he spoke about the difference between the eighth grade and the tenth grade when there is a drastically changing relationship between self-esteem and GPA. He called it dis-identification. In particular, Black males dis-identify with school between eighth and tenth grade. I think that's an important point in the concept of de-segregation. When you approach the complex processes being described here, I would think to some extent it's (i.e., the dis-identification) protective.

We at CHANGES (Center for Health Achievement Neighborhood Growth and Ethnic Studies) have conducted our own research with high-performing and marginally performing students. Among other things, our research is concerned with understanding how identity processes can affect educational outcomes. Among the measures that we used was the Multi-Dimensional Inventory of Black Identity. There's a construct in the measure that is important to this discussion. It is the Oppressed Minority ideology. The concept represented is not exactly as the name implies. The person who endorses this ideology believes that Blacks are oppressed, that there are other minority groups who are also oppressed, and that these groups should come together to address these issues. Ironically, endorsement of that ideology is associated with higher self-esteem. And when you think about this finding with respect to Black males who dis-identify with school between eighth and tenth grade, there are important implications. What this suggests is that either on their own, or with the help of some more sophisticated peers or adults, they learn to make meaning of these dissonant experiences that could potentially cause them to dis-identify with school. In order to protect their sense of self, they had to give some meaning to these dissonant experiences. From the point of view of the young Black male, if I understand some systematic things are going on, then I will not internalize this dissonance that I'm experiencing.

It's also important that this distinction be identified between the United States and South Africa in that they acknowledge Apartheid in many ways, in formal ways. As Dr. Jones said, the relevant historical experience of Apartheid informed South African development. I think that's a critical difference, and any intervention here needs to take that into account. We need to help make meaning of what they (students of color in the United States) are experiencing, whether it involves research activities or not. Hopefully we can.

Addendum

Since this presentation was delivered, Dupree, Spencer, and Fegley (2007) published a chapter entitled, "Perceived social inequity and responses to conflict among diverse youth of color: The effects of social and physical context." Extending the analyses discussed in my response to Dr. Jones' lecture, we found that high academically performing youth of color were more likely than marginally performing youth of color to endorse the Oppressed Minority Ideology (e.g., acknowledge that oppressive processes underlie racial disparities). These findings relate to my previous suggestion about integrating cultural meaning-making into interventions for youth of color. Specifically, the findings suggest that the complexity with which youth are culturally socialized to think about personally relevant social issues (e.g., Apartheid, segregation, oppression, etc.) may reflect the complexity and depth with which they are encouraged to think more generally. The same cultural socialization processes that encourage and/or give youth the ability to think about racial disparities in more complex ways may also be the processes that encourage them to interpret academic challenges in more complex ways that support and sustain motivation for higher academic performance. In contrast, allowing simplistic views of complex social issues to prevail encourages stereotypic thinking and discourages in-depth understanding. Cultural socialization matters.

References

Dupree, D., Spencer, M. B., & Fegley, S. (2007). Perceived social inequality and responses to conflict among diverse youth of color: The effects of social and physical context on youth behavior and attitudes. In R. K. Silbereisen & R. M. Lerner (Eds.), *Approaches to positive youth development* (pp. 111–131). Thousand Oaks, CA: Sage.

10. Lifetime Effects of Participatory Preschool Education

LAWRENCE J. SCHWEINHART
HighScope Educational Research Foundation, Ypsilanti, MI

The mission of the HighScope Educational Research Foundation is *lifting lives through education*, and we think these words capture all we try to do. HighScope combines research, publishing, communication, teacher training, and curriculum development. But mainly, we combine public policy and practice with research. Day to day, practitioners and researchers collaborate. This is the essence or genius of HighScope that affects all our curriculum development and research.

Design of the HighScope Perry Preschool Study

Now, let us go back to the past. I can talk about preschool programs' effects over all of this time because our studies were *experimentally designed*. The HighScope Perry Preschool Study (Schweinhart, Montie, Xiang, Barnett, Belfield, & Nores, 2005) started out with a group of young African American children living in poverty and atrisk of school failure; 123 of them were identified between 1962 and 1965, one class at a time. Then, with each of these classes of 20 to 25 children, we randomly assigned children either to the program group or the no-program group. The scientific value of this study comes from this random assignment, essentially a flip of the coin that placed children in one group or the other.

Each of these 123 young children had an equal chance of either being in the program or not being in the program. That led to initially similar program and no-program groups. The groups were alike in almost every way, except for the fact that one of them had a preschool program and one did not. Nobody chose to be in the preschool program; rather, they chose to be in the study. The families in the program group did not differ from those in the no-program group in how much they valued education or how much they wanted their children to have a good early childhood educational experience. Such differences would constitute selection bias that would raise questions about whether a group difference in outcomes might have been due to preexisting group differences in disposition. But these children were randomly selected and put in one group or the other, so the differences between the two groups are most likely due to the program.

Here is one description of the program: Four teachers with bachelor's degrees held a daily class for 20 to 25 three- and four-year-olds and made weekly home visits. We will talk about that in more depth. Another way to describe the program is by its process. Children participated in their own education by planning, doing, and reviewing their own activities—very different from education as we remember it and as we typically experience it. In other words, active participation was not limited to the teachers and parents; the children themselves participated actively by planning, doing, and reviewing their activities.

Results of the HighScope Perry Preschool Study

Here is a summary of all the findings over time. The age 40 effects did not just appear from nowhere and would not be very credible if they did. Rather, they developed over time. In Figure 10.1, the gray bar represents the program group, the white bar represents the no-program group, and the difference between them is the program effect. In the first comparison, without the program only 28% of the children were ready for school; but

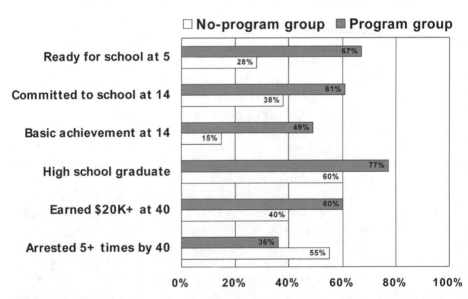

Figure 10.1. HighScope Perry Preschool Study: Major findings over time.

with the program, two-thirds of the program group were ready, twice as many. Readiness was identified here by a measure of intellectual performance. There has been a lot of talk about the fadeout of effects on intellectual performance. But IQ tests are not particularly good tests of the effects of early childhood programs, except perhaps at ages four and five. Their utility was primarily in showing that children were better prepared for school.

The next two findings involve *Commitment to school at age 14*, and *Basic achievement at age 14*. They are the glue that carries the effects through schooling. When you enter school, if you have success you get more committed to it and consequently have more success. If you fail, you get less committed to it and fail more. It is a principle of life in general. My favorite personal example is about me and rollerblading. I am a failure with rollerblading, an unqualified failure. One time at a nearby park, I had access to free use of rollerblades so I figured, "Well, I'll give it a shot, I've never done that before." It was very difficult for me to move, and I remember this little girl saying to her mother, "Why did that man fall down?" and her mother said, "Well, look, it's okay, he's getting up, see, he'll be alright." These kinds of experiences do not make you want to do stuff again, and in fact, I have never tried to rollerblade again. Now you take that same kind of experience, day in and day out with your performance in school, you can see how this cycle goes one way or the other. The idea here is to help children be more ready for school so that they are more successful when they start school. Success breeds commitment, commitment breeds success, and it goes all the way through school. You can see the evidence at age 14, nine years later, that children were more committed to school, that is, they did more homework, they were more likely to talk to their parents about school, and they had a more positive attitude towards school. Regarding *Basic achievement test at 14*, only 15% of the no-program group passed the test as compared to about half of the program group. This was the biggest effect on school achievement we found.

We found smaller effects on school achievement at first, second, third, fourth, and fifth grades. Then, eighth grade came along, and that is about the time that I joined the study and analyzed these data and found a great big effect. The intellectual performance effects did not explain the achievement effect because it had disappeared by then. It turns out that the age 14 test was a lot harder than the previous achievement tests. Children were coasting through the earlier tests, but now that they faced the harder tests, it was not their intellectual performance that carried their day, but rather their commitment and motivation. Their desire to do well on their tests helped them to do better on the tests. Another factor was the difference in special educational placement, particularly for educable mental impairment. Basically, fewer program group children than no-program group children needed treatment for mental impairment. Put these three things together and you can see the differences in school experiences that eventually lead to differences in the *High school graduation* rate, 77% versus 60%.

Then we have *Earned $20,000 or more at age 40*: 60% for the program group and only 40% for the no-program group. *Arrested 5 or more times by age 40* went down from 55% to 36%. These findings show, unfortunately, how poverty predicts a lot of failure in people's lives. Parents of study participants averaged a ninth grade education and were unemployed or had unskilled jobs. These factors predict so much about their children's lifetime earnings and how many crimes they were going to commit, with 55% arrested five or more times. The preschool program helped some of the children break loose of this crime that was rampant in their neighborhoods.

Let's take a closer look at some of the age 40 findings starting with educational attainment. In Figure 10.2, the dark gray is *College attendance*, and it is twice as much as the program group, but not many attended college. Then, in light gray, you have *Graduated from high school* and you have 68% plus 9% in higher education for the program group, so 77% graduated. You get the total graduation from high school for the no-program group (55% plus 5%), which adds up to 60%. Looking at *High school dropout*, in white, we have 23% of the program group versus 40% of the no-program group. So, one out of five preschool program kids have dropped out of school as compared to two out of five in the no-program group.

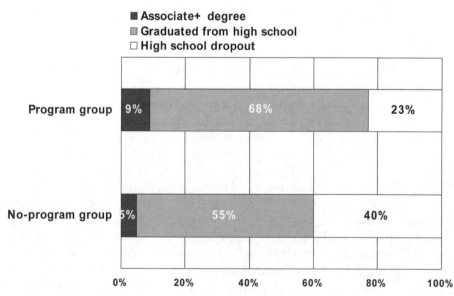

Figure 10.2. HighScope Perry Preschool Study: More high school graduates.

Now, let's look at employment and earnings, Figure 10.3. The data are so consistent at ages 19, 27, and 40. More of the program group than the no-program group were employed at age 40 and at age 27, a persistent edge in employment rate that lasts through life, lifetime effects. Now look at the earnings, which are consistent with the employment findings—a $5,500 advantage at age 40, a $2,000 advantage at age 27, again suggesting higher earnings throughout lifetimes.

The only difference between these two groups is that one had a preschool program and the other did not.

Here are several perspectives on the crime findings. There is about half as much crime, half as many arrests, in the program group as in the no-program group. That generalization applies to violent crime, drug crime, and property crime, and you can see in Figure 10.4, that there are substantial reductions in each of those. Violent crime reductions were mostly in assault and/or battery, threatened assault, and disorderly conduct. Drug crime, basically drug dealing, was cut by half from 34% to 14% by participation in the preschool program. Property offenses dropped from 58% to 36%, and that was mostly larceny, that is, stealing. Looking at specific types of crime does not reveal some underlying pattern that is not in evidence in the broader types. The program group certainly has greater impulse control. This program is preventing anti-social behavior in a variety of manifestations.

There are some other findings regarding family relations, shown in Figure 10.5. This first finding is interesting because it was so unexpected. Looking at the males only, we crossed *Ever had a child* (a biological child) and *Ever raised a child*. Remarkably, we found that almost twice as many of the

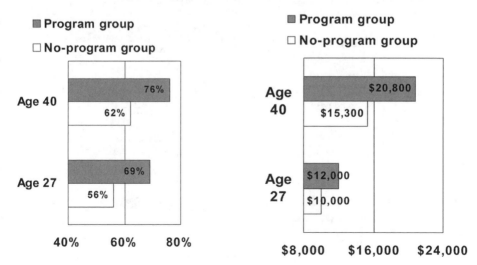

Figure 10.3. HighScope Perry Preschool Study: More employed, higher earnings.

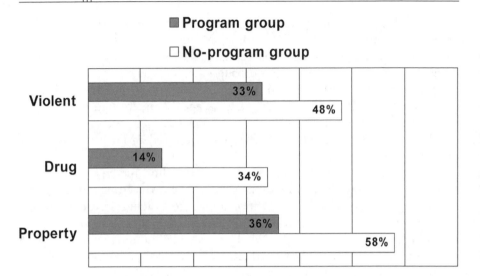

Figure 10.4. HighScope Perry Preschool Study: Fewer arrested for various types of crimes.

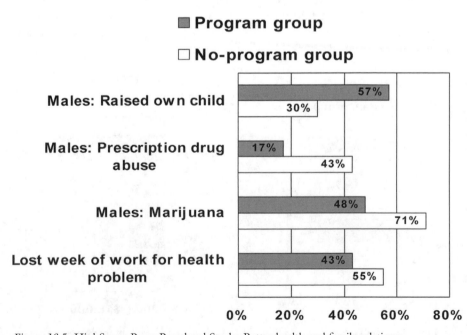

Figure 10.5. HighScope Perry Preschool Study: Better health and family relations.

program males were raising their own child as compared to the no-program males. We found differences for the males in *Prescription drug abuse* and *Marijuana* usage that are all consistent with the drug finding that I told you about earlier. The one general health finding, *Lost a week of work or more for health problem,* fell from 55% down to 43%. All of these differences that I am presenting here, by the way, are statistically significant with a probability of .05 or less. We did not find many group differences in health, but then, this was not a health intervention. To explain such diverse findings, you have got to look not only to the differences in schooling, but also to the general socioeconomic differences and quality of life that might account for things like better health.

Does the program affect males and females differently? This preschool program had strong effects on females and strong effects on males, as shown in Figure 10.6. But, because male and female socialization is different, the effects manifested differently for males and females. So let's look at the strongest effect on each. The high school graduation rate difference between program and no-program females is actually one of the largest effects in the study, 88% versus 46%. Most of the program females graduated from high school and fewer than half of the no-program females graduated from high school.

Now why is that? Let me give you two or three ideas here. The first one that you will think of is probably teen pregnancy. Obviously, teenage pregnancy is a very different issue for males and females, so you think maybe fewer program females got pregnant and dropped out of school? There is such a difference in teen pregnancy, but it does not account for much of the high school graduation rate difference. What accounts for most of the difference is differential placement of girls in special education or grade repetition, and the girls who went to the preschool program were less likely to

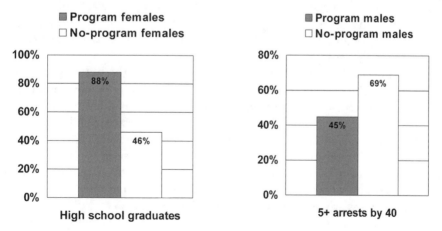

Figure 10.6. HighScope Perry Preschool Study: Different effects on males and females.

repeat a grade or be placed in special education. It may not be a dropout sentence to be retained in grade or placed in special education, but if you are so placed, chances are pretty good you are going to drop out of school. All 17 of the girls in the program group who had regular education graduated, and 10 of the 12 no-program girls who repeated a grade or were placed in special education dropped out of school.

Although we found a large program effect on the high school graduation rate of girls, we found no such effect on boys. I suspect the reason is that teachers having children repeat a grade or join special education classes focus on the academic performance of girls, but the antisocial behavior of boys. The biggest program effect difference for males was the reduction in those with five or more arrests from 69% to 45%.

This is one of the big effects of the study and represents an enormous economic saving, in fact, the major factor in the cost-benefit analysis through age 40. Michael Anderson at MIT thinks that the program had no effect on males through age 27, but here by age 40 we are looking at one of the big effects of the program. As I said, it appears to me that the preschool program had strong effects on females and strong but different effects on males.

Return on Investment

Now, let us talk about the return on investment. This has been a topic of great interest lately because economists have become interested in this project, and they have a way of getting attention that the rest of us do not. A good cost-benefit analysis is rooted in a good evaluation. A good evaluation lets you compare the costs and benefits of the program group and the no-program group and identify the differences between them as the outstanding program costs and benefits, and that is what we were able to do. What I am going to present to you is in constant dollars for the year 2000, discounted at 3% annually. The discount rate is comparable to a real interest rate over and above inflation.

In Figure 10.7, the top bar represents benefits, and the bottom bar represents costs. The cost per child of the preschool program is $15,166. That is based on the cost of 13 children who attended the program for one year and 45 children who attended for two years, so the cost per child per year was $8,540. Administrators and accountants must constantly focus on costs and seldom get a glimpse at economic benefits. Out of sight is out of mind, and cost-cutting can become the dominant economic perspective. The choice seems to be to save money by cutting back on $15,000 per child. But larger economic benefits are more important, even if they are also harder to discern. The true choice may be to reap huge economic benefits by spending $15,000 per child or to reap smaller, or no, economic benefits by spending less.

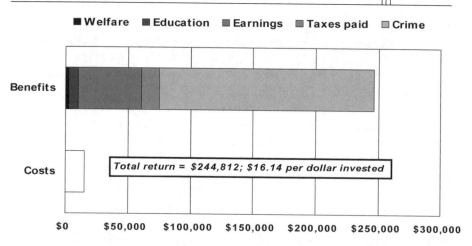

Note—Per participant in 2000 constant dollars discounted 3% annually.

Figure 10.7. HighScope Perry Preschool Study: Large return on investment.

Here are the economic benefits that flowed from that expense. There is a small welfare savings of $3,000 per person. Education savings of $7,000 per person come from reduced need for special education classes. Each program participant has $50,000 more in lifetime earnings and pays $14,000 more in taxes. The biggest benefits come from crime reduction. Criminal justice system savings are $100,000 a person, and crime victim savings are $71,000 a person. Add it up and you get $245,000 per person returned to society, all for a $15,000 investment. That is $16 per dollar invested in total—$13 back to taxpayers and $3 to each program participant.

That is an enormous return on investment. To the extent that we are not investing in such programs, we are choosing to spend 13 times as much as we would need to spend to provide them, and that is the obviously foolish choice we make over and over again. Talk about fiscal madness! Investing in these programs is the truly frugal, conservative fiscal policy.

Five Ingredients of Effective Preschool Programs

But it's not enough simply to spend the money. To get what we got, you've got to do what we did. Here are the five key ingredients of what we did.

First, teachers help children participate in their own education. Both teachers and children plan their own activities. Second, teachers lead classes of three- and four-year-olds, including those at risk for school failure, with an adult for every eight children. These classes can be open to all children, but the returns will be greatest for those at risk of school failure. Similarly,

Perry was a part-day program, but the same curriculum could take place in a full-day program. Third, teachers visit the families frequently to discuss their children's development. The Perry teachers visited families every week. In a subsequent program we ran, teachers visited families every two weeks with similar results to Perry. Teachers might visit with families in the classroom rather than their homes, but that would sacrifice the affirmation of the home as a place for learning that comes with home visits. The point is to approximate what was done in the Perry program, to come close, if not to replicate exactly. If you do something completely different, you can't expect the Perry results to apply; another study is needed.

The fourth ingredient is qualified teachers—a teacher with teacher certification based on a bachelor's degree leading every classroom along with a second teaching adult. The Perry program actually had four certified teachers for a class of 20 to 25 children. This unusual configuration does not need to be replicated exactly, but the principle of having a certified teacher in each classroom is based on it. The fifth ingredient is ongoing teacher training, supervision, and assessment to support the participatory educational approach. It is important for teachers to be held accountable in terms of participatory education. But it undermines the program if training, supervision, or assessment holds the participatory educational program accountable in terms of direct instruction. The two approaches often conflict with each other. All teachers need to have a plan and to know what they are doing. Participatory education teachers focus on empowering children in classrooms and empowering parents through home visits.

In the HighScope participatory education model, the classroom is arranged into activity areas rather than rows of desks. In the daily routine, children plan, do, and review their learning activities and engage in small-group and whole-group activities. Teachers help children grow by treating them with respect, engaging them in conversation, and supporting their key child development experiences. Such a classroom is very different from the commonplace teacher-directed classroom, with teachers talking 70% of the time.

Let's consider how this model prevents crime. Crime is adult antisocial behavior for which perpetrators can be arrested, tried, and sentenced. One explanation for how a preschool program prevents crime is that it prevents the antisocial behavior patterns or habits that begin in early childhood and grow into adult criminal activity. The difficulty of preventing crime with programs in adolescence or adulthood could well be due to the persistence of antisocial habits that began in early childhood. What, then, did the Perry program do to prevent young children's antisocial behavior? Clearly, it taught them to anticipate consequences, take responsibility, and take a planful approach to their activities. It taught them to resolve conflicts with other children peacefully rather than with aggression. Regrettably, we don't have data in early and later childhood to support this hypothesis. But neither do we have data to refute it, and it is the parsimonious explanation. Surely, program participants' improved school success also helped prevent their criminal activity, but this seems to be a supplemental explanation.

When I present the powerful effects of the Perry program, sometimes I think of myself as a prospector coming down from the hills with news of the discovery of gold. Everyone is intent on going about their business unless I can convince them that the gold is really there. Well, it really is. This study has high internal validity because of random assignment and low attrition. We can trust these findings, and because we can trust them, we need to use them to change public policies.

The HighScope Preschool Curriculum Comparison Study

We conducted another study that sheds further light on early childhood curriculum. It is called the HighScope Preschool Curriculum Comparison Study (Schweinhart & Weikart, 1997a, 1997b). In the study we compared three different curriculum models: the High/Scope Curriculum, which we have discussed; the Nursery School approach, in which children made their own choices and teachers provided passive support; and the Direct Instruction program, in which the teacher followed a script and asked children to provide correct answers to frequent questions. Other than curriculum, the programs were exactly alike—daily classes, biweekly home visits, the same supervisor—and the randomly assigned groups of children were quite similar in background characteristics. We found that all three of these approaches were pretty effective in helping kids to get ready for school, the Direct Instruction program a little more effective than the others.

But as children grew older, we found big advantages for the HighScope and Nursery School groups over the Direct Instruction group, as shown in Figure 10.8. Almost none of the children in the HighScope and Nursery School groups were ever treated for emotional impairment or disturbance, whereas almost half the Direct Instruction group received such treatment. Similarly, two out of five members of the Direct Instruction group were arrested for a felony by age 23, as compared with less than one out of five of the other groups. These findings suggest that preschool participatory education offers a great opportunity to prevent antisocial behavior and crime, that preschool direct instruction does not.

I was just in the Netherlands last week visiting a school that was using HighScope, and what struck me was how interesting it is to watch children engage in activities and conversation with each other as opposed to watching them just sit there listening to the teacher.

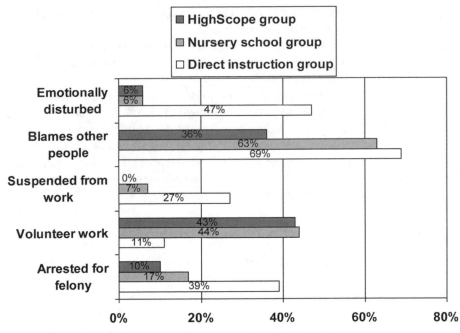

Figure 10.8. HighScope Preschool Curriculum Comparison Study.

The Training for Quality Study

We have been training and certifying HighScope teacher trainers since 1983, and these trainers have trained over 16,000 early childhood teaching teams throughout the U.S. We also have training institutes and centers in eight other countries—two in Canada, Indonesia, Ireland, Korea, Mexico, the Netherlands, South Africa, and the United Kingdom. We conducted a study to see if HighScope training led to participatory education in preschool classrooms (Epstein, 1993). In the study we found that classrooms with trained HighScope teachers have better learning environments, daily routines, adult-child interactions, and overall implementation. We were accomplishing what we wanted to accomplish in these classrooms. We looked at the children in some of the classrooms and found that they had better initiative, social relations, creative representation in arts and music, and overall development. The ultimate goal of all teacher education is to change children's outcomes in classrooms, but this is one of the only sets of studies that traces effects from teacher training through teachers' classrooms to children's outcomes.

Other Studies Finding Long-Term Effects and Return on Investment

The HighScope Perry Preschool Study is not the only study that has found long-term benefits and return on investment. Another is the North Carolina Abecedarian Project that found such effects for high-quality versus typical childcare (Campbell, Ramey, Pungello, Sparling, & Miller-Johnson, 2002). This study looked at programs operated during the late 1970s and involved random assignment of children. "Abecedarian" is a word derived from the ABCs, the basics. This study shows the value added to child care by high quality. In the Perry study, David Weikart directed both the program and the research. In the Abecedarian study, Craig Ramey directed both. While this combination may raise a question about research objectivity, it also gave the director a very clear idea of what the program needed to accomplish and thereby contributed to the program's effectiveness.

Another study that found long-term effects and return on investment was the Chicago Child Parents Center Study (Reynolds & Ou, 2011; Reynolds, Temple, White, Ou, & Robertson, 2011). This study did not involve random assignment of children, but involved rigorous statistical analyses. It complements the other two studies in that it was much larger, throughout Chicago in fact, and the research director did not administer the program. David Olds has also found long-term effects and return on investment for nurse home-visit programs, one of the few home-visit programs that has been found to have long-term effects (Olds, Kitzman, Cole, Robinson, Sidora, Luckey, et al., 2004). All these programs involved trained professionals—teachers working with children and visiting parents, or nurses visiting parents.

HighScope in Head Start

One question that comes up with our work at times is, so you did this study a long time ago, but what about today? How do these programs work in a real-life situation? Head Start's Family and Child Experiences Survey (FACES) has data regarding this question (Zill et al., 2003). Both regular Head Start classrooms and those that used HighScope were associated with improvement in children's letter and word identification, an important literacy skill. But the improvement in regular Head Start classes was only about half a point while the improvement in HighScope Head Start classes was 1.6 points. It appears that the teachers who were doing HighScope were better focusing on letter and word identification than the others. Findings were similar for improvement in children's cooperation and reduction of their hyperactivity. HighScope Head Start classes were better at helping children become more cooperative and less hyperactive.

HighScope and Literacy

HighScope has lately developed its focus on language and literacy. The High-Scope Perry Preschool Study shows that the program improved children's language and literacy from early childhood into adulthood. But literacy researchers have more recently identified specific skills that are antecedents of reading ability—phonological awareness, the alphabetic principle, concepts about print, vocabulary, and comprehension. We have been concerned that some early childhood educators were focusing on these skills but not the teaching practices that led to them, conditions favorable to teachers lapsing into a direct instructional approach. So we tied the HighScope participatory education approach to these skills and developed the Growing Readers Curriculum, with small-group times focusing on the skills, and the Early Literacy Skills Assessment (ELSA) assessing the skills as children listen to a story and answer questions about it.

The IEA Preprimary Project

HighScope also coordinated the international IEA Preprimary Project over the past decade or so in a dozen nations. Research teams in each country collaborated to develop and select instrumentation and to collect data from early childhood settings and young children around the world. We collected data from children at age four, and again at age seven, and carried out hierarchical linear modeling analysis to make sense of the data (Montie, Xiang, & Schweinhart, 2006). We arrived at four major findings, four preschool characteristics that predicted children's language or cognitive performance in all these different countries. First, free choice in participatory learning activities contributes to children's ability more than other types of activities such as preacademic lessons. Second, having fewer whole-group activities contributes to children's ability. Third, the amount and variety of materials contributes to children's ability. The more materials you have in preschool classrooms, the more children learn, although a teacher-directed approach might view these materials as distractions. Fourth, teachers' schooling contributes to children's ability. Throughout the world, in all these different countries, in Europe, Africa, and North America, free-choice activities, an absence of whole-group activities, amount and variety of materials, and teachers' schooling contribute to children's language or cognitive ability.

Conclusion

All the studies I have talked about lead to a few general conclusions. First, high-quality preschool programs for young children living in poverty have long-term effects and return on investment. These programs have such effects when they engage in participatory education in which both teachers and children make choices about activities. HighScope training has been shown to help teachers implement such programs so that they contribute to children's development. Use of HighScope in Head Start classrooms helps children develop literacy and social skills. Participatory preschool education contributes to children's development throughout the world.

References

Campbell, F. A., Ramey, C. T., Pungello, E. P., Sparling, J., & Miller-Johnson, S. (2002). Early childhood education: Young adult outcomes from the Abecedarian Project. *Applied Developmental Science, 6*(1), 42–57.

Epstein, A. S. (1993). *Training for quality: Improving early childhood programs through systematic inservice training.* Ypsilanti, MI: High/Scope Press.

Montie, J. E., Xiang, Z., & Schweinhart, L. J. (2006). Preschool experience in 10 countries: Cognitive and language performance at age 7. *Early Childhood Research Quarterly, 21*(3), 313–331.

Olds, D.L., Kitzman, H., Cole, R., Robinson, J., Sidora, K., Luckey, D.W., et al. (2004). Effects of nurse home-visiting on maternal life-course and child development: Age 6 follow-up of a randomized trial. *Pediatrics, 114*(6), 1550–1559.

Reynolds, A. J., & Ou, S. (2011). Paths of effects from preschool to adult well-being: A confirmatory analysis of the Child-Parent Center Program. *Child Development, 82*(2), 555–582.

Reynolds, A. J., Temple, J. A., White, B., Ou, S., & Robertson, D. L. (2011). Age 26 cost-benefit analysis of the Child-Parent Center Early Education Program. *Child Development, 82*(1), 379–404.

Schweinhart, L. J., & Weikart, D. P. (1997a). *Lasting differences: The High/Scope Preschool Curriculum Comparison Study through age 23. Monographs of the High/Scope Educational Research Foundation No 12.* Ypsilanti, MI: High/Scope Press.

Schweinhart, L. J., & Weikart, D. P. (1997b). The High/Scope Preschool Curriculum Comparison Study through age 23. *Early Childhood Research Quarterly, 12*(2), 117–143.

Schweinhart, L. J., Montie, J., Xiang, Z., Barnett, W. S., Belfield, C., & Nores, M. (2005). *Lifetime effects: The High/Scope Perry Preschool Study through age 40. Monographs of the High/Scope Educational Research Foundation No. 13.* Ypsilanti, MI: High/Scope Press.

Zill, N., Resnick, G., Kim, K., O'Donnell, K., Sorongon, A., McKey, R. H., et al. (May 2003). *Head Start FACES (2000): A whole-child perspective on program performance—Fourth progress report.* Prepared for the Administration for Children and Families, U.S. Department of Health and Human Services (DHHS) under contract HHS-105-96-1912, Head Start Quality Research Consortium's Performance Measures Center. Retrieved from http://www. acf.hhs.gov/programs/opre/hs/faces/reports/faces00_4thprogress/ faces00_4thprogress.pdf

11. *What Do We Expect From Girls? Confronting the Performance Gaps in Math and Science*

Pamela Trotman Reid
Saint Joseph College, Hartford, CT

I read Dr. Clayton's biography, and I really feel a strong affinity to her mission of educating urban children, and to the challenges she faced as an Educational Administrator. In fact, as I read through her biography, I noticed some striking similarities between us. Her first research efforts were with Head Start here in Philadelphia, known as Get Set. My first job in Philadelphia was as a Get Set teacher. And my master's research was with children in my research center. She attended Philadelphia's High School for Girls and I also attended an all-girl high school. She played the cello in high school and went to concerts. I played the violin and was introduced to opera. Her mother told her she could do anything. My mother also believed strongly in my abilities to succeed. She was an obedient little girl who loved to read—me too. I actually believe it is not trivial or coincidental that there are similarities between Dr. Clayton and myself. And I would venture that a number of other women who have achieved greater-than-usual success in both non-traditional and traditional ways would share some characteristics with us. That is the point of this paper, to look carefully at how girls may become successful woman.

Focusing on the Successes of Girls

First, of course, let me acknowledge that society still has a lot of problems and issues that have not been dealt with in respect to boys. I know I have to say that because there is always someone out there worrying—what about the boys? But this program is really focused on the girls because there is still a need to attend to the success of girls. Perhaps it seems obvious that as an African American woman I will pay particular note to the disparities for girls of color, but I actually think it reflects more on my personal experience than my personhood. Not only did I attend an all-girl high school, as I mentioned, I also matriculated at a historically Black university, Howard University in Washington, DC. Seeing girls and Black students play all the roles, as they can when they are in a single-sex or single-predominantly race environment—not just the ones that are prescribed in the co-ed or more mixed settings—enabled me, in fact maybe forced me, to become aware of how stereotypes in our society can limit us, mislead us, and maybe distort our sense of reality in a number of ways.

Organizing Ideas and Concepts for the "GO-GIRL" Program

Before describing my working model of "GO-GIRL," the intervention program for middle school girls, let me make clear that I have a number of organizing ideas. Here are some conceptual assumptions.

The Construction of Social Identity

First, each social identity is constructed within the context while simultaneously creating a context. So, whether we are talking about gender, social class, or ethnic identity, our construction and understanding of that identity occurs within the unique context of our family, our community, and the larger society. For example, being poor is more than just economic deprivation. It colors the lens through which a poor person sees the world. And at the same time, that deprivation shades how the world views a poor person. Socialization and social identities prescribe the set of responses to which individuals have access. So, within that community and family, we learn how to behave as male or female, as a White person or as an African American person, as a poor person or as an affluent person, or as whatever those identities may be. The negatively constructed identities that persons may have will diminish their capacity, both directly, and indirectly through the expectations and the context inherent in the physical and social environments. So, for example, as a girl, I encountered gender stereotyping when friends' parents articulated their norms for girls' behaviors. Some parents thought that girls clean up the kitchen but boys mow the lawn. Growing up as the oldest of three girls with no brothers I actually was expected to do both. I learned about racial and ethnic stereotyping in a predominantly White parochial school, as the teachers held lower expectations for me compared to my White classmates. So I was left to ask myself, well how come the teacher isn't saying, "Pamela you should be doing better" when she would say that to other people. And I knew I should be but I was not. Clearly, my experiences occurred decades ago and don't count. But sadly many girls and women today are still living by standards that may restrict their visions of potential futures and limit their possible selves.

Persistent Gender Biases and Lower Societal Expectations for Girls in Science and Technology Fields

I would like to suggest that the limits on girls are in large part due to persisting gender bias in education and low expectations by society. The expectations for achievement are particularly low for African Americans, Latinas, girls in poverty, and Latinos. These groups are disproportionately shut out of the most promising professions, the ones they call the STEM fields—science, technology, engineering, and math. Why the focus on math and science? This comes not only from my personal interest but also from the understanding that our system of preparing students in math and science is woefully lacking. Three different reports have come out just within the past month addressing this issue about the crisis in math and science preparedness in our country. The first, from Kirsch, Braun, and Yamamoto (2007), is called *America's Perfect Storm*.

The second is a proclamation to Congress sent by a group of distinguished business and education leaders, and the third is from the National Academy (2007). They all agree that much more is needed to raise our math skills, and they suggest that to ignore this need threatens the actual economic viability of the entire country. The National Academy Report, especially, discusses the gender inequities. This report notes that "women remain underrepresented in the professorate, in advance research labs, and in major scientific forums."

Although women are now a majority of the students at most college campuses and university campuses, the National Center for Education Statistics reports that women continue to be concentrated in fields that have historically been dominated by women. So yes, there are many, many, more women on campuses, but they are in the same fields that they were in 25 years ago. In education, for example, in 1996, 75% of education degrees went to women, the exact same percentage that went in 1970. There has been a little progress in engineering. Women went from less than 1% in 1970 to 16% in 1996—better, but still not equity. We can see that even when women do enter challenging math fields, the rewards they receive are still not equitable.Women earn less in jobs such as engineering manager, chemical manager, pharmacist, and information systems manager. We can see that the profession of chemical engineering has a $15,000 gap between men and women. Perhaps the rewards are not equitable in the classroom either. Girls are less likely to persist in science, math, and engineering courses. Their decision to abandon math may actually be encouraged by those who do not see a future for girls in these fields. A few years ago, a study by the National Science Foundation indicated that 34% of high-school age girls reported being advised by a faculty member not to take senior math. The reality, though, is that the performance of girls has reached parity in the classroom, yet they remain behind. Even though we have as many girls taking AP Physics and going on to take these classes, they remain behind in their confidence in math self concepts and achievements. Girls continue to have lower expectancies and to score lower than boys, especially on high-stakes tests. For the verbal SAT, except for Hispanic boys, there are only a few points separating girls and boys. For math, however, boys in every ethnic group outperformed girls in double digits. In fact, except for African American boys who only surpassed the girls by 18 points, all the other boys surpassed their female counterpoints by more than 30 points.

Understanding the Cultural Context

We recognize that verbal skills may be influenced by the books and materials that our family provides, and we are only beginning to learn what impact accessibility to new technologies may have on children. We do know that poor students and ethnic minority students have lower levels of exposure, and fewer opportunities to catch up with their peers. Children from homes with computers and who can use the Internet for exploration may develop a comfort level and skill sets that we have not yet examined. This is all a preface to the fact that the problems of girls and math and the achievement gaps were seen as an issue back in 1999, when my colleagues and I at the University of Michigan felt we could address these problems with a model problem for girls.

Our underlying theoretical perspectives, as mentioned previously, incorporated the need to understand culture as a part of context. Thus, we felt strongly influenced by both Bronfenbrenner's ecological views and Vygotsky's socio-cultural perspective. My own view about intersectionality, the understanding that social roles are complex and intertwined so that no one role may be accurately viewed as independent from the others, was also incorporated into our model program.

Background and Description of the GO-GIRL Intervention Program

Just to give acknowledgement, the first part of this program was actually piloted at the University of Michigan with Abby Stewart, and we worked on the initial program, which was called UM GIRL—"Using Math." It was cute because we all know what "UM" means. It was different in a number of significant ways, but I really wanted to move the program into a more urban setting, so we did. I moved it to Detroit and collaborated with Dr. Sally Roberts at Wayne State University within their College of Education. The College of Education was very amenable to providing resources and support for this program to take place, and it was housed there as well. And in the past few years we have also had partners in other institutions that have taken the model and made it their own. They are not just replications, they are really modifications in terms of what fits into their community. As to our sponsors, we have received a lot of support from the Michigan Department of Education, the National Science Foundation, and some smaller grants from Hewlett Packard and so on. In fact, our program even got a CompuWorld Innovation Award for Education.

Linking Math Skills to Social Science Research

Now I will move on to a description of the program. To address the math issues, we developed a program that would encourage math skills by linking them to social science research. The data show that people, girls especially, are more interested in social kinds of questions than abstract, deconceptualized math. So we said, "What about creating a program where girls learn about social science research?" So we morphed our curriculum eventually from just teaching statistics to actually allowing the girls to construct and conduct a survey, and then they analyzed their own data using both descriptive and inferential statistics. It is a lot of fun for them to see all that progression.

We also wanted to facilitate girls' exploration with education and career goals related to math and science. This included having talks from visiting scientists and researchers and taking field trips to places such as the College of Pharmacy Labs and the Ford Motor Company, as well as attending lessons conducted by university librarians in how to search the Web about careers. Another objective was to promote their interest, obviously, and their achievement in math by demonstrating that there are interesting uses for math skills in helping them to gain success. I was just looking at a magazine recently and it said people are more likely to like people who like them. Well, people are also more likely to like activities in which they experience success.

The "FFF" Factor: Fun, Food, and Friends

To give the girls success was obviously something that we felt would also raise their interests in mathematics. The development of our curriculum was not a simple one. We were not trying to fail, we wanted to put in and use all of the data that has been out there to help and to set an environment that would promote success. We wanted the students to feel empowered and valued, so we offered learning, but not play. It was not a camp, but it was a very relaxed atmosphere. Sally Roberts, my collaborator at Wayne State, loves to quote one of the girls who, when asked "Why do you like the program?" said, "It's the FFF factor—fun, food, and friends." So we had all of that.

I think our afterschool/Saturday program was a very successful contrast to the typical large classroom, especially in Detroit, where it was much more structured, and where the average middle school student is in a class of 35. So even though we had a large class, it was broken into small learning groups. The groups comprised four or five girls and two mentors. That is a very nice ratio. We had math intensive activities. All sorts of math games leading them up and through learning how to use descriptive statistics such as mean, median, and mode, which are, by the way, in the seventh grade curriculum, but we took it a little bit further and let them do testing on the means with T-tests. It is interesting, even though they might not be able to turn around and explain it, that when children can be lead through the process, they can do this pretty sophisticated analysis, and it was something that they were acutely aware of. The technology skill-building included learning PowerPoint for those who did not already know it.

Schedule, Structure, and Sustainability of the GO-GIRL Program

The whole program took place on a university campus that was in the middle of downtown Detroit, but a campus that a lot of these students had never really visited, no less been invited into a building of, and on a regular basis at that. It was a 10-day experience but in this case spread over 10 Saturdays. So every Saturday morning for about five hours from 9:30 to 2:00—if it was a field group it would even be later—the students were together.

We actually constructed two environments because we had service learning courses as well as the enhancement program. Sustainability is so important. You know, across the county there are hundreds of programs that have been developed for girls and boys, minority students, and poor students, to try and get them to engage in math and science. So sustainability is important. Why take all of this money and then develop a program that when the money is gone, there is no more program and there is no more influence? So, creating the Service Learning Course was an important part for sustainability. We actually had two courses, because Sally Roberts is a Professor of Math Education, and I am a Developmental Psychologist. I had an undergraduate course that I developed that was called Middle School Girls Theory and Practice. It was an adolescent development course focused on girls and achievements. Sally's courses, she actually had two courses, were math and education.

How to teach middle-school math? What is the feature? It was a methods class and a skills-building class. Both of the classes combined theory analysis and practicum, so we brought these university students into the lives of our seventh graders because they were the mentors. That was part of the class; it made it sustainable. Knowing that even though the university wants to do something for the community, it still has to serve its students, I said to these administrators, here is a class that can be a service to students as well as bringing tens of girls to Wayne State. Where up to now we have been doing it with about 80 girls a year—40 each semester—now it is one semester, but there are 60 girls enrolled, and this is the fifth year at Wayne State.

The close and intense interactions with the girls allowed the university students to understand middle school girls' lives in a way that reading and observing could never accomplish alone.

The enhancement program, as I said, was a great success. The students chose a research topic and we figured out a strategy for how to get 40 people to decide on one topic. That was very exciting; a brainstorm just came to me. Each small group decides on a topic, gets together, talks about it and chooses a topic. Then each group gets up and presents their topic to the others, and then they all vote on which one they want. Then everyone goes back and designs survey questions with their mentors. We put all the survey questions together into one big survey. In fact, there are some surveys coming up now. If anyone can find Wayne State's GO-GIRL Program, you can see the survey, because the students put it up on the Web and when it goes on the Web, hundreds of people from all around the country, the world, can respond, so then they have real answers to the questions that they have posed; it is not just an abstract activity. At the end of the 10 weeks, they give a PowerPoint presentation. They analyze the data and present their findings to their parents and to each other.

We put these all together and wanted to see if it worked. Does this program really enhance girls' math confidence? We were not trying in 10 days to change what has to happen across the whole of seventh- and eighth-grade math. But, we did want to know if there would be some improvements in math abilities, and if the girls would change in terms of thinking about careers. And we wanted to know about the university mentors—of what benefit were these activities for them?

The Girls Who Participate: What We Know—Pre- and Post-Program

Let me tell you a little bit about the girls who are in the program. Over the past five years, since 2002, I think we are now up to over 300 girls who have participated in this program, which is a lot for a small program run by two people and their graduate assistants. It really does not touch the thousands of students in Detroit, but you know, you have to do something. The students are seventh-grade adolescent girls from all over the Detroit area, not just in the city. Although many of them are from Detroit Public Schools, they are also from suburban and parochial schools. About 75% of the students are African Americans from different socioeconomic groups. So it was not only that the African American students were participating or not affluent. There are affluent African American students who are participating and a variety of other ethnic group students as well. But, the predominance was African Americans, which really surprised a lot of parents when they came to the orientation meeting, where we invite everyone's parents, we have a big lunch, and everyone comes.

The university is not predominantly African American, and therefore, when White parents walk in, sometimes they are sort of shocked that they all of a sudden find themselves in a setting that is predominantly African American. My favorite anecdote is about this one little girl. Orientation is the opportunity for us to do a lot of pretesting when the students are there, and we get the parents to sign all the permissions. This one parent, a mother, was sitting there and she looked a little distracted. I said, "Is everything okay?" And she said, "Well my daughter is in the bathroom on the cell phone begging her father does she have to stay?" And she said, "But I told her, look around, there are no guns or metal detectors." That was her reassurance to her daughter. Her daughter came out and her eyes were all red from crying and her father said, "Yes, she had to stay."But in the end, she loved it. She loved the program and at the final activity, where we have a whole ceremony and everything, she did not even sit with her parents for lunch. They were left there sitting by themselves and she was sitting with her friends!

We wanted to measure with some confidence participants' interest in math, and so we used the Fennema-Sherman Math Attitude Scale and compared both pre- and post-test means for the subscales on math competence, math utility, and motivation, using paired sample T-tests. We also constructed our own pre- and post-math skills tests based on the eighth-grade Michigan Tests to meet the aptitude test that they give, and I think almost every state gives. We had open-ended questions for the student mentors; for the participating girls we used measures of educational and career aspirations, and measures of attitudes towards the program and towards math. We also did some surveys and open-ended questions; we gave some to the parents and the mentors, and also had spontaneous discussions with the parents and did interviews and focus groups later with the mentors.

We did not find any difference in math motivation.It is, obviously, a pre-selected group. We had to do pre- and post-tests because when you are doing an implementation program such as this, even though we wanted to and we thought about how we could have a comparison group, it was not that easy to do, especially since the students were coming from all different schools and different places. So we used a math confidence scale and it was significant for the students. We did this Fennema-Sherman Test, a confidence test, on different groups; we did it multiple times and we always got a significant increase in math confidence. When we did it as a compressed program in two weeks, we got improvement. This program was over 10 weeks and we got improvement. In support of these quantitative findings, qualitative interviews revealed that the girls who participated reported that they were more confident and that they had more positive perceptions of their math skills.When we talked to teachers who had some of these girls in their classrooms, they also reported that the girls were more confident and spoke up more in class. When one girl was asked about the program, she remarked, "I think it helped me 'cause, like now in math class we learn things that we're reviewing now and it's, like pretty easy." Many of our girls reported their confidence and interest in math had increased, and their parents also reported that it had increased and that they saw marked improvements in their daughter's motivation and confidence even in school as a whole, but particularly in math. A quote that we liked from one parent said, "She's constantly finding mathematical things to do." In addition, many of the parents felt that the program not only increased their daughters' confidence but also their participation seemed to increase their actual mathematical abilities. We thought in the beginning that if you like something, and you have more confidence in your ability, you will do it more, you will stay at it, and you will get better grades. Your persistence ensures you will do better. In fact, the parents reported that the grades did get better, did get stronger.

We had an application format for students to be accepted. We actually accepted everyone that we had space for, but because it was a free program, we had funding so students were not paying. We wanted them to feel that this was important, that there was a level of importance and gravity attached in coming, and so we had them apply. They had a little application form where they had to make a statement about coming and it was on their honor that they were B-minus students. We thought we should set some standard—B-minus. But later we found out that people came who were not B-minus. Our skills test that we made up looks like it is not that much of a difference, and in a paper that we published recently, we give the real range because the range was broad. There were students who came in who were getting almost zero on the test and these were all seventh graders. So they are all in the same grade, but some of them are in public schools, and some of them are in affluent private schools and parochial schools, which are smaller and more select. So we parceled it out and it turns out everyone increased, everyone did better, and the students who were low had significant increases in their math scores. We were very pleased with that. Now you know it is pre- and post- and they were in seventh grade, so it was not like they were not doing anything. Here is where the control group would help us to know. I would have to tell you that our skills tests included eighth-grade math, so we did not make it so that anyone could reach the ceiling. No one could reach the ceiling as they were may be answering things that they had not learned in their class.

Follow-up reports from the parents and the girls indicated that they felt they were doing better. They could see the difference in themselves, a sense of accomplishment. If you look at those MEAP scores, there is a lot of overlap in math and social studies. As I went into this as a social scientist, as a psychologist, as a researcher who uses statistics, I acknowledged that we were teaching them applied math. Applied math are all the things that are on those exams, such as how to read graphs and how to understand the differences, and that is exactly what they were doing. The girls reported attitude changes as well. One of the scales that we had asked "How important do you think being good at math and science is to your success?"—we saw improvement in that area. There were slight increases in their educational and career goals, but not so great, really, because you can imagine that students who would come on a Saturday morning are motivated, or their parents are motivated, so they already had pretty high goals. They expected to go to college, and they expected to have achievement, but we did have a shift in terms of math. So, 37% as opposed to 28% were thinking about medical degrees.We had a medical researcher come in and talk to a couple of groups. Double the number but still small, 8% as compared to 4%, said that they were going to engineering areas. Eighteen percent talked about mathematical before as well as after. So the shifts in the careers seemed minimal. But we also did qualitative follow-up using journaling. We had girls write on a regular basis, in response to a prompt. I do not know how many people have close familiarity with 12-year-olds. They are not always the most forthcoming. So we decided rather than just give them a blank page, to ask "What do you think about this part of the program? Tell us what you really think."And these qualitative analyses showed that they felt that there were a lot of positive impacts on the girls.

Diversity was something that I will have to admit we really did not have a good way to measure, but these were diverse groups of students and the diversity goes both ways. You know we so often think about White students getting exposed to students of other ethnicities or socio-classes, but students who grow up in an urban school where it's 100% or 99% African American also may not be comfortable with diversity, and so this was an experience for these students. There was not only diversity in ethnicity but in social class. They were feeling more confident in technology, they had higher expectations of good grades in math, and that was one of our measures.

We do not have good ways to measure anything that is really sensitive to what the change means. Something we did not measure, but I have to say we saw, was a significant difference in communicating with adults and peers. We think that participation in this program gave girls the opportunity to also interact with adults differently. As I tried to reflect on this opportunity, it reminded me of how different the experiences are for middle-class students, particularly affluent students who go to private school, and the kind of interactions they are used to having with adults as opposed to lower-income students and how they interact with adults. I was talking with some students earlier today and I gave the example of my granddaughter who is in a pretty expensive private school. She is in first grade, and her teacher's name is Sally, and I could not quite get my mind around a seven-year-old calling her teacher Sally. One time I was saying something about "Oh, and how is your teacher Miss Sally?" "It's not Miss Sally, it's just Sally." "Okay, I got it." But you know how much different it is in public schools. My experience, because it was just such a powerful one, is in a Newark school where a little boy was trying not to leave the library where they had a Science Fair. The teacher was trying to get the class to all line up and she finally, in a very angry tone said to him, "You wait for me. I don't wait for you." I do not think he calls her "Sally."

GO-GIRL Mentors—Adult Pre-Service Teachers and the Service-Learning Experiences Enabling Friendships With Their Girls

In our program, the mentors were all adults. There were some undergraduate students who were young adults, but some were graduate students in the MAT program at Wayne State, they were adults changing careers and so they were not young adults. We had a whole discussion very early on, and some of the "teachers to be" were not that happy, but our decision was that the students would go with the mentors and that we were not re-creating school.It was not school and they were not "Miss" and "Mr."

The importance of the mentors was really underscored in the journals and in the comments by the girls when we followed up, because we did have some follow-up with one group about a year later at the end of two semesters, at the end of the term. The importance was that they, the mentors, were guides. They talked to the girls about school, helped them with their lessons, helped them with the activities, and gave them career guidance. The girls felt that they were friends. Over and over, the thing that the 12-year-olds wanted to say was, "They listened to me. I could come to them and they would listen."And that I think was a really critical part of the intervention program. This relationship with the mentors challengedthe status relationships, and in a really different way than most of these children were used to.

Mentors were not exclusively female. We had some male mentors. It is a public institution, and so we could not restrict the classes, right? The service-only classes were open to everyone. By the way, you might want to know that Proposal Two in Michigan, the recent proposal that was just passed banning the use of race and gender and so on and so forth, threatens this program because we are still running it but everyone is wondering should we be running or scrambling or waiting.We are trying to figure out. Everyone, including boys, can come in it if they are willing to be called "GO-GIRLS." I do not think too many 12-year-olds would do it. But, you know there will be some parents who will put them in.

The mentors as a group really directed the group activities, and I want to say that the mentors really were important in a lot of ways. Let me talk about what they got out of the program as well, because we focused on the girls in our research. We did focus groups and surveys with the mentors. And the mentors, I think, benefited immensely. One student said, "From being a mentor, I have gained a greater understanding of what middle schools are like. For example, since I was in middle school, I had forgotten the incredible energy that youngsters of that age have." Think about 40 of them all together. That is palpable. The student said, "This will help me keep students motivated as a teacher. I have also gained some insight into what types of challenges urban girls have to confront at a young age."

The quality of analyses suggests that as Wayne State University increased service, teachers emerged feeling better prepared for their student-teaching, which most of them pursued the following semester after taking this course. In other words, the College of Education would say, we will allow students to substitute this course for the course that they typically use, which is just going into a classroom and observing. Even though this is not as many hours, it is much more intense. So instead of just going in and watching a teacher manage her class and just sitting on the sidelines, these pre-service teachers were sitting there with these girls having to convey and convince them to be interested and engaged. And if you think that that is a piece of cake with just four or five girls, you have forgotten what 12-year-olds can be like; sometimes they are not engaged. They will tell you when they are bored. They will put their heads down and fall asleep when they are bored with whatever it is that you are doing. The co-requisite teacher-education course that went with the one on math education indicated that the teacher candidates gave valuable insights, and that it helped them develop as culturally confident and academic-achievement focused.

The university students indicate that the service-learning component facilitated experiential learning of the course material where the real-world context informed their academic work, and vice versa. According to one student, "From this experience, I am recognizing that even though you know the right theories and studies, actually applying them and understanding them in terms of real girls is completely different." When discussing how the service-learning component benefited their education, students often mention the reciprocity with the experience. They mentored seventh-grade girls, but they learned from them as well, and they valued the opportunity for the self-reflection. One student said, "It taught me a lot about myself and adolescent girls." Another girl actually related it to her adolescent sister whom she said she had lost touch with—she had a much younger sister whom she did not really feel connected to—but having gone through this experience, she was energized. Now she had new strategies and understandings to help her to try and connect with her sister. The involvement in the Mathematics Enrichment Program, along with the course reading, spurred the undergraduate students to think about their own middle-school experiences. The self-reflection that accompanies good service-learning experiences is very rewarding. One student said, "Through this class I found myself revisiting some of my own experiences in middle school and reevaluating why they occurred and how they affected me in the long run."

Other students talked about the appreciation for diversity as well. With the undergraduate students, by the way, it varied. Most of the undergraduate students in the first three years were from the University of Michigan. So they were traditional undergraduate students living in Ann Arbor, and they were very motivated; they had to get up very early in the morning and get a van and drive the van down to Detroit. It's about 40 minutes, if you drive very fast. One student said, "An increased comfort with diversity. The experience has given me a different perspective on students from Detroit. The media has portrayed them as angry, troubled, and lacking in ambition." This student said, "Through this experience I've had the opportunity to meet girls from urban schools who are eager to learn, are polite, and have the desire to improve themselves." So here are stereotypes that maybe are even reinforced when we just take unprepared students and unprepared White students, or a student who is not familiar with urban environments, who is not comfortable with African American children. What do we do with these unprepared students? They have gone through all the methods classes, we put them right into a classroom, and maybe their worst fears are confirmed because they are not seeing these children as individuals. Here they have to because they are just dealing with them as individuals. Another student even said she felt more comfortable with diversity at work, with some of the changing environments.

I have to just make one more point about the comfort with diversity— the impact on the teachers. Even when we first started the program in Ann Arbor at the University of Michigan, we were doing it with in-service teachers, with teachers from the schools, because we really thought this would be of value, to work with these teachers, to help these teachers, and to prepare these students as they go into seventh grade. We thought that this would be a real benefit, but we had many roadblocks to success. But even with the roadblocks to success, which made me abandon doing it with in-service teachers and go to pre-service teachers who are not so set with their repertoire and what they are going to do in class, and are more open to these new experiences, even the experienced teachers came back and said, "I've been a teacher in that school for eight years and for the first time, the African American students are coming to me with their problems." So, was it that the students just changed, or maybe this teacher who had been there all these years felt more comfortable with his students and sent out a different kind of message in his interaction with them? We think that the mentors got this understanding of the adolescent experience, coupled with diversity, and of real pride. More than half of the students expressed the pride they felt in really making a difference in the community. Not just giving back, but doing something that was of worth, that gave a sense of satisfaction that they would be able to boost.

The Importance of Skill-Building in the GO-GIRL Program

In addition to the conclusion that we drew from this program, that mentors are so important, we also drew the conclusion that building skills is important. There are a number of programs that I have seen or read about from time to time where people just say this program is about building self-confidence. We are going to build the self-confidence of these children. Well, self-confidence does not occur in a vacuum. Why are you confident? Building skills, we think, builds people's confidence because now they have something that they are proud of, and that they can feel successful at. We are moving away from this, but we used to have graphs and calculators as part of the activities. We taught the girls how to use graphing calculators. We found out, unfortunately, that in the middle schools in Detroit they were not using them. They had a skill without a distinct use and no place to go with it. In the Ann Arbor schools, the more affluent communities, they always use graphing calculators, and when the girls came in, having been tutored in how to use them, we gave them high-school level TIA 84s when they finished the program. Teachers and parents were saying the girls were teaching the other people in their class. When you give someone a skill, then they can lead others. They have something to lead with.

The small groups were very, very effective, and I think teachers use this in a lot of classes; this is the new pedagogy. But a lot of people feel like in some urban schools, there is not the room, and they are not constructed to facilitate small groups. So I will say to the teachers, it is so much easier to keep four or five students engaged with each other, to make them responsible, and to move toward that constructivist model. Many people spout constructivist rhetoric, but one of my doctoral students some years back was part of a major project that was going on in the New York City public schools. The entire district adopted a constructivist approach to teaching math, and all of the teachers wanted to train, all of the principals wanted to train, and my student's research was to go around and do some initial observation. She picked four teachers who were trying, who were using it to some extent with their math, and four teachers who were clearly not using it with their math. Using the constructivist approach made a difference, a big difference, for girls. It did not make much of a difference for boys. But it made a difference for girls. Why do you think? Adult attention cannot be overemphasized. The reason is, that the constructivist approach in math education says that the students have to talk about it. They have to come up with the solution. When the teacher actually allowed that to occur, it gave girls license to talk and to be in there, and to think through their insecurities, and to find out—because it is more comparative with the other students—that they did know something, that they were competent and that they could have more confidence. Since boys will talk out no matter what rules you are under, it did not really influence them. It influenced the girls.

Concluding Comments: University-School-Community Partnerships With the GO-GIRL Program

Connecting universities, schools, and communities is one of the benefits that I feel this program also brings, which is why I was so happy to find colleagues willing to take this to other universities. The University of Pennsylvania, for example, reaches out, even the buildings sort of look toward the community instead of being a little enclave in and of itself, and it creates a different atmosphere. When the communities are invited onto campus, when the students see that this is someplace that they can aspire to, it starts to make a real difference, and it makes a difference in the university too as we have to do these cooperative programs.

One thing about doing any kind of cooperative program with the community is that you have to enter into some kind of partnership. I will have to say that the partnerships in our major project at Wayne State University have really been with the parents and with the teachers directly. We do not go through the public schools. Public school bureaucracies are hard everywhere. We recruit students and we get more students than we can serve, unfortunately. We go directly to the students and to teachers because teachers want their students to be involved and they know what students will benefit and will take advantage of the opportunity. We go to ministers who have youth groups and youth activities and also, as I told Dr. Slaughter-Defoe, I was on the radio for about five minutes, as even parents who want their children to attend may not hear about it, and so parents will contact you directly. In conclusion, today the GO-GIRL program is still going strong. We have 60 students enrolled in this semester at Wayne State, students here at Penn in the Penn GO-GIRL program, at Illinois Wesleyan, at Roosevelt University, and at Howard University—those are the five operating sites in 2006–07.

Addendum

Since this paper was written, the author has chosen to provide the following update: "The need to encourage girls, particularly those considered at risk for academic failure, remains strong. With the burgeoning of information technology and social media, the opportunities for career advancement depend on higher education. Increasingly we see scientific and mathematical skills becoming intertwined with humanities and social sciences. The results of the program efforts, both anecdotal and quantitative, compel us to continue to deliver high-quality, skill-based, out-of-school enrichment activities as a means to expand girls' confidence and leadership abilities. Additionally, the program serves to mediate the equity gaps that continue to exist for underrepresented populations in STEM areas. Since this paper was written, the GO-GIRL Program at Wayne State University, now directed by Dr. Sally K. Roberts, continues into its 12th semester. More than 600 seventh-grade girls have been served since the program was launched with students from the first GO-GIRL cohort completing their third year of college."

References

Committee on Maximizing the Potential of Women in Academic Science and Engineering, and Committee on Science, Engineering, and Public Policy (2007). *Beyond bias and barriers: Fulfilling the potential of women in academic science and engineering.* Washington, DC: National Academies Press. Retrieved from www.nap.edu/openbook.php?record_id=11741

Kirsch, I., Braun, H., & Yamamoto, K. (2007). *America's perfect storm: Three forces changing our nation's future.* Princeton, NJ: Educational Testing Service. Retrieved from: www.ets.org/stormreport

Reid, P. T., & Roberts, S. K. (2006). Gaining options: A mathematics program for potentially talented at-risk adolescent girls. *Merrill-Palmer Quarterly, 52*(2), 288–304.

Reid, P. T., & Stewart, A. J. (2002a). *Using Math: Girls Investigate Real Life (UM-GIRL)—A report on the 2000 summer program and the 2000/2001 follow-up activities.* Ann Arbor, MI: University of Michigan Institute for Research on Women and Gender.

Reid, P. T., & Stewart, A. J. (2002b). *Using Math: Girls Investigate Real Life (UM-GIRL)—A report on the 2001 summer program and the 2001/2002 follow-up activities.* Ann Arbor, MI: University of Michigan Institute for Research on Women and Gender.

12. Thoughts on Improving the Intellectual Life Chances of Adolescents: The Case for Tool Design

Louis M. Gomez

University of California, Los Angeles (UCLA)

Whenever people have an opportunity to give lectures like this one, that are named for someone who is quite notable, they always say things like, "Well, I'm honored or it is a pleasure," and I am, and it is. Giving this lecture *is* personally very meaningful to me because, at the end of the day, I think of my work, and the work of my colleagues, as being about school improvement and leveraging design to make the lives of people better. So, to be asked to come and have a conversation with you by means of a lecture in honor of someone whose work has been deeply centered in school improvement is very special. I am indeed honored, to be here.

Theories of Educational Instruction

It is useful to think about what the lions of our field have to say about education and its purpose. In Dewey's (1916) words, *"The aim of education is to enable individuals to continue their education . . . (and) the object and reward of learning is continued capacity for growth"* (1966 ed., p. 107). Benjamin Bloom and colleagues (Krathwohl, Bloom, & Masia, 1964) focused on a lifestyle of intellectual development and described a taxonomy of levels of expertise associated with the internationalization of values associated with a consistent lifestyle for intellectual depth and growth. Building on Bloom's 1956 Taxonomy, they characterized the Affective Domain (Bloom's Taxonomy: Affective Domain) as "pervasive, consistent, predictable, and most importantly characteristic of the learner"(Krathwohl et al., 1964; Anderson & Sosniak, 1994). From the ideas expressed by Dewey and characterized in Bloom and colleagues' Affective Domain taxonomy, it seems clear, that Bloom and Dewey are advocating that we radically aim to change people's lives through inculcating and helping each person to create new and effective habits of learning. Unfortunately, it is our enduring problem that we tend to find most of our success in radically changing the lives of a few, while failing the many. We need to make more progress than we have. Making progress in using school as a vehicle to improve lives is a multifaceted task. Part of making progress involves having better tools to make progress at the disposal of teachers and learners. This is the subject of my lecture.

I would recommend for your reading a really nice piece that Lauren Resnick and colleagues (Resnick, Lesgold, & Hall, 2005) wrote recently titled *Moving from the Schooling We Have to the Schooling We Need*. Resnick and colleagues aim to help the reader understand what the developmental, cognitive, and learning sciences, and the social sciences have to say about how we might go about the job of arranging schooling to help make people productive and happy members of the 21st century world. Resnick et al. (2005) spend considerable time helping us think about what competence really is. What does it mean to be competent? What is the nature of knowledge? What is the nature of intelligence? And should the nature of instruction be to build competence for the modern world? They argue that the schooling we have (with lots of exceptions certainly) fails to get the job done. If you were to look at what we do in school today you would think that we believe that learning is all about acquiring sets of automated skills, as if there were some catechism out there that all students were meant to learn. Rather than a fixed catechism, the aim ought to be confident and competent learners. It is probably the case that confidence, in learning, is about understanding explanation, engaging in inquiry, and argumentation. The thing we should want people to be able to do is to understand how to engage in explanation, inquiry, and arguments. The task of being confident in such abilities is something that is acquired and performed through interaction with people in groups. Most schools, it would seem, if you look at what happens within them, consider knowledge to be a list of facts rather than structured schemes of relationships. It seems that we believe that there is a small canon of knowledge that can help make us self-confident, rather than many sources of information. Even further, looking inside most of our schools might lead you to believe that knowledge is a thing to be controlled rather than a developmental process growing in an unbridled fashion, and that it, i.e., knowledge, is bounded rather than exploding and emerging.

Continuing with this example, if we were to look inside today's schools, we would also think that intelligence is an entity to be possessed rather than a skill to be incrementally performed and improved. We behave as though intelligence is limited thing rather than learnable, with effort. We would think that some of us have it, and some of us do not. We would think that instruction should be largely about unguided practice, about the transmission of knowledge, about opening heads and stamping in, or about opening heads and taking, out rather than talking about interpretation and explanation. But construction of knowledge, as John Dewey and Benjamin Bloom would both argue, is about creating "lifelong learners" who understand how to monitor and manage their own growth. All people should know how to work in learning settings that are designed to be social and collaborative.

In today's conversation I want to talk about why *these* aims of instruction and education and why *their* import to today's adolescents. I will discuss why schooling, as currently structured, is perhaps inadequate to transformational challenge. I will consider why a more design-focused approach is important to transformation learning and teaching. To make that argument more concrete, I want to offer a couple of examples from work that my colleagues and I have been involved in, and then talk again about the importance of this process.

Contemporary Demands Upon the Aims of School Instruction

We are living in a perfect storm right now. We live in a world that is demanding more of all of us, but especially from the young people in our midst. We have what I think of as misplaced expectations, for those young people. We place them in school organizations that are not well equipped to help them meet genuine expectations of the modern world.

The way I want to talk about the new demanding world comes from Frank Levy and Richard Murnane's new book *The New Division of Labor: How Computers Are Creating the Next Job Market*. Published in 2004, Levy and Murnane make an argument about how computers are changing the ways of work and how the ways and expectations of work are changing around us. They suggest that you can take the world of work, as it has been done for the last many decades, and break it up into four forms. The first form is something they refer to as routine cognitive work—filing and bookkeeping. The second form is routine manual work—assembly line work. The last two are what they refer to as expert thinking— problem solving—and finally, complex communication—the eliciting of information and conveying it to others.

It is important to understand one very important thing about their proposition. They are saying that the categories of work called expert thinking and complex communication, over the last couple of decades have been the places where all the jobs are, and they are arguing that the other two categories—the two routine categories—are the places where the jobs are not. However, they are not arguing that jobs, in these two top categories, are restricted to people who run corporations, for example, and the other two are restricted to other forms of work. They are arguing, instead, that absolutely most of the work that people in this century and beyond will be asked to do, if our economy is to be productive, is in the top two categories. So, if you are the person who runs Target Corporation, to pick an example at random, or if you are the person who stocks the shelves at Target, they would argue that for you to be successful personally, in either job, and for your organization to be successful commercially, you will have to engage in some form of complex communication and expert thinking. And they ask the question, "How do we prepare a world where more young people are able to engage in these forms of work no matter their station in that work, or in the world?"

Expert thinking in Levy and Murnane's (2004) conception is about developing well-organized information about problems, seeing patterns and complex information, taking the initiative, employing better cognition, and thinking about the work that you do in a reflective way. Complex communication is about observing and listening and listing critical information, making sense of information, and telling others about the information. It is important to note that Levy and Murnane (2004) are not the first scholars to recognize that this is what important learning is about. John Dewey (1916, 1933, 1938) argued that the sort of learning that Levy and Murnane (2004) are calling for is really the nature of important learning.

At the same time that our world is getting more and more demanding, in terms of the work asked of all of us, we have misdirected the expectations of our students. We ask students to learn about domains rather than working within them. For example, we rarely ask students in school to explore consequential problems with results that have meaning beyond school. We socialize students that the most important thing is to get an answer rather than to build evidence. And as a result, I think that little ambitious learning goes on, and accountability is often framed around minimal accomplishments.

I think that this is, in part, because of the ways that schools are organized as loosely coupled communities where teaching practice is a private thing. Schools are not really strong professional communities and (as a result), as I said earlier, little ambitious learning goes on there. I think part of the problem is that such conditions lead to a lack of organizational coherence, and therefore no real convergence around activity. And I think this is partially because we view the organizational problem in schooling, as Pfeffer and Sutton (1999) would argue, as filling the ignorance-knowledge gaps. We need to, instead, make sure that students are prepared to work to fill what they call "the knowing-doing gap." These authors' claim that while learners often need facts, the bigger problem is that we do not have the right structures to allow people to engage in concerted action with those facts to solve problems. So, we do not have good ways to create common vision, shared beliefs, and thus concerted action to solve problems in most organizations, including schools.

One way to depict this as a "coherence challenge," as it relates to schools, is with the idea that you pick a reform and different people in the same school organization see that reform through different eyes. One way to think about the consequence of these differing perceptions is to pick any reform you like, and think about that reform making its way to a school organization. And those of you who have worked in schools, teachers, administrators, will say, "Oh, I do that!" Whatever the educational task or approach is, people will say, "I do that." And I do not think this is a problem with the local actors, I think it is a problem that has more to do with our inability to couple actions to ideas; we have weak theories of change and vastly underspecified reforms.

In education, we have a kind of command-and-control logic of reform. For example, we are in the habit of telling teachers that every teacher has to be a teacher of reading. But we do not really help people understand how the work is to be executed. The typical practice under-specifies the actions that need to change. Reform regiments of almost any stripe are better designed to tell people *what* to do rather than telling them *how* to do it. So the challenge of coordination, then, is that school actors need to know how to do the right things at the right time. Therefore, teachers who are given a reform agenda need to know what specific actions to do with their students, and at what precise times. School leaders need to know what particular set of things they do with teachers and other staff, and at what particular time, to meet the goals of the reform agenda. I believe the important work is about establishing *organizational routines*—adaptable, repeatable, recognizable, patterns of actions that are shared among a group of people.

If we want to address this coherence problem in education, we need a new metaphor for intentional action. If you want to solve this coherence problem, you might ask yourself, "How do we catalyze teams?" I want to talk about the importance of design as one metaphor to guide our work. I want to argue that a lot of what we do in this business of education should be thought of as a kind of Design Science. Design is a very powerful metaphor for sets of activities. I think that the work of the Colleges of Education exists at the nexus between practice and research. I ask, "How do you bridge that chasm?" I think design helps us to do that, when we engage in design, with the intention to restructure the work. Designers might say that it means school actors and research actors should co-construct the new routines around problems, to guide practice in providing concrete routines for organizational actors, including students, for action.

This perspective places the problem of implementation at the center of our work. Often we in education think the most important goal of our work is novel theory. It is, when you think about it yourself, only as "theory driven researcher," that the coin of the realm is novel theory-centered ideas.

Theory driven research is important. But, when we think in the implementation realm, the raison d'être becomes getting stuff done—on-the-ground improvement. What is important about implementation thinking is that you think about designing things and systems that work, you think about engineering them, and you think about looking at what happens and trying to figure out what to do next to make the next iteration better.

Alan Schoenfeld (2006) has a great piece that he published a few years ago in the *Educational Researcher* where he made this argument masterfully. A characterization of Schoenfeld's argument is that our tasks—knowledge-building and improvement—have at least three big categories. First there is the task of uncovering novel ideas with the promise for improvement. Here is where most of us think of the world of basic research. Then there is the task of, "how do I make ideas effective in practice?" and finally there is the work of, did it really work?"—that is, can some regimes produce statically better effects than a control in experimental conditions Schoenfeld (2006) argues that there is a growing amount of educational work in this last —for example, there is a growing call for more randomized field trials. He goes on to argue that as a field, we invest very little effort in the "how do I make it work" category. In essence, we value showing effects over working toward effectiveness in practice.

The work of education is about practice; the work of design is about making things work. I think more research and development effort in education needs to be in the "how do I make it work bucket," which is the task of implementation. And I think this is connected to the problem I started with, because tools are how people get things done.

Tools as Design Artifacts

Tools are design artifacts that help individuals and organizations do work. And let me be clear, when I use the word "tools" here, I do not simply mean computer- or technology-based things, I also mean paper and pencil things. A simple paper and pencil tool that is an important tool for any organization is the calendar. A calendar is a tool that tells people where to be and who from the organization is joining them. When I want to use the word tool, I want to talk about things that are purposefully made, and thoughtfully constructed to help people do work. A tool is highly public to the work of an organization, and tools are embedded in things that we want to call identifiable patterns of activity. To recap, it is the *lack* of those identifiable patterns of activity, vis-à-vis any reform, or most reforms, that causes reforms not to gain the kind of attraction that they can have. Why? Because tools help create specificity, regularity, and persistence. They help keep goals in view. Therefore, they become at least part of the vehicle to coordinate human activity.

I want to talk about a design approach to a couple of complex problems devoted to supporting complex thinking and expert communication. I want to talk about two programs of work that my colleagues and I are working on. The first is the Adolescent Literacy Support Project (ALSP) that we have been engaged with for the last several years; the second is a project called the Space Project. Space is embedded in a larger research effort that my colleague, Tony Bryk, and I (2008) have been working on that we call the Information Infrastructure System (IIS) project. The IIS considers the issue of how we could build tools that are evidence centered, to re-instrument and rethink the infrastructure of schooling. And in both cases, ALSP and IIS, I want to talk about (a) the goals of the work and the challenges associated with them, (b) the tools that we made as a part of the work, and (c) our experience thus far.

The Adolescent Literacy Support Project

The aim of the Adolescence Literacy Support Project is to build explicit support for literacy instruction in science. Those of you who work in high schools have probably heard acknowledgments regarding the deep challenge of low levels of literacy for many high school students, no matter what domain. But some domains, such as science, in particular, are devilishly hard, and I have had a curriculum supervisor say to me recently that the literacy demand of freshman biology is very tough for kids.

In addition to the science concepts, the language of science just blows them out of the water. When confronted with students with low literacy levels who must successfully complete challenging domains, such as freshman biology, oftentimes—and this is a bit pejorative and a little over the top—school systems will say that every teacher needs to be a teacher of reading. In their private moments, teachers will say, "Well, yeah, what do I *do* to do that?" So our goal is to create learning environments that help teachers and students use language more purposefully to acquire knowledge. We want to study learning and build theory around that. So we want to help address the sinking feeling you get when you have been trained for a whole career to be a teacher of science and someone in authority says, "Well you know you're a literacy teacher too." We want to work on that problem.

The people who work on this problem—before I tell you about the work— are a long list, because about half or a third of them are teachers, then there are faculty colleagues, and students as well. The complex collection of people that it takes to do work of a design sort, to have real traction, and to get the work done are, necessarily, very diverse. Practicing teachers really understand classrooms, and even the research scientists, who were teachers, do not understand classrooms in the ways, and to the extent that currently practicing teachers understand classrooms.

ALSP is a very large project. It includes working with several high schools with several different science curricula. This work on literacy and science would not be possible if the people who published the Investigations in Environmental Science (IES), and the people who published the biology curriculum, BSCS (The Biology Studies Curriculum Simple) were not our partners in this work.

The essence of our work is that we aim to be tightly coupled to the work that people want to do, in this case teaching the curriculum. The challenge of supporting adolescent reading and science is also a multifaceted one. There is a mismatch between students' reading abilities and the requirements of text and science.

The language demands of science curricula pose a great challenge to students. Students are asked to read very diverse text, and science teachers do not necessarily take ownership of the problem of supporting literacy. Our responses to these problems are often inadequate—they are frequently overly focused on professional development. We sort of lose contact with the content mostly, and often times our approaches to solving these problems are overly general. Reading in science is a bit different than reading in social studies, and other disciplines are in turn different. There are a lot of similarities, but you have to recognize the disciplinary differences, and you have to have design techniques that force learners to come to terms with them.

An example from a science lesson might include the word "ecological," as in, for example, "Ecologically productive land is land that is fertile enough to support forests." In this case, ecological refers to the ecological footprint, i.e., the measurement of the ecologically productive land that a person's lifestyle requires. So in that small space, that sentence, you find connector words, and you find special-purpose words, and in lots of cases, science students are stymied by texts like that. Science teachers and science students do not have specific instructional teams to deal with such texts, and at the same time to keep the science in the first position. So the problem with practice is that the texts and language are not deeply connected enough to support a student's knowledge acquisition in science. We have few techniques to couple conceptual understanding to procedural activities around science, and few specific skills to read science text as part of inquiry.

We have been exploring a specific tool-based response to provide tools and routines that teachers and students can use to work in a coordinated fashion on confronting texts such as those, to acquire information about science. So we have been trying to change how teachers work with literacy and language by enhancing the interaction with the content knowledge and by purposely coupling literacy and language to the content by doing things such as collaborative analysis of the text.

What does that look like? It looks like sitting down with a professional teacher and saying, "Where in these texts are the big ideas that kids need to understand?" and then trying to understand what would make those big ideas prominent to kids. The subsequent recommendations include specific literacy strategies to deal with those concepts and recommendations for analyzing and explaining charts and displays. If you want to be surprised sometime, take any popular science textbook, open it up, and look at the array of figures and charts in that textbook. See how complex they are in trying to convey information. This is not to say that the figures and charts should not be there. This is not to say we should simplify them. This is simply to say that they are difficult, and we need specific routines to deal with them.

We have taken teaching strategies and coupled them to specific parts of science text, and we have suggested what kind of text analysis should be applied. We have also recommended specific teaching strategies to address specific content elements. And, I want to underscore, this would be impossible if we did not do this work in collaboration with practicing science teachers.

Another example is that we try to provide specific teaching notes for talk about the purpose of instruction for the science lesson and the kinds of misconceptions that kids might encounter as they are confronting the text in a lesson. So what we are trying to do, through tools such as these, is to inculcate specific instructional routines around the texts, while at the same time keeping the content in the primary focus, or as we say in the ALSP, content forward. We want to integrate specific text strategy recommendations and to bridge the conceptual knowledge to the text to make it really specific and concrete for learners. So we have worked specifically in building tools to help teachers help learners recognize the structures in text, to be reflective about what they are reading, to have a place to document their reflections, and to help them do a better job at capturing the gist of text.

One concrete instantiation of tools is text annotation. We built a set of tools to help teachers annotate text and to help students annotate text. We designed a set of tools that enabled teachers, either while they were teaching or prior to teaching, to mark up a PDF file of text in certain ways. We also encouraged students to mark up the text in certain ways. Now something that should not go unsaid is that a core piece of the work is that we do require kids to own text. It seems like a simple thing, but in most schools, you do not *own* the text you work on. In our first attempt at doing this work, our grant paid for a set of textbooks that the school planned to use for instruction, but that model (purchasing textbooks) was not sustainable. What was sustainable, and is sustainable, is to form partnerships with publishers that allow you to make PDFs of all their texts. In this approach, students own the text in the sense that they can annotate the text using pencils or pens. Some schools still buy the books, but the work of learning is done in another place. So we try to provide specific instructional routines for teachers to tell them how to use annotation in their instruction.

We also do things such as creating wall posters that keep the problem *in front* of kids' eyes, and we build electronic tools to help teachers and kids do the same work. For example, with a certain mark-up tool you can import the text that you are reading, and then decide the type of annotation (e.g., for vocabulary, transitions, arguments) that you want to use. You can then click to select the text, indicate your annotation type, do the annotation, and then based on your current understanding of the text, you can write a summary of the text. Now the reason we began building electronic tools to do this sort of marking up of text was because teachers constantly pushed back on us about literacy activities taking huge amounts of time in science classrooms. Building electronic tools, such as this, enables it to be the case, at least in some environments, for this kind of activity to be much easier to employ in classrooms.

So what do we know so far? We know that when teachers consistently use these tools, we see small, but reliable, pre- to post-test increases in learners' DRP (reading test) scores. Learners are better able to understand science and to engage in classroom science discussions. And this makes sense, because in order to engage in the classroom discussion effectively, you have to have something to talk about, and to have something to talk about you have to be able to confront the text. Our results indicate that use of this tool correlates with science achievement on essay questions at about the same level as prior reading scores. When we look at tenth graders who use these tools, they understand the content, and they do a better job than their ninth grade peers who did not have a year's worth of advantage in using the tools.

What do teachers and students think about this process? Well, my favorite anecdote is that my wife, Kim (Dr. Kimberley Gomez), was interviewing a child and he said, "Oh, I don't really like all that marking up stuff you make us do! But I'm going to show my younger sibling, who's going to show up in this school next year, how to do that." Teachers tell us that they think that students read text more purposefully as a function of having engaged in these exercises. And students tell us that when they are not compelled to annotate text, as a part of a classroom assignment or activity, they do it anyway. When most people get to university, they cannot survive unless they have deep expertise around the way to make text friendlier. We think that annotation as a tool provides students with a means to make text more accessible.

The implementation challenges in this work continue. We ask students to annotate many different structural and semantic features of text. Students are pretty good, for example, at isolating main ideas and supporting arguments. They are really terrible at recognizing inferences and talking about the inclusion of implications. That raises a question: How do you get them to do stuff like this and what is their developmental trajectory?

We have only made the slightest progress in creating electronic tools. We have a lot of work to do in order to understand things such as how you automatically capture and score students work. Those of you in the world of computer science might know about automatic essay grading technologies and the technologies that are a part of our work that is about the summary. Yet, we need to find better ways to automatically get information from things such as annotations and double-entry journals.

Supporting Projects Through Authoring, Critique, and Exemplars (SPACE)

SPACE stands for *Supporting Projects through Authoring, Critique, and Exemplars.* Ever since Dewey (1916, 1933, 1938), people have been trying to get students to learn through project-based learning. This effort has been particularly focused on science learning. Our aim is to have students do open-ended, consequential, investigations in all subjects. As educators, we have not succeeded, on the whole, in helping teachers and students know more about how to do project-based learning really well. There are several great hot-house examples where really extraordinary project-based learning has occurred. Some teachers are willing to stay up until all hours of the morning to create great project-based learning opportunities, or to figure out how great project-based learning happened for others.

But it should be the case, if inquiries are important, that regular, everyday people should be able to design good opportunities for learners to engage in project-based inquiry. One conjecture on why they do not is that we do not have a tool structure to help get it done. Essentially, right now, the teacher has to be an amazing person who can juggle 20 balls in the air at the same time, to keep track of everything that needs to happen to make project-based inquiry work well. Most educators are scared to do it because of the amount of time it requires, and the multiple elements that have to be attended to.

The work I am going to describe next was done by Ben Shapiro, one of my graduate students. SPACE was part of his dissertation. Other graduate students have also contributed a lot to our thinking about SPACE and the research associated with it.

What makes inquiry so hard to teach? Well, there are cognitive expectations, cognitive demands, representational difficulties, and coordination and feedback challenges. Inquiry requires students to interconnect many skills. Consider a classroom teacher supervising students' better-than-average science fair projects: students are analyzing data, there are methodological challenges, information has been assembled from a large number of places, and the teacher has to be reflective about what she is doing and what students are doing. It is hard for one teacher, even two, to keep track of everything and do it all well, particularly with classrooms of upwards of 30 students.

Successful inquiry-based project teaching is very difficult. It requires specific and concrete details about what lots of students are doing. It is very different from live-step instructions. The teacher must keep up with students' work, which increases in difficulty as projects become more open-ended. In live-step instruction, everybody reads the same article. If the teacher is trying to get learners to engage in inquiry, chances are that if the teaching, and learning, is done well, many, if not most, of the students are going to be using different sources of information. How does the teacher keep track of their work when there are multiple sources in play? How does the teacher know that students are drawing effective conclusions? It goes on and on.

It is because of this that I think inquiries are a shining light in the world of education. It is common thought that students' tasks are discrete; that they build when everybody is doing the same thing. There are a small set of hypotheses that suggest that reasonable supports pull in just the opposite direction in inquiry-based activities when students do different projects on different subjects, with different readings and so on.

So part of the technological solution is weaving into the inquiry the SPACE tool. Basically, SPACE is a database that automates much of the tedium associated with doing projects. So it helps create routines for teachers and kids. Teachers focus on instructions, not bookkeeping, and the prep work with SPACE encourages teachers to think about, and be articulate about, assignments and how things link together for students.

SPACE lets students quickly see what they have to do, and teaches them to focus on work being done whether by individuals or by a group. Assessments that the students do are emailed to teachers, this builds, for teachers, a complex network of data about the products on which students work. So when students come to SPACE, on the computer, they get to see a quick dashboard of their assignments and the kind of thing they are meant to do, and over what time period. They get a product overview so they get to see all the tasks they are asked to do and their deadlines. Students work on the tasks, and get to see, in one place (in the tool), the things they are being asked to do, and how they are going to be evaluated for doing it. Teachers can get student views or class views, and have information about where these tasks are in the process of project development. So, they can see who does what and what they are waiting for and what kind of progress the kids are making.

In one sense, these are the common tools for other kinds of instruction, and one of the reasons I think that other kinds of instruction proceed well is that those tools exist. So to make a different kind of instruction proceed well, you need tools for that instruction. Teachers and students can quickly assess student work and ask for revisions. And behind SPACE there's a rich database of the standards that students are working towards, a list of their assignments, what individual students have done, and which students have worked together in doing their work. So, SPACE becomes a reference source for doing the work of inquiry.

Among the things that we have learned in doing this work is that it gives us an interesting view of the organizational state. Teachers are constantly asking students to critique other students' work. Well, when you have many students doing critiques, it is very hard to keep track of all of them. We worked with several teachers who thought their students were pretty good at doing critiques. But, actually, by our judgment, the students were pretty awful at doing critiques. Having a tool such as this exposes for the teachers, and the students, the real state of play in their organization; the tool exposes a kind of hidden complexity. Having data such as this also drives professional development. Teachers find a lot to discuss in the evidence and space of each others' practice. It brings, and has brought literacy, social studies, and science teachers together, and has exposed common flaws in the ability to build an argument that cuts across domains.

We'd like to develop, in the ongoing refinement of SPACE, a way to support grouping. We'd like to have a means to capture and display a record of who works with whom and about what. We hope to be able to mine this kind of data to help teachers build better grouping strategies within project-based classrooms. So, we hope to be able to see records of which young people are good at which kinds of tasks, and, based on what they are good at, and also using social network data, based on their friendship structures, help teachers build groups better. Now in elementary schools, the task of grouping is core to the day-to-day work. But by the time you get to late middle school and high school, the task of grouping becomes a lost art. Some people are very good at it but there really are no useful core tools that underlie the task of doing grouping. So we hope that social network data can help teachers figure out how to put groups of students together. Teachers can leverage students who get along and can do work together.

Conclusion

I think that design is important because it is a vehicle to catalyze change. Design serves as a window for an organizational state. Design catalyzes change. It is a vehicle for moving organizations from one stable place to another stable place. Now one of my favorite little acronyms is that belief follows practice, not the other way around. And I think that designed artifacts catalogue practice and reform agendas are often about beliefs. If you want to move beliefs, you have to give people the cognitive tools to get there. I think that tools support coherent and common actions of instructions, but through persistent representations. I think that one way we can capture what is going on here is that design artifacts, in this world of coherence, are what some scholars call *value objects*. These artifacts are things that can inhabit multiple worlds.

The reason that I think design works so well for us in our research group is that design artifacts are boundary objects. They live well in a research world and they live well in a practice world. They inhabit multiple places. They allow us to talk about the same things using the same language. And these boundary objects create a common temporary perspective on our problems, especially in design mode. So, one way to think about boundary objects such as SPACE, Annotation, and social networks is that we all get to see the proper improvement through a common lens. Boundary objects serve as connectors in school improvement.

In summary, I think design is very important in bringing order to chaos. Schooling can be isolating and chaotic. The chaos and the isolation are reigned in, just a little bit, by having better tools. All actors and all organizations need coherent contexts to work within tools. For the work of education to be more of a design science, I believe that part of the problem we all face has to do with concerted action. Tools can provide a context for that action.

References

Anderson, L. W., & Sosniak, L. A. (Eds.). (1994). *Bloom's taxonomy: A forty–year retrospective*. Chicago: University of Chicago Press.

Bloom, B. (1988, March). Helping all children learn well in elementary school—and beyond. *Principal, 67*(4), 12–17.

Bloom, B. (1976). *Human characteristics and school learning*. New York, NY: McGraw-Hill.

Bloom, B., et al. (1956). *Taxonomy of educational objectives: The classification of educational goals*. New York, NY: McKay.

Bloom's Taxonomy: Affective Domain (Internalizing values-characterization). Retrieved from http://www.nwlink.com/~donclark/hrd/bloom.html

Bryk, A. S., & Gomez. L. M. (2008). Ruminations on reinventing an R&D capacity for educational improvement. In F. M. Hess (Ed.), *The future of educational entrepreneurship: Possibilities of school reform* (pp. 181–206). Cambridge, MA: Harvard Education Press.

Dewey, J. (1916). *Democracy and education. An introduction to the philoso-phy of education* (1966 ed.). New York, NY: Free Press.

Dewey, J. (1933). *How we think. A restatement of the relation of reflective thinking to the educative process* (Revised ed.). Boston, MA: D. C. Heath.

Dewey, J. (1938). *Experience and education.* New York, NY: Collier Books.

Krathwohl, D.R., Bloom, B.S., & Masia, B.B. (1964). *Taxonomy of educational objectives: The classification of educational goals. Handbook II: The affective domain.* New York: Longman, Green.

Levy, R., & Murnane, R. (2004). *The new division of labor: How comput-ers are creating the next job market.* Princeton, NJ: Princeton University Press and Russell Sage Foundation.

Pfeffer, J., & Sutton, R. (1999). *The knowing-doing gap: How smart companies turn knowledge into action.* Cambridge, MA: Harvard Business School Press.

Schoenfeld, A. (2006). What doesn't work: The challenge and failure of the What Works Clearing House to conduct meaningful reviews of studies of mathematics curricula. *Educational Researcher, 35*(2), 13–21.

13. Perceived Messages From the 2008–2010 Clayton Lectures: Overhauling Urban Education Through Developmental Science, Interdisciplinary Teamwork, and Even Litigation

Laura C. Murray
University of Pennsylvania

I am honored to be invited to summarize my recollections and reactions regarding the three most recent Clayton Lectures. After attending the 2010 and 2009 Clayton Lectures, and reviewing a tape of the 2008 lecture, I have concluded that these speakers are true pioneers whose wisdom and leadership guides the next generation of educational scholars as we navigate this second decade of the 21st century. Their insights contribute not only to change and innovation today, but also lay the groundwork for future researchers as we conceive and prepare for our own additions to the intersecting fields of developmental science and education.

Although Margaret Beale Spencer (2008), Sharon Ramey, Craig Ramey, John Fantuzzo, and Vivian Gadsden (all in 2009), and V. P. Franklin (2010) represent diverse academic fields (e.g., psychology, history), social perspectives (young children, adolescents), research trajectories (e.g., human development, psychological sciences, history) and expertise, I believe their remarks converge around the sad truth that we have not yet fulfilled the promise of quality public education for all of America's children. Dr. Sharon Ramey (2009) reminded us that "parental aspirations for children to be happy, healthy, and contributing citizens" are universal. "Although they may manifest differently in different cultures," she explained, "they are *universally shared* as goals for the next generation." If so, then much work remains to be done if we are to be, as Dr. Spencer has challenged us, "proactive in our responsibility to educate not only our *own* children around the dinner table, but also other people's children as well."

Synopsis of 2008 Clayton Lecture: Margaret Beale Spencer: Youth Identity and Development in the "Colorblind" American Context Post Brown 1954

Just a few days before the historic election of President Barack Obama, and in her final semester as a professor here at Penn (before returning to the University of Chicago, where she completed her doctoral training), Dr. Margaret Beale Spencer gave the 2008 Clayton Lecture, entitled, "Youth Identity and Development in the 'Colorblind' American Context Post *Brown* 1954." Dr. Spencer's remarks displayed her contagious commitment to the study of youth (particularly youth of color), and to understanding and supporting their identity development and resilience by openly addressing race in learning. As she eloquently explained–and with her own data from over 30 years of research to back it up—"color still matters in this country." Her lecture powerfully positioned race as central to human development, foregrounding the concept that acknowledging race is *essential* if educators are to provide all youth with the opportunities needed to reach their full potentials.

She positioned her own academic and professional development against the backdrop of cogent educational, psychological, and historical advancements from the *Brown* decision onward; and she clearly articulated her primary influences and the motivations behind her persistent research trajectory. Mamie and Kenneth Clarks' seminal 1940s "doll experiments" on children's racial attitudes sparked Dr. Spencer's intellectual interest, and she chose to replicate the Clarks' work as her master's thesis at the University of Kansas. This project in the late 1960s launched a course of research that she continues to this day.

In her talk, Dr. Spencer shared that it was her doctoral advisor at the University of Chicago, Dr. Edgar G. Epps (1999 Clayton lecturer), who first challenged her to think about how children's color and skin tone preferences might affect their *self-esteem*. In a groundbreaking departure from the assumption underlying the *Brown* decision (namely, that children's color preferences profoundly impact their self-esteem), Dr. Spencer initiated a line of research that was entirely original. "Since the Clarks, the assumption had always been that if Black children chose the White doll, then Black children must hate themselves," she explained. "That was imposing adult reasoning on children's meaning-making . . . and the assumption was, in fact, not accurate." In the 1970s and 1980s, she hypothesized that "using 1940s social science to undergird the *Brown* decision was a continued *misinterpretation* of psychological processes, and *potential*, in Black children."

In an effort to move past the common practice of studying Black children from a "deficit" or "pathology" perspective, she instead focused on normative development and on children's resilience and capacity to successfully achieve identity in the face of ubiquitous discrimination. Her countless studies of children's color preferences (with dolls, puppets, drawings, and even charts with different skin tone options) all lead to consistent results: (a) that color and race are discernible by preschoolers, (b) that race and skin color matter for ego identity processes beginning in middle childhood, (c) that children's racial attitudes do not necessarily affect their global self-esteem adversely, and (d) that adolescents' capacity to shift from earlier "informally learned" social stereotypes to an "own-group cultural identity" and orientation allows for profound protection against institutionalized racism. These revolutionary findings continue to have compelling implications for the design of teacher training efforts, educational policy recommendations, and social-service strategies today.

After explicating her own theory of human development (the "Phenomenological Variant of Ecological Systems Theory"—aka P-VEST), and emphasizing that "how an individual thinks and makes sense of the world *matters*," Dr. Spencer circled back to the pioneering legislation that initially ignited her interest in race and education. "It seems to me," she said, "that if the Brown decision were truly designed to right the wrongs of history, a still nagging need is to acknowledge the fact that humanity generally ignores the problem of risk and vulnerability associated with White privilege, and that these issues *continue* to be ignored."

In closing, she invited the audience to work toward accommodating the diversity of experiences of *all* youth, and to commit to creating programmatic educational efforts and supports that actually make a difference. "Remember," she said, "if 'supports' are not adequate and reality-based, they may not be experienced by youth as, indeed, supportive."

Dr. Spencer's tenacity and commitment to scientific inquiry is an inspiration to emerging scholars. Her decades of work and personal commitment to the complexities of one over-arching research question—how race affects youth development—highlight the importance of what she herself, terms "dogged research persistence." Dr. Spencer reminds us that, regardless of our research focus, we must ultimately use developmental science and empirical data to improve the human experience and push against the barriers that harm or divide us. In fact, one of the great paradoxes of human development, and one that we might never have recognized without Dr. Spencer's work, may be that the more we are able to identify with others "in our group," the greater our capacity to tolerate—and even celebrate—difference.

Synopsis of 2009 Panel Discussion: Craig Ramey, Sharon Ramey, John Fantuzzo, and Vivian Gadsden, moderated by Diana Slaughter-Defoe: Early Education Forum: Is Early Childhood Education a Realistic Strategy for Urban School Reform?

In 2009, the Clayton Lecture took the form of a panel discussion among four eminent scholars in the field of early child development: Drs. Craig and Sharon Ramey (guests from Georgetown University), and Penn GSE's own Dr. John Fantuzzo and Dr. Vivian Gadsden. The title of their conversation was "Early Education Forum: Is Early Childhood Education a Realistic Strategy for Urban School Reform?" It was a privilege to hear these four nationally renowned experts engage in an animated discussion ranging from brain plasticity and individual differences, to the importance of cultural competence when working with parents of young children, to the many challenges of actually *implementing* interventions in school settings. A key component of the discussion was, of course, the Rameys' landmark longitudinal "Abecedarian Study," in which they followed children from birth to age 30, documenting the myriad positive effects of an intensive preschool program on children's later outcomes.

Craig Ramey opened the discussion by winning over the crowd of educators in admitting that he "couldn't think of any instrument that we have to help us control our future that is even *close* to the power of education." Sharon Ramey concurred, foregrounding the necessity of "infusing our schools of education with more of the science of human development."

After receiving applause, Craig Ramey went on to discuss recent advances in brain scanning technologies (such as functional magnetic resonance imaging) and the excitement of "finally being able to see brains in action *in real-time.*" After explaining that experience truly does alter brain structure and function, he shared a real-world example of an effective and systematic intervention to "grow brains"—his own *Abecedarian Study.*

Begun in North Carolina in 1977, *Abecedarian* was a randomized controlled trial investigating the potential benefits of early childhood education for poor children. Four cohorts of individuals, born between 1972 and 1977, were randomly assigned to either the early educational intervention group or the control group. Children from low-income families received a full-time, high-quality educational intervention in a childcare setting from infancy through age five. Activities focused on social, emotional, and cognitive areas of development, and the children's progress was monitored with follow-up studies conducted at ages 12, 15, 21, and 30. Dr. Ramey catalogued "a whole cascade of positive effects" for the children who received the intervention, including improved reading and math achievement all the way through high school; a threefold increase in the likelihood of going to college; fewer special education placements and grade retentions; and higher education levels, job status, and earnings at 30 years of age.

Championing these dramatic results, and the multiple replication studies that the Rameys have conducted over the past several decades, Dr. Fantuzzo commented that "we now have solid knowledge about *what* needs to be done," but added that "where we go bump in the night is the 'how' and 'with whom.'" He highlighted the importance of forming relationships with stakeholders across disciplines, and argued that "complex structural equation models and diagrams locked in academic texts won't help us." Dr. Sharon Ramey agreed that research-to-practice is key, claiming that "the new challenge is trying to get people to implement what we *know* works." As a tangible example of the importance of partnership and teamwork, Dr. Ramey then recounted the *National Transition Demonstration Study* (for which she and Craig Ramey were the primary investigators). This longitudinal study was designed to test the value of extending comprehensive, Head Start-like supports through third grade. Between the 1991–92 and 1997–98 school years, 11,000 children in 31 sites throughout 30 states participated.

"What we learned," Dr. Ramey said, with a measure of disappointment, "is that all of that extra stuff didn't seem to make as much of a difference as we had hoped." She explained that despite "good intentions and hardworking people," there were too many obstacles to implementation at the vast majority of demonstration sites. "People just couldn't adequately implement their programs in the way that they wanted. . . . And this is a major challenge to our field: money and good intentions are simply not enough to make transformation happen."

Dr. Gadsden reminded those in attendance to remain optimistic, however, and advised "although we may not be able to transform *everything*" in terms of context and culture, "we do have the opportunity to transform the lives of the children right in front of us." She also suggested that both the *Abecedarian* and the *Transition* studies were instrumental in turning the idea of "school readiness" on its head. Citing (Stanford University School of Education Professor) Deborah Stipek, Dr. Gadsden eloquently reminded us to "worry less about getting children ready to learn, and more about getting schools ready for children."

The discussion among these four scholars was rich, timely, and varied; its focus, however, was clear: academics and practitioners across disciplines must work together—and include parents and families—to bring the latest scientific research to bear on the actual practice of teaching young children. Collaboration that prizes translation, dissemination, and successful execution of programming to improve early childhood education is vital.

Synopsis of Clayton Lecture 2010 by Dr. V. P. Franklin: "A Freedom That Feels Like Love": Reparations, the Testing Industry, and the Promise of Freedom Schooling

Dr. V. P. Franklin, Professor of History and Education at the University of California, Riverside, gave the 2010 Clayton lecture, entitled " 'A Freedom That Feels Like Love': Reparations, the Testing Industry, and the Promise of Freedom Schooling." With the ferocity of a preacher, the eloquence of a storyteller, and the detail of a historian, Dr. Franklin wove together what might at first glance appear to be three wholly unrelated themes: reparation lawsuits for people of color in the U.S., the harmful assumption that standardized tests can actually assess innate ability, and his own vision for alternative urban schooling. He seamlessly constructed a case for what he calls "Freedom Schools" (theme-based schools that shun standardized testing and prize "mastery learning" and cultural diversity), while indicting high-stakes testing and promoting litigation as a vehicle to fund school reform.

Dr. Franklin used his own 1978 *Teacher's College Record* article (written with Ronald Batchelor), "Freedom Schooling: A New Approach to Federal-Local Cooperation in Public Education" to launch an exploration of 30 years of inequality in U.S. primary and secondary education. Quoting that early article, he shared that "having witnessed the high rates of academic failure in traditional public schools, and having participated in highly successful and innovative programs created in urban magnet schools" he and Ronald Batchelor called for Freedom Schooling. This approach was to be "a new relationship or partnership between the federal government and local school districts to introduce alternative educational programs, practices, and structures into American public elementary and secondary education." Their recommendation was that the federal government evaluate alternative programs and institutions, providing financial assistance to public school systems actively involved in successful alternative education.

The original Freedom Schools were opened in various parts of the American South during and after the Civil War as a way to provide basic literacy skills to formerly enslaved African Americans. In addition, Civil Rights workers and volunteers during Freedom Summer (1964) opened multiple Freedom Schools in Mississippi for Black children who had previously been deprived of educational opportunities. Since 1995, The Children's Defense Fund has adopted and expanded the model. "In 2009 alone," Dr. Franklin explained, "The Children's Defense Fund reported that they served 8,500 students, worked with 970 student leader interns at 134 sites, involving 99 organizations and 79 cities in 27 states. So Freedom Schools do indeed remain."

After describing the impact of Freedom Schools—both past and present— Dr. Franklin sketched a picture of magnet and charter schools as comparison. In the 1970s, the Office of Education, through appropriation of Title VI, made funds available for the opening of magnet schools; the goal was to attract White students back into predominantly Black and minority public school districts. Different schools specialized in various areas, such as performing arts; music; science, engineering, and technology; foreign languages; and sports and athletics.

Dr. Franklin reported that on the basis of what he witnessed at early magnets, and on what was reported by the schools themselves, he concluded that their specialized and innovative content lead to increased motivation among students. He explained that in states where comparisons were made in the academic achievement levels of Black and White, magnet and non-magnet students, researchers found that African American and Latino students "made greater gains in math and reading than did their fellow students who stayed in the traditional urban schools." In addition, White students attending the magnet schools "outdid their peers at traditional suburban, and generally much whiter, schools, too."

Pointing to 30 years of data on the success of magnet schools, Dr. Franklin ended this section of his lecture by reiterating what he and colleagues advocated in 1978: "Freedom Schools similar to magnet schools, but not solely for the purpose of school desegregation."

Following this foundation, Dr. Franklin offered a forceful critique of charter schools and the recent media attention and acclaim that they've garnered. He denounced the 2010 documentary film *Waiting for Superman* on the grounds that it unduly demonized teachers' unions, and dangerously exaggerated certain charter schools' successes. "Have unionized public school teachers in the past produced high levels of student engagement, parental involvement, and academic achievement in public schools similar to or better than that attributed to the Kipp Schools, the Harlem Children's Zone Promise Academies, and the Summit Academy?" he asked. "The answer is *yes*, but in the film the narrator only mentioned once the high demand for the limited spaces in public magnet schools." Franklin again offered his conception of 21st century Freedom Schools (built upon successful magnet school models) as an alternative to both traditional public schools *and* charter schools.

Next, Dr. Franklin linked recent increases in school dropout to the No Child Left Behind legislation and its high-stakes testing mandates, claiming that standardized tests and accountability measures "push kids out of schools." Eight years after the institution of NCLB, he said, "we are dealing with severe cases of educational malfeasance." Here he segued into a description of the "pipeline from public school to prison," and gracefully indicted "the private prison industry" as well as "big-business standardized testing agencies" for causing undue harm to minority children. The damage done by the testing industry, he claimed, was due to the fact that their products claimed to measure *innate ability*. ETS and College Board instruments, he said, were falsely used as "proof" that minority children did not have the same abilities as White children. This flawed assumption, he said, was then used to "justify" under-resourced schools and inadequate instruction for minority children, culminating in a widespread denial of the complex social factors behind disparities in academic achievement. This denial, Dr. Franklin explained, undergirded our collective refusal to allocate tax-payer dollars to improving infrastructure and pedagogy "to *those* children" who were, apparently, incapable of learning.

Concluding his polemic on standardized testing, Dr. Franklin returned to Freedom Schools, and ended his remarks with a powerful plea to concerned citizens everywhere to launch "reparations lawsuits" against the myriad agencies that stand in the way of quality education for children of color. "And what would we *do* with the money won in these class-action lawsuits?" he asked with a smile, "we'd open Freedom Schools!"

Whether one agrees with Dr. Franklin's thesis regarding litigation as a funding mechanism for alternative schooling or not, his premise that urban public education needs a systems overhaul cannot be denied, and his passion for reform is inspiring. He reminds us that access to quality education is a legal right for children in the United States, and his argument forces us to think critically about whether, and when, we do and do not fulfill this mandate.

Conclusion

Although, as stated earlier, I believe that these lectures "converge around the sad truth that we have not yet fulfilled the promise of quality public education" for all of America's children, I also believe that each presentation offers hope for the future. In 2008, Dr. Spencer reminded us that, historically, psychology and education have framed African American students as "less than" or somehow not equipped to succeed. However, her research powerfully refutes this misconception. Our job as the next generation of scholars is to continue to disseminate her important findings, assisting educators in developing culturally competent programming, curricula, and supports for children. These supports should acknowledge race and give young people the opportunity to openly discuss race and ethnicity in school settings and beyond. How can youth begin to unpack the complexities of these issues if we, as caring adults, remain too anxious to initiate the conversation?

The 2009 panel, after reminding us of the challenges of collaboration and implementation when jump-starting early education interventions, also ultimately leaves us optimistic. In the last decade, we have seen unprecedented advances in neuroscience, and today, early childhood is broadly recognized as a critical period for development. We understand from Drs. Sharon and Craig Ramey that brains are elastic, and that just as developing minds can be harmed by neglect or deprivation, they can also be nurtured and enriched with adequate resources and scaffolding. The next decade will no doubt prove to be just as rich with new information and new challenges; and as long as we put equal effort into empirical research *and* effective program implementation, just as the Rameys and Drs. Fantuzzo and Gadsden have done, we can and will make great strides in supporting children's optimal development.

Although there is arguably no single or "best" way to offer quality education to urban youth, Dr. V.P. Franklin made the important point in his 2010 lecture that we must continue to test new formulas for success, and that, indeed, a "successful" school in one context or community may not see favorable outcomes elsewhere. His remarks seem more a call to arms than anything else. We must keep searching for strategies to educate youth and promote healthy academic, social, and emotional development in diverse settings. And, of course, we must be creative—revolutionary, even—when envisioning ways to sustain such positive change.

I believe that broad—and consistent—economic disparities keep some schools and students in a state of "concentrated disadvantage." Until we address these seemingly intractable financial obstacles with systemic policy change, it's doubtful that *any* school, curricular, or pedagogical reform will stick. The persistent question remains: "Who will *pay* for all of this?" We don't yet have a comprehensive solution, but we do know that the answer cannot continue to be "the children." They have clearly paid enough already.

In closing, the Clayton lecture series has stood not only as a tribute to Dr. Constance E. Clayton's legacy as an administrator and educational reformer in Philadelphia, but also as an important addition to the training that we graduate students receive. Over the past 13 years, countless students like myself have benefited from the wisdom and insights shared by visiting scholars. And I humbly speak for fellow researchers-in-training by sending a heartfelt "thank you" to all of those lecturers, and also to my mentor and advisor, Dr. Diana Slaughter-Defoe, for making this series a reality.

Author Note

As a doctoral student in Interdisciplinary Studies in Human Development at the University of Pennsylvania's Graduate School of Education, I am honored to have been invited to summarize my recollections and reactions regarding the three most recent Clayton Lectures.

14. March 22, 2011 Interview with Dr. Constance E. Clayton: "Reflections on the Clayton Leadership Era in the School District of Philadelphia"

CONSTANCE E. CLAYTON AND DIANA T. SLAUGHTER-DEFOE
University of Pennsylvania

Slaughter-Defoe: I must tell you, Dr. Clayton just how excited and pleased I am to conduct this interview with you. All people have dreams and one of my dreams was to do something before I retired that—would honor you, even if only in a small way, for the difference that you made in my own life. And so doing this volume and being able to include this interview in it is such a pleasure and such a treat. Thank you so much for agreeing to do this interview.

Clayton: Well you're very kind; however, as I've said to you on numerous occasions Diana, it was a privilege to have [you] as the Clayton Chair Professor. We were honored and I was very, very excited when you were selected because I knew the experience and the commitment you brought to the work of education.

Slaughter-Defoe: Thank you so much . . .

Clayton: I think that you need to reconsider retiring.

Slaughter-Defoe: [*Laughs*] Well we're here to talk about *your* legacy. And I have my questions and I'm going to move forward with them because I know that each one of these could be the subject of a long monologue.

Your legacy, in my opinion, includes an exemplary record of educational and human service to Philadelphia citizens. When you were creating and molding your legacy, and I'm sure you weren't thinking necessarily about it like that at the time, why did you choose to invest your life in urban educational reform?

Clayton: That is a very interesting question and I must admit I wasn't thinking about it at the time. I think I was really very concerned that the language that is usually [used] to depict urban school children is the language of failure. And so that gave me concern because it's been my experience that children want to learn, their parents want them to learn, and children can learn. All children can learn and be successful.

Slaughter-Defoe: I think your article here in *The Nation*[1]

Clayton: Yes.

Slaughter-Defoe: . . . really starts to address that (i.e., Dr. Clayton's firm conviction that all children can learn and be successful) doesn't it?

Clayton: It really does. We can educate all children is my—the article in *The Nation.* And then of course I quote Ron Edmonds (in *The Nation* article) just briefly when he says " . . . *whenever and wherever we choose, successfully we can educate all children; it's a matter of deciding whether we really want to do it.* " And I just have not been convinced that there is that kind of pledging commitment to educate all children.

Slaughter-Defoe: In some ways I worry that we might even be going backward with the retrenchment in State budgets now . . .

Clayton: Well there's an assault on education.

Slaughter-Defoe: Yes; yes. We are so fortunate that you committed your life to urban education. In fact, you did such a good job at it that you were, just for the record, the first African American woman in history to have an endowed chair named for her at a major, predominantly White American university. Now you may not have known this but I knew it. And that is why I left Northwestern University to come to the University of Pennsylvania. I was quite satisfied with my professorial status at Northwestern. Evanston is a beautiful community and at the time that I interviewed I had been there almost 20 years. Before being contacted by Penn, I had every intention of ending my career at Northwestern University.

But I realized at the time that I had never heard nor had known of an endowed chair at any university of the stature of the University of Pennsylvania named for any African American woman. And so I told myself, I've got to leave my "cushy little life" in the Evanston suburbs and come to Penn because I want to be part of this history.

There were 69 donors who made large and small donations to your chair. Can you tell me in retrospect what you remember about how this extraordinary honor came about?

Clayton: I really need to give that a lot of thought. I distinctly remember Dr. Bernard Watson who was then the President of the William Penn Foundation and a long-time family friend and a former Deputy Superintendent of the School District of Philadelphia, and Bernie knew that—and I've often said to people who were kind enough to think of me—in giving me awards, that I didn't need any more plaques and that we needed to find a way to do something, do something for children.

And so of course the then Dean at the School of Education and Dr. Watson and others determined that that's the way they would do it. They don't give ladies wristwatches I don't think [*Laughs*]—and I certainly didn't need any more plaques.

Slaughter-Defoe: Well, this is a wonderful, wonderful legacy. I should mention that since that time when your chair was endowed there have been other endowed chairs named in honor of African American women: Ida B. Wells Barnett at DePaul University in Chicago, IL, Sarah Lawrence Lightfoot at Harvard University, for example. But for the record, as far as we know, yours was the first. Since I have been at Penn, this fact was called to my attention once again by a librarian at Fisk University.[2] That is quite a distinction. And at the time that the chair was endowed, I think you had been Philadelphia's school superintendent for 13 years before retiring.

Clayton: Eleven years, which was the record for a Superintendent.

Slaughter-Defoe: Eleven years?

Clayton: Yes.

Slaughter-Defoe: Wow! How did you do it? What did you understand about it? Why did they want to do this? This is a big thing; why did they want to establish this chair in your name at the University of Pennsylvania?

Clayton: Well I think the persons who were responsible wanted to indicate the importance of urban education and the fact that children can learn, and we needed to really stop articulating that children are our most important resource when we don't back that up with human and/or fiscal resources.

Slaughter-Defoe: I know that every Clayton lecturer that I invited over the past 13 years was genuinely honored by the invitation to lecture at the University of Pennsylvania in deference to your contributions. Now we never did invite you to lecture because we didn't want to put you to work, but if you had been invited, what would you have talked about and why?

Clayton: Well it would not have been putting me to work; it was just a continuation of my work. I'm still working as a matter of fact, as you well know. I would have lectured on probably Early Childhood Education and the importance of it, but of course you had a splendid lecturer do that anyway. And I would have lectured on probably what I wrote in the *Nation*, that we can educate all our children. I'm absolutely unflinching in my determination that we see children as children of value. So, that probably would have been my lecture.

Slaughter-Defoe: Several scholars have documented—and I think I hear some of that in your emphasis on the importance of children— have documented a strong activist tradition of leadership among African American educators, especially in the pre-*Brown v. Board of Education* era.

So, historically speaking, in your opinion, have African American educators been particularly optimistic in addressing pervasive educational problems?

Clayton: I think that they have been active to a degree but not as much as we need to be. There's always room for improvement and always room for expansion because the issues confronting children, be they African American, or of any ethnic or racial or religious group, are really of enormous proportions. And so I think that African Americans have been very active in addressing educational disparities, but there's certainly room for expansion.

Slaughter-Defoe: You've always been a Northern educator. Would you make any distinction between activism among the Northern, versus Southern, educational leaders, that you've encountered?

Clayton: Honestly I haven't done any research in that regard; however it would appear just on the surface that Southerners have been very much involved in being activists in terms of addressing pervasive educational issues. I think it has started—I think it begins with the African American family—the Southern family, the Southern churches, and the educators, and I think the Northerners could learn from them.

Slaughter-Defoe: Do you even see yourself as an activist educator?

Clayton: I do. Absolutely.

Slaughter-Defoe: Absolutely—so would you elaborate on that? What is an activist educator?

Clayton: Well for me personally it has been not sitting idly by and being silent when I see the injustices, the omissions, and the negativity as it pertains to urban children. I've taken several different stands in that regard. I must admit that within my own School District, some of my Board Members did not see the importance of Early Childhood Education. But my own research here at this University, at the University of Pennsylvania, was done in terms of the carry-over effects of Early Childhood Education.

Slaughter-Defoe: Right.

Clayton: And so therefore I could clearly define my findings and they were really very positive in terms of the longevity of children staying in school and not dropping out, better academic achievement . . . but I distinctly remember thinking—having a Board Member [ask] why was I paying— that paying for Early Childhood Education for a child was as much as a college tuition. Evidently they [i.e., persons like the Board Member] don't understand the cost of ignorance, [of] allowing it to manifest itself.

Slaughter-Defoe: If I'm not mistaken wasn't it during your Administration that Project Head Start and other related early childhood programs were brought to schools in the School District of Philadelphia?

Clayton: Actually prior to my becoming Superintendent, I wrote the first historic grant for the City of Philadelphia for the School District. And we received a quarter of a million dollars to initiate Head Start, but I did that years before I became Superintendent. So I've had a long commitment to Early Childhood Education. But during my tenure I expanded early childhood services and increased the School District's contribution to daycare. We expanded daycare and had daycare in every section of the City.

Slaughter-Defoe: And it's still there today?

Clayton: It is still there.

Slaughter-Defoe: So you put in place something that is still in existence today?

Clayton: Well I think today there is recognition of the importance of early childhood. And I think people have become more vocal and articulate on the value of early education.

Slaughter-Defoe: Uh-hmm.

Clayton: Let me indicate another way that I might be an activist. I insisted that teachers with young children were credentialed. Play is important; however, it's also been proven that children learn very early and so therefore, we had credentialed and certified teachers working with our children in daycare programs, in childcare programs, and in Head Start.

Another way that I was an activist was when I introduced the breakfast program for children. We had the lunch program—but children who are hungry don't learn as readily as others and I distinctly recall the Federal Government wanting me to give children tickets if they were eligible, poverty stricken; they would go through the line to get a breakfast but also have to hand in a token or a ticket of some kind. I refused. And they said, "Well Dr. Clayton we will—we might have to remove the program." I said, "No; you won't—you can't do that. Why don't you come to Philadelphia and see my kids?" And they did; I invited them to meet me at a school (long pause) . . .

Slaughter-Defoe: Take your time; take your time . . .

Clayton: I invited them to meet me at a school at 7:30 in the morning and they did. And here were these little kids walking through lines to get some breakfast. It had occurred to me that if I had been a student in line and my family was able to afford breakfast for me but the kid in back of me could not . . . you know children can be unkind to each other.

Slaughter-Defoe: They can be very unkind indeed.

Clayton: And so that [i.e., having a token or ticket] says: "You know Susie Smith is poor, and look, she has to have her breakfast paid for." That didn't make sense to me. They [the visitors from the Federal Government] were convinced and they allowed me to continue the program.

Slaughter-Defoe: Yes; it hurts to think that people have to be shown things like that. They should be able to figure it out on their own shouldn't they?

Clayton: Well they really should. But that's what I said; they don't see all children as children of value.

Slaughter-Defoe: I remember reading an interview on school reform with you and Michelle Fine and another gentleman from Penn (Robert Schwartz),[3] and in that interview you were talking about initiating some work with the high school students too. That was another initiative that you began just before you retired. You were trying to make the point that just because you're an older child doesn't mean you're—

Clayton: Well you don't give up on children ever. That was my philosophy then and it still is. Who are we to pre-judge the ability and the accomplishments that children may make? And how many children have been cast aside and how much have we lost as a nation because we didn't see the benefit and give children the chance to learn at different paces and in different styles. Our children are not to be thrown away.

Slaughter-Defoe: Uh-hmm . . . What lessons should younger generations of African American educators be paying attention to as they observe the legacy of previous generations of African American educators now? It seems to me that's one strong lesson isn't it—not to ever give up on children?

Clayton: You don't give up on children.

Slaughter-Defoe: And see all children as children of value?

Clayton: Yes, as children of value, and not to take anything for granted. I mean I must admit that I think African Americans thought with the election of President Obama that we had reached a pinnacle, but the truth of the matter is it was a step on that mountain trail. I think if they really would take time to analyze it, they can see that. If they listen very carefully and analyze how people are treating President Obama today, [they say that] "He's too professorial." I mean are we asking for mediocrity?! The overt racist attitudes that I'm observing, and the lack of respect for him as a person, as an African American, and as the President of the United States, is just unconscionable.

And so I think the younger generation needs to look at that and not assume that because Mr. Obama has reached the pinnacle of high office in this country that every wrong will be righted and that things will—that the struggle is over. The struggle is not over.

Slaughter-Defoe: There's much to be done . . .

Clayton: That is right. I think they have to take—I think young African Americans in the coming generations have to take more than a "can-do" attitude; they have to take a "will-do" attitude. It's always been a case where minorities, some minorities have had to prove themselves over and over again. Jesse Jackson says "You know we can do." I take it beyond "*can do*" to what we "*will do.*"

And I think if they look at the people like Mary McLeod Bethune, who began a University [Bethune-Cookman College], if we look at Geoffrey

Canada, a contemporary gentleman [and educator] who created his own School in Harlem, and if we look at Leon Sullivan [founder] of Opportunities Industrialization Center [OIC], . . . I mean there are many, many role models, and I would like to see our younger generation take a look at those people and understand the struggles that they had but [also] see their determination and their perseverance.

Slaughter-Defoe: Well you certainly have been a role model. I believe from what I read of your background, you worked at every level in the system. You were a teacher—

Clayton: I was a classroom teacher. I've been a supervisor, and then Deputy Superintendent, Associate Superintendent excuse me, and then the Superintendent. And I applied for all of my positions. I didn't have anybody give them to me. I didn't grow up in a family where the expectation was that you were entitled. You worked for it.

Slaughter-Defoe: Uh-hmm. What is the capacity of African American educators in the post-20th century Civil Rights Era to forge alliances, and to transform public education for African American children?

Clayton: Well I think the capacity is self-defined. I mean if they set the bar low then that's where it'll be. But if you believe that "I have unlimited capacity and I will exhaust that capacity in terms of working for future generations," anything is possible. I think it's very clear that we need to forge alliances. I hear people often say that it takes a village and I think that statement need not be mere rhetoric. You have to align yourself with people of like thinking and philosophy and determination—and remove yourself from those who are not allies.

Slaughter-Defoe: Yeah, it seems to me that if you looked at it as just a technological problem, future generations have more capacity than ever to be networked—

Clayton: That's right.

Slaughter-Defoe: —and come together and communicate.

Clayton: Well we're seeing that. We've seen that all over the world in terms of what they're calling now "social networking." And the younger generations are very, very skillful, very astute, and readily identify with the social networking [capacities of the] Internet.

Slaughter-Defoe: So it's a matter of whether they have the will isn't it?

Clayton: It's a matter of the will; yes. But I think we have to also constantly show them that they do have the will and the capacity. We have to stop speaking to our children in terms of what they cannot do. As a matter of fact, I've said to children and to teachers, delete the word *can't* from your vocabulary.

Slaughter-Defoe: Uh-hmm . . . [*Laughs*] do you personally see the potential for contemporary urban youth to lead the Civil Rights Movement, particularly to address pervasive educational inequalities that are relevant to their generation? Please elaborate if you can.

Clayton: I'm going to say hopefully yes. [*Laughs*] I think they—I think they have the potential. I'm beginning to see young people make very potent statements about what they feel their rights are but I think I want to hear them talk about responsibility as well. And I want to see them take the same unflinching interest in education as they take in rap music [for example] and other things.

Slaughter-Defoe: [*Laughs*] Reflecting back now on your tenure, and it's an 11-year tenure as the Superintendent of the Philadelphia Public Schools, is there any initiative you would have implemented yet were restrained from doing at the time due to unlimited money and resources?

Clayton: There were always money constraints. I inherited a system that had a $165 million deficit.

Slaughter-Defoe: Hmm.

Clayton: But I left the system with an $11 million surplus and that was without cutting Art, Music, or Libraries or Early Childhood Education.

Slaughter-Defoe: Oh?

Clayton: Much to my dismay, I found on the payroll of our school system 1,200 people for whom there were no personnel dockets. One of the things that I did find was that—and I don't want to make—and I will not make a generalized statement—people were given, literally given, jobs. I made it very clear in my inaugural statement of October 1982 that the children come first. The school system was there for the children; we were not there to give jobs to the friends of politicians or the friends of anybody, for that matter.

And so it became very clear during my Administration that I expected people to apply for a position, to sit for an exam for the position, and to be successful in it and to come with their credentials. In fact, one politician in a publication in Philadelphia was quoted as saying "We would have given Connie Clayton more money but she wouldn't have known what to do with it."

Let me tell you what that really means. It meant that I would not have given him money to do what he wanted to do and to hire his friends and his cronies, and I stood by that even to the point where one time in my office he asked me if he had to go to my Board President. At that point I said, "Don't threaten me ever, because you know I'm not going to acquiesce."

I mean there were some folks who thought I was a little bit arrogant and you know, that I was the "Black [queen] bee," but that's all right. I mean, I was named by my parents. I was never confused about my name. But if I had had more money I think I would have given every child sets of books to take home: Literature books, books related to their academic subjects as well. Children need—

Slaughter-Defoe: A library at home.

Clayton: —they need a library at home. I even found when I went into office that some of the libraries in the schools were closed. And I visited every school during my tenure.

Slaughter-Defoe: *Every* school?

Clayton: Every school. I visited every school. People would say to me this is the first time we've seen a Superintendent. And I said, "Well, get used to it because you will see me."

It was interesting; the Principals often said, "Dr. Clayton, just a minute and I will take you around the building." And I replied, "No; I'm a citizen first and then I'm a Superintendent. I know my way around buildings." And so I would go in and visit, because I didn't want "show and tell." I wanted to see the classrooms; I would go in and sit down and sit in the back of the room to see if I could read the handwriting or the printing on the chalkboards, and I would look at the bulletin boards to see what kind of papers were posted on the children's lessons. Had they been up there for two months, or did they reflect ongoing learning?

Then if I sat in the back of the room I could see how the teacher interacted with children, who she called on and who she didn't call on, because we have a way of demeaning kids. If their hands are raised, they think they know the answer, and probably do, and [some] are never called on. There are many, many ways to demean kids. That's why I say that *all* children are children of value. And even if they have the wrong answer, the fact is that they were trying to answer and wanted to answer.

So I would probably give books away and I'm going to speak in a few minutes about how I did give my money away because I had a Superintendent's contingency fund. I would probably have afterschool classes, particularly for hobbies, so the children could develop hobbies. When I was growing up—

Slaughter-Defoe: Uh-hmm—Find their talents.

Clayton: That's right. When I was growing up you know I had many interesting things that I wanted to do, and of course I had a very supportive family so I was able to. . . . But children . . . have all kinds of interesting things that they want to do and can do [e.g., stamp collecting], so they could. . . . I would use my money that way.

Speaking of using the Superintendent's money, you know it's very easy to honor kids who are academically proficient. And we started off with honoring the top 10 highest academic kids in every school. So one morning I went into my Cabinet meeting and I said, "You know it's easy to do that. Why aren't we honoring children for a variety of reasons?" And they said "For what, Connie; What do you mean?" I said "How about the kid who showed improvement or the kids whose attendance was poor but began to come to school?"

And so we did; and we had an Evening of Excellence. And we moved it around the City and I would write a letter to ask the teachers and the principals to give me the names of kids who had shown definitive improvement. And they did. But what I didn't tell them was what we were going to do. We had a speaker—we used to have a speaker, a motivating speaker to talk to them. And the children were to come with their parents. And I'll never forget one night I gave $250 to every child. And a parent said—came down the aisle. I thought what did we do wrong? And she was so upset. She said "Dr. Clayton; you've given my child some money—$250 . . . I had to borrow a car to get him here tonight."

Slaughter-Defoe: Lord have mercy . . .

Clayton: So those are the kinds of things—and we gave awards to children who helped senior citizens and had done service work in their communities. And there were some kids who because their parents had gone to work early, they were really the "responsible adult," the older sibling who saw the children off to school—things like that. We just don't even understand how children make it in spite of the society in which they live.

But I had one Board member who said to me, "Dr. Clayton, you're giving this money to these families?" I replied, "It's in the budget for my use." And so of course he didn't raise the question anymore, but it [i.e., the question] was a clear lack of sensitivity regarding the needs of families and children.

Slaughter-Defoe: You know when I first came to the University, my first Administrative Assistant was a young woman who went to Philadelphia's schools; she told me that she was so happy to work with me because she remembered that you had written her a letter of congratulations and she still had the letter.

Clayton: Well I wrote—I do hear that today.

Slaughter-Defoe: I don't know whether she had improved or—

Clayton: Yes. I hear that today. Nobody signed my letters for me. I wrote them myself—I wrote all of them.

Slaughter-Defoe: It was personal.

Clayton: It's a personal letter.

Slaughter-Defoe: A personal letter.

Clayton: As a matter of fact I even wrote—I wrote the teachers and the children. And I had teachers who would say to me, "Dr. Clayton, you signed the letter." I said, "Of course, I signed the letter," because I wouldn't allow a name stamp to be used. The only name stamp was on checks that paid, you know, the payroll. But I used to sit in meetings with a stack of letters and I would write and I would use blue ink so it didn't look printed. And I meet people in the supermarket today who still have pictures or letters.

Slaughter-Defoe: Well my administrative assistant told me. Her maiden name was Williams; she's married now but she told me that she had gotten one of those letters. You sent it—She had maybe made progress in her work in school. I don't know what the circumstance was, but she prized that letter. It was as if she had gotten a plaque (prized award). She prized it and she told me so; it was one of the very first things that she told me.

Clayton: Well a Superintendent can't be a Superintendent or an educator or care about kids and staff by sitting in an office somewhere. You just cannot do that. There was another thing that we decided to do: I decided to invite people to have dinner with me. And they were—they couldn't believe it. And I said to the Personnel Office, " . . . just randomly select every third name," which is what they did. And so we sent a letter to every third name from our list of staff members in the District and they would come down to the Board of Education, to have dinner and there were no constraints. They could ask any question and I had the Cabinet there to respond to them. Small gestures like that mean a lot to people.

Slaughter-Defoe: Yes, they do. And here's another question. How would you like your legacy as an educational leader to be remembered? Let's put it this way, it will clearly be remembered. This is understood, and we know that, but—how would you *like* it to be remembered? That's the question.

Clayton: As valuing children and their right to be taught and to learn and as valuing and respecting them and their families. I'd like to be remembered for integrity. And of course for making incremental academic progress which is what we did. Our test scores didn't shoot up overnight because I don't think that's honest. But incrementally our test scores did go up because we were honest and we tested all children—special needs as well as children in regular classes.

[And] I'd like to be remembered for having courage.

Slaughter-Defoe: Under pressure—under great pressure.

Clayton: Pressure particularly from politicians—some politicians. Again I don't want to generalize—from some politicians. But I must admit, I had an excellent working relationship with my Unions and I had seven.

Slaughter-Defoe: Seven?

Clayton: Yes, we had seven Unions and I am pleased about the fact that prior to my Administration there were five strikes in seven years and when I calculated it children had lost a full year of school. And in my 11 years we didn't have a single strike, because I met with the Union and I indicated particularly to the Teachers Union that without the children there's no need for you or for me.

Slaughter-Defoe: What made you so clear that education and schools are about the children? I ask that because I've spent most of my years [career] in schools of education. I was in the Department of Education part of the time at the University of Chicago. I was in Northwestern University's School of Education and Social Policy. And then I've been here at Penn now 13-and-a-half years as of this coming June. And I would go so far as to generalize and say 90 percent of the educators that I have encountered have stopped at the point of curriculum and do not understand that education is about the children.

That may be an extreme statement but I've seen people who love to teach; they love to teach a subject matter because they want to share their love of it. So they might be an English teacher. And they really became an English teacher because they love literature, English literature or American literature. And they want to share their love of that subject matter with the children. But the children are only a means to an end of sharing what they really like. It might be math; it might be something else. But you seem to have been so very, very clear for such a long, long time that education is about the children.

Clayton: It never occurred to me that it wasn't, and part of that was family. Education was very important in my household. I was an only child, and I had so many opportunities; I traveled extensively. I had—oh, I had a room full of books. I had some standards that I had to meet; the expectations of me were high. And I think my family thought that there wasn't anything that I couldn't do. I was disciplined. For example, Saturday was the day to help clean. But after that I knew that I could go to the theater, to a museum, or to the movies. I always had an allowance. I could buy things that I wanted.

Slaughter-Defoe: Uh-hmm.

Clayton: I was extraordinarily fortunate.

Slaughter-Defoe: So basically you were "paying it forward" as they say.

Clayton: Yes.

Slaughter-Defoe: Thank you so much. I wish more people would do that . . . just pay it forward—

Interviewer Notes

This audiotaped, and subsequently transcribed, interview originally took place in a private room at the Faculty Club on the campus of the University of Pennsylvania. Laura Murray, doctoral student in the Graduate School of Education, arranged for the taping and assisted with it during the interview. Laura's assistance in editing this manuscript is also very much appreciated.

Lead interview questions were either verbatim or adapted from:

Loder, T. L., Principal Investigator. (2005). *Bridging the tradition of activism and professionalism within the context of contemporary urban education: Perspectives from Birmingham educators born pre- and post-Civil Rights Movement.* [Grant Award #200500140]. Chicago, IL: Lyle K. Spencer Foundation, and

Loder-Jackson, T. L. (2010). Bridging the legacy of activism across generations: Life stories of African American educators in post-civil rights Birmingham. *The Urban Review*, 43(2). DOI 10.1007/s11256-009-0142-1.

Notes

1. Clayton, C. (1989, July 24/31). We can educate all our children. [Special issue: Myths, realities, a program for action—Scapegoating the Black family—Black women speak]. *The Nation,* 132–135. Reprinted in: W. Ayers & P. Ford (Eds.). (1996). *City kids, city teachers: Reports from the front row* (pp. 137–146). New York, NY: The New Press.
2. According to the 10th Edition of *The African American Almanac,* "By 2007, twenty-two Chairs have been identified as endowed and named for African American men and women, including . . . Constance E. Clayton . . . Grace Towns Hamilton . . . Willa B. Player. . . . At least 186 African American scholars scattered through the country now hold endowed chairs . . . " (p. 765). Three of the 22 names mentioned

were names of females: Clayton, Hamilton, and Player. The Grace Towns Hamilton Chair was created at Emory University in Atlanta in 1990. Grace Towns Hamilton had been the first Black woman elected to the Georgia Legislature and the first Black female to serve as a state legislator anywhere in the Deep South. Likewise, the Willa B. Player chair was created in the South at Bennett College where Dr. Player had been the first Black female President of a four-year college. In contrast, Dr. Clayton's endowed chair was established in 1993 at a major, predominantly White, private, Northeastern "Ivy League" university, a historic first for an African American woman. This information was forwarded to Diana Slaughter-Defoe on February 28, 2008 by Jessie Carney Smith, University Librarian and Cosby Professor, Fisk University, Nashville, TN. The 10th (2007) edition of the *Almanac* was edited by Brigham Narins and published by Thomson-Gale in Farmington Hills, MI.

3. Schwartz, Robert (1994, Winter). Restructuring Philadelphia's neighborhood high schools: A conversation with Constance Clayton and Michelle Fine. *Journal of Negro Education, 63*(1), 111.

15. The Generational Challenge for African American Educators in the Post-Civil Rights Era

TONDRA L. LODER-JACKSON
The University of Alabama at Birmingham

I was first introduced to the legacy of Dr. Constance E. Clayton when I became Dr. Diana Slaughter-Defoe's 2002–2003 post-doctoral fellow in the Graduate School of Education at the University of Pennsylvania. Dr. Slaughter-Defoe's interview with Dr. Clayton in this volume presents a coveted opportunity for an African American educator, with a prolific record of urban educational leadership, to offer pearls of wisdom to a contemporary generation of African American educators, particularly those who will lead in urban K-12 schools and districts.[1] As noted by Schwartz (1994), Dr. Clayton "is generally credited with having restored fiscal health, educational purpose, and public confidence to an ailing system during her tenure as superintendent" (p. 111). Dr. Clayton's positive record as an urban superintendent between 1982 and 1993 should be viewed as no small feat, especially when examined within the context of the post-*Brown* era of urban educational leadership, which placed many of the "first" African American superintendents and principals between a rock and a hard place (Loder, 2006). In the aftermath of *Brown*,

> Urban school districts across the nation experienced severe economic, fiscal, and social problems caused largely by the loss of middle-class White and African American students and families who were formerly invested in urban schools, coupled with a rise in the enrollment of students who are socially and economically disenfranchised, shrinking financial commitments from state and federal governments, and the bombardment of negative press coverage of the so-called urban school crisis. (Loder, 2006, p. 70)

The fact that Dr. Clayton's tenure as superintendent of the School District of Philadelphia (SDP) spanned 11 years, when the average tenure for urban school superintendents is estimated to be roughly two years (Buchanan, 2006), tells a story in and of itself.

Dr. Slaughter-Defoe's interview with Dr. Clayton gets at the heart of a personal and empirical question I have been grappling with for several years: what is the leadership capacity of successive generations of African American educators to forge alliances, in order to advance the aims of African American education in the post-*Brown v. Board of Education* era (Loder-Jackson, 2011)? V. P. Franklin (2009) reached a sobering conclusion regarding this question in his historical review of African American educator-activism from 1795 to 1954. He concluded that African American educators in the post-*Brown* era have failed *as a collective* to address the problems confronting contemporary public schools.

> During the 1980s and 1990s, as numerous interest groups raised their voices in support of the campaigns to improve public educational conditions for a "nation at risk," noteworthy for its absence from the chorus of proponents for change was the collective voice of African American educators. (Franklin, 2009, p. 48)

Recent perspectives on the status of African American education post-*Brown* suggest that African American educators have lost ground with respect to preparing younger generations of critical thinkers who are equipped to transform the persistent reality of separate-but-(un)equal schooling (Christensen & Loder, 2005). Chronicling the evolution of political and educational ideas among African American educator-activists in the 1960s and 1970s, Perlstein (2002) documented how "activists developed, abandoned, re-created, and again abandoned open-ended progressive approaches to the study of social and political life" (p. 249). In the wake of the waning Civil Rights Movement and Black Panther activism these once cutting-edge Black Power schools, designed to help students become critical observers and world-changers, eventually morphed into more traditional and less ideologically threatening curriculums focused on reading, mathematics, writing, self-concept, and a global understanding of the world around them (Perlstein, 2002). And with the enactment of the polarizing No Child Left Behind (NCLB) law in 2002, African American educators have found themselves especially constrained with respect to delivering critical pedagogy. In light of this context, do today's African American educators, as a collective, possess the leadership capacity to address educational inequities that disenfranchise today's African American children? Or has the post-Civil Rights era ushered in a more individualistic, heroic, and smaller-scale response to educational problems heralded by salvational figures such as Chicago Preparatory Schools founder, Dr. Marva Collins (Collins & Tamarkin, 1990), and more recently, Harlem Children's Zone founder, Geoffrey Canada (Tough, 2008)?

I have written previously about the need for a closer examination of the role that generational and historical location may play in facilitating or impeding opportunities for intergenerational dialogue, mentoring, and ultimately, collective action among African American educators born during the pre- and post-Civil Rights Movement eras (Loder, 2005a, 2005b, 2006; Loder-Jackson, 2009, 2011). African American educators from different generations have a lot to share with one another, but they are often worlds apart experientially. This generational divide tends to breed isolation and misunderstanding, both of which could stifle opportunities for constructive intergenerational conversations and collaboration (Loder-Jackson, 2011). Reflecting on Dr. Clayton's professional experience is an instructive strategy for inspiring younger generations of African American educators to perpetuate the activism modeled by her legacy (Levine, 2002).

Constance E. Clayton's Charge to the Next Generation: "Don't Give Up on Children of Value!"

African American educators have a long-standing legacy of *professional* activism (Loder-Jackson, 2011). In the era that ushered in the 1954 *Brown v. Board of Education* Supreme Court case, African American educators instilled a strong sense of racial pride in their students, led efforts to liberate Blacks through literacy, fought for equality of educational opportunity, and were looked upon as leaders in the community (Anderson, 1988; Fairclough, 2001; Siddle Walker, 2000, 2005). Dr. Clayton situates herself squarely within this activist tradition.

In her interview, Dr. Clayton identifies herself unequivocally as an "activist educator," which she defines as "not sitting idly by and being silent when I see the injustices, the omissions, and the negativity as it pertains to urban children" (Clayton & Slaughter-Defoe, 2012, p. 204). Dr. Clayton describes several activist stands she took as an urban school superintendent. Unlike the acts of activism commonly heralded during the latter-20th century U.S. Civil Rights Movement (e.g., marches, boycotts, sit-ins, and strategic arrests), African American educators who came of age during this era typically fought their battles behind the closed doors of classrooms and schoolhouses (Loder, 2005b; Loder-Jackson, 2011). The activist examples cited by Dr. Clayton are characteristic of the professional activism displayed by many African American educators, both past and present (Loder, 2005b; Loder-Jackson, 2010, 2011).

When asked to describe her activist contributions during her tenure as the superintendent of the SDP, Dr. Clayton cites her role in perpetuating and establishing several early childhood education initiatives to grant African American children success from the very beginning of their schooling experiences. She recalls being criticized by an SDP board member for investing as much money in early childhood education for urban children as someone might pay for college tuition. But it took courage and keen foresight, supported by her doctoral education preparation at the University of Pennsylvania, to make these unprecedented monetary and programmatic investments in the early education and development of urban, and very often, poor, African American children in the 1980s and 1990s.

Dr. Clayton also recounts a defiant stance she took with the federal government, in which she emotionally portrays her insistence on enacting the free breakfast program in a manner that would convey compassion toward, and preserve the dignity of, urban school children. She recalled that federal officials required students who received a free breakfast to use an identifiable voucher ticket to cash in for their meal. This ticket, she believed, demeaned children in the free breakfast program by openly identifying them as poor and needy to their peers, and thereby exposing them to hurtful taunts. Dr. Clayton not only refused to comply with this requirement, but she also invited the federal officials to her school, to see for themselves the demoralizing consequences of this policy. The federal officials' visit convinced them that Dr. Clayton was right.

When asked what lessons younger generations of African American educators should heed as they observe the legacy of previous generations of African American educators, Dr. Clayton states emphatically: "You don't give up on children" (Clayton & Slaughter-Defoe, 2012, p. 206). She also reiterates her deeply ingrained philosophy that all children should be seen as "children of value," a view represented in her 1989 publication that was subsequently reprinted in 1996 (see Clayton, 1989, 1996). Dr. Clayton goes on to say that younger generations of African American educators should not rest on the intermittent achievement of laurels and racial victories, citing the historic election of President Barack Obama as a case in point. Reflecting on what she deems to be the disrespectful treatment of President Obama by the political establishment and many U.S. citizens, Dr. Clayton warns, "The struggle is not over" (Clayton & Slaughter-Defoe, 2012, p. 206).

Finally, Dr. Clayton insists that younger generations of African American educators assume "more than a can-do attitude," but rather a "will-do attitude" (Clayton & Slaughter-Defoe, 2012, p. 206). Citing historical and contemporary educator-exemplars such as Mary McLeod Bethune, founder of what is now known as Bethune-Cookman University (Loder-Jackson, 2010), and Geoffrey Canada, founder of the Harlem Children's Zone, recently touted as the model for the Obama administration's Promise Neighborhoods grant competition for educational reform (Tough, 2008), Dr. Clayton urges younger African American educators to "take a look at [these] people and understand the struggles that they had" (Clayton &

Slaughter-Defoe, 2012, p. 207). In the midst of these struggles, she points out that they maintained "their determination and perseverance" (Clayton & Slaughter-Defoe, 2012, p. 207). Dr. Clayton is cautiously optimistic about the capacity for urban youth to lead their own Civil Rights Movement, noting that they have the highest potential to do so, but must cultivate the same love for learning that they have for hip-hop music and culture.

I was struck by Dr. Clayton's critique of the empty rhetoric implied by some who flippantly quote the African proverb, "It takes a village to raise a child" (Clayton & Slaughter-Defoe, 2012, p. 207). Admonishing that this proverb "need not be rhetoric," she calls for younger generations of African American educators to align themselves with like-minded individuals in order to forge alliances to advance the aims of African American education (Clayton & Slaughter-Defoe, 2012, p. 207). Her charge leads me to reflect on my journey to higher education, with the Constance E. Clayton Postdoctoral Fellowship being a pivotal career point. I offer a firsthand account of what I deem to be the invaluable role of intergenerational mentoring between African American scholars in higher education.

Intergenerational Mentoring

I met Dr. Slaughter-Defoe in 1996 when she was involved in a professional group of Chicago-based African American women in higher education, the Black Women's Education Network, whose earned-doctorate membership decided to reach out to an emerging generation of African American women scholars. A former mentor whom I met at The University of Chicago, Dr. Gwendoyn Laroche, introduced me to this auspicious group of women, whose mission reflected the "lifting as we climb" motto of 19th and 20th century African American women's clubs (Hine & Thompson, 1998). Out of the Black Women's Education Network, co-founded originally by Drs. Geraldine Brownlee, Gwendolyn Laroche (later Laroche Rogers) and Slaughter (later Slaughter-Defoe), whose members came of age primarily during the Civil Rights Movement or shortly thereafter, was birthed a spinoff group, made up of post-Civil Rights Movement-born "Generation X-ers." Led initially by Dr. Kimberley Williams (now Williams Gomez), we named the newly formed group fittingly, The Anna Julia Cooper Society, after a founder of the National Association of Colored Women's Clubs, a doctoral graduate of the Sorbonne University in Paris, and only the fourth African American woman to earn a Ph.D. in the United States (Johnson, 2010). This offspring Society proved to be an invaluable venue for me and other emerging women scholars to find intellectual, social, and emotional support throughout our doctoral experience.

As I came to know Dr. Slaughter-Defoe, I was intrigued by our parallel professional trajectories. She and I both attended the University of Chicago, but during strikingly different historical periods: Dr. Slaughter-Defoe, during the 1950s and 1960s, and I, during the early 1990s. African American women born on opposite sides of the Civil Rights Movement confronted vastly divergent opportunities and constraints for "what [they] could be and do" (Shaw, 1996, Title page). Coming of age academically and professionally during these divergent eras could have presented a barrier to our cultivation of mutual understanding and appreciation for our respective journeys (Loder, 2005a; Loder-Jackson, 2009, 2011). But our shared positionality as African American women in higher education helped us to bridge this generational divide (P. H. Collins, 2000).

Shortly after meeting Dr. Slaughter-Defoe through the Black Women's Education Network, our paths crossed again at Northwestern University in 1997. I entered the doctoral program in Human Development and Social Policy (HDSP), housed in the School of Education and Social Policy (SESP), a few months shy of her transition into the endowed position as the inaugural Constance E. Clayton Professor of Urban Education at the University of Pennsylvania. Dr. Slaughter-Defoe was the coordinator for HDSP in 1997, and notably, my former mentor, Dr. Laroche received her degree from Northwestern University. Even though Dr. Slaughter-Defoe's time with me at the SESP would be brief, she took the time to orient me to the higher education profession. Five years later we reconnected during our mutual pursuit for post-doctoral program involvement. I sense that Dr. Slaughter-Defoe encouraged me to come to work with her as a postdoctoral fellow partly because we had so little time to really interact in these earlier contexts. During the 2002–2003 academic year, I became Dr. Slaughter-Defoe's fourth and final Constance E. Clayton Postdoctoral Fellow in Urban Education.

Our relationship represents the kind of professional relationship I believe African American educators must intentionally pursue in order to advance the aims of African American education. As a product of the Civil Rights era, Dr. Slaughter-Defoe was able to share a unique and critical perspective about the hard-fought gains for equity and excellence among African Americans in academe. Her sound advice about academic professional preparation, particularly the promotion and tenure process, has spanned critical turning points in my career from mid-career professional to doctoral student; doctoral student to post-doctoral fellow; post-doctoral fellow to assistant professor; and eventually, assistant professor to associate tenured professor. Our mutual professional interest in investigating and advocating for the equitable education and development of African American children has resulted in a series of conversations and collaborations over the years that have advanced our scholarship and service to African American education respectively. Dr. Slaughter-Defoe has always reminded me, through her professional modeling and wise counsel, about the importance of being uncompromising in one's professional mission to advance the aims of African American education.

"Pay It Forward"

During her interview, Dr. Clayton spoke of her intention to do for other children what her parents had done for her during her own childhood—as a child, she had many advantages that enabled her to become an effective learner and disciplined student, and to later develop into an educational leader. She wanted to, in effect, "pay it forward" (Abrams & Leder, 2000) by offering as many of these same opportunities as possible to all children for whom she subsequently became responsible.

Dr. Clayton could never have known that having an endowed professorship named in her honor at her alma mater would serve as a means to reconnect me to an African American woman scholar with whom I had previously crossed paths. Her noteworthy legacy as an urban educator and leader paved the way for two African American women scholars, whose lives and work bridged the pre- and post-Civil Rights generational divide, to more deeply invest and engage ourselves in scholarship, teaching, and service in the fields of urban education and African American education. Writing this book chapter brings me full circle by affording me my first opportunity to concretize Dr. Clayton's role—by virtue of her legacy and namesake—in linking two generations of African American educational thought and mission. It is my intent to pay this honor forward by continuing her tradition of intergenerational mentoring and pursuit of excellence in education.

Notes

1. The author's recent publications referenced in this chapter related to African American educator-activism, including some of the interview questions presented in Dr. Diana Slaughter-Defoe's interview with Dr. Constance E. Clayton, are derived from a Small Research Grant project funded by the Lyle K. Spencer Foundation (200500140) and a Comprehensive Minority Faculty Development Award from The UAB Office of Equity and Diversity.

   Correspondence regarding this chapter may be sent to the author at The University of Alabama at Birmingham, EB 232-H, 1530 Third Avenue South, Birmingham, Alabama 35294-1250. E-mail: tloder@uab.edu.

References

Abrams, P. (Producer) & Leder, M. (Director). (2000). *Pay it forward* [Motion picture]. United States: Warner Brothers in association with Bel Air Entertainment and Tapestry Films.

Anderson, J. D. (1988). *The education of Blacks in the South, 1860–1935.* Chapel Hill: The University of North Carolina.

Buchanan, B. (2006). *Turnover at the top: Superintendent vacancies and the urban school.* Blue Ridge Summit, PA: Rowman & Littlefield.

Christensen, L. M., & Loder, T. L. (2005, November). *Keeping the dream alive through in-service and pre-service teacher education: Alabama educators' reflections on teaching an innovative Civil Rights Movement course.* Presentation at the National Association of Multicultural Education Conference. Atlanta, GA.

Clayton, C. (1989, July 24). Children of value: We "can" educate all our children [Special issue]. *The Nation 249*(4), 132–135.

Clayton, C.(1996). Children of value: We "can" educate all our children. Reprinted in W. Ayers & P. Ford (Eds.), *City kids, city teachers: Reports from the front row* (pp. 137–146). New York, NY: The New Press.

Clayton, C., & Slaughter-Defoe, D. T. (2012). March 22, 2011 interview with Dr. Constance E. Clayton: Reflections on the Clayton leadership era in the School District of Philadelphia. In D. T. Slaughter-Defoe (Ed.) and J. Alston (Series Ed.), *Messages for educational leadership: The Constance E. Clayton lectures 1998–2007* (pp. 201–213). New York, NY: Peter Lang.

Collins, M., & Tamarkin, C. (1990). *Marva Collins' way.* New York, NY: Penguin Putnam.

Collins, P. H. (2000). *Black feminist thought* (2nd ed.). New York, NY: Routledge.

Fairclough, A.(2001). *Teaching equality: Black schools in the age of Jim Crow.* Athens: The University of Georgia.

Franklin, V. P. (2009). "They rose or fell together": African American educators and community leadership, 1795–1954. In L. Tillman (Ed.), *The Sage handbook of African American education* (pp. 35–51). Thousand Oaks, CA: Sage.

Hine, D. C., & Thompson, M. (1998). *A shining thread of hope: The history of Black women in America.* New York, NY: Broadway Books.

Johnson, K. A. (2010). Cooper, Anna Julia Haywood (1860–1964). In K. Lomotey (Ed.), *Encyclopedia of African American education* (Vol. 1) (pp. 184–186). Thousand Oaks, CA: Sage.

Levine, D. (2002). The Milwaukee Platoon school battle: Lessons for activist teachers. *The Urban Review, 34*(1), 47–69.

Loder, T. L. (2005a). On deferred dreams, callings, and revolving doors of opportunity: African-American women's reflections on becoming principals [Special issue]. *The Urban Review, 37*(3), 243–265.

Loder, T. L. (2005b). African American women principals' reflections on social change, community other mothering, and Chicago Public School reform. *Urban Education, 40*(3), 298–320.

Loder, T. L. (2006). Dilemmas confronting urban principals in the post-civil rights era. In J. L. Kincheloe, K. Hayes, K. Rose, & P. M. Anderson (Vol. eds.), *The Praeger handbook of urban education* (pp. 70–77). Westport, CT: Greenwood.

Loder-Jackson, T. L. (2009). The confluence of race, gender, and generation in the lives of African American women principals. In L. Tillman (Ed.), *The handbook of African American education* (pp. 223–236). Thousand Oaks, CA: Sage.

Loder-Jackson, T. L. (2010). Mary McLeod Bethune. In K. Lomotey (Ed.), *The encyclopedia of African American education* (pp.71–74). Thousand Oaks, CA: Sage.

Loder-Jackson, T. L. (2011). Bridging the legacy of activism across generations: Life stories of African American educators in post-civil rights Birmingham. *The Urban Review, 43*(2), 151–174.

Perlstein, D. (2002). Minds stayed on freedom: Politics and pedagogy in the African-American freedom struggle. *American Educational Research Journal, 39*(2), 249–277.

Schwartz, R. (1994). Restructuring Philadelphia's neighborhood high schools: A conversation with Constance Clayton and Michelle Fine. *The Journal of Negro Education, 63*(1), 111–125.

Shaw, S. (1996). *What a woman ought to be and to do: Black professional women workers during the Jim Crow era*. Chicago, IL: The University of Chicago Press.

Siddle Walker, V. (2000). Valued segregated schools for African American children in the South, 1935–1969: A review of common themes and characteristics. *Review of Educational Research, 70*(3), 253–285.

Siddle Walker, V. (2005). Organized resistance and Black educators' quest for school equality, 1878–1938. *Teachers College Record, 107*(3), 355–388.

Tough, P. (2008). *Whatever it takes: Geoffrey Canada's quest to change Harlem and America*. New York, NY: Houghton Mifflin.

16. Conclusion: Looking to the Futures of Urban School Children

DIANA T. SLAUGHTER-DEFOE
University of Pennsylvania

As promised in the Introduction, in this concluding chapter I have chosen to discuss a prominent theme of Dr. Clayton's life noted by Dr. Watson, but not addressed in the Clayton Lecture Series: the arts. With Dr. Clayton, I also believe children must discover through education the pleasures and joys associated with the humanities, both mainstream and intra-cultural, if they are to reach adulthood as whole persons. For example, for years as a member of Northwestern University's faculty, 1977–1997, I happily taught a course for graduates and undergraduates entitled the "Role of Play in the Development of the Child." I fondly recall the centrality of Jerome Bruner's 1974-edited volume on *Play: Its Role in Evolution and Development* (New York: Basic Books), and his lengthy article on tool use in that volume. In his prescient commentary on the nature of the human condition and the role of tools in that process, Bruner anticipated many of today's contemporary concerns about the potential adverse impact of increasingly restrictive educational environments on the overall development and learning of children, including lower-income and African American children.

Yet even as I am drafting this concluding chapter, the School District of Philadelphia is projecting retrenchment in arts education, an education that typically begins very aggressively in the earliest childhood years. An article in the *Metro Philadelphia News* dated April 28, 2011, states:

> The School District of Philadelphia yesterday announced cuts of nearly 16 percent of its work force, including more than 1,200 teachers, eliminating full-day kindergarten and scaling back art and music spending to close a $629 million budget deficit. . . . The moves come as the district tries to . . . follow up eight consecutive years of improving test scores. The Philadelphia Federation of Teachers was expectedly angered with the planned layoffs, particularly the hit to kindergarten. "We are outraged by the short-sighted and indiscriminate cuts the school district is making to balance its budget. Targeting preschool

programs that are proven to prepare youngsters to be successful in school is unconscionable," PFT President . . . said in a statement. . . . (p. 2)

Since the 2008 recession, increasing attempts have been made to balance state and local budgetary shortfalls by slowly and systematically reversing commitment to one of the few initiatives that have proven beneficial to the long-term educational development and learning of urban children: early childhood education and intervention.

Even before the recession, however, contextual and social concerns in urban communities have been linked to a reduction in actual opportunities for urban children to engage in any form of play behavior, including elimination of "recess" in many city schools (Pellegrini, 2005; Pellegrini & Bohn, 2005; Pellegrini & Holmes, 2006). Further, for some, play is considered to be diametrically opposed to learning and development; for others, there is just no time for play. Research by Stipek (2004, 2006), and by Hamre and Pianta (2005, 2007) and their colleagues suggests that teachers of lower-income and ethnic/racial-minority young children appear to stress linear development of skills, possibly at a cost of attention to elaboration of children's conceptual and imaginative abilities. The approach of these teachers is consistent with recent American educational policies that deemphasize the value of social and pretend play for both cognitive and social-emotional development in the education of younger children, in support of stronger emphases on basic skill acquisition (e.g., No Child Left Behind).

Nonetheless, however important such academic skills are to school success in urban schools and other urban educational environments, I believe it is also important to reaffirm a research tradition that emphasizes the significance of varied approaches to developing literary and social competence during the early childhood years, preschool through grade 4 (e.g., Bowman, Donavan, & Burns, 2001; Bradley & Szegda, 2006; Hirsh-Pasek, Golinkoff, Berk, & Singer, 2009; Singer, Golinkoff, & Hirsh-Pasek, 2006; Welch, 2006; Zigler & Bishop-Josef, 2006). This tradition stresses the existence of close ties between social and pretend play behaviors and children's emergent linguistic and social competence. In addition, overarching ecological factors linked to prevailing assumptions about early childhood pedagogy prevalent in the contemporary American cultural context (Bloch & Kim, 2010), and the critical importance of the arts (broadly defined: pictorial and visual, theatrical, musical, etc.) point to their importance for urban children's academic learning and development (Brown, Benedett, & Armistead, 2010; Gadsden, 2008). Scientific research clearly points to the important contribution of play and the arts to the learning and development of all children, regardless of their socioeconomic status, race, or ethnicity.

In summary, this literature indicates that opportunities to have free time to explore, play in, and with, the arts, and opportunities for artistic expression, are beneficial to children's social-emotional *and* cognitive development and learning. Further, there is every indication that structured experiences in art appreciation and artistic expression are as beneficial to children from lower-income families as they are known to be to children from middle- and upper-income families. For example, we have reason to believe that children's identity development is enhanced when the opportunities include time for the appreciation of both the child's own cultural heritage as well as the heritages of other children. In a nation as socially diverse as ours, within the ecological context of frequent and sustained contact with a global and international world as consequence of our contemporary technology (Goncu & Gaskins, 2007), I think we continue to narrowly focus on academic skills as the crux of urban education at our own future peril, quite simply because a "house divided against itself cannot stand."

References

Bloch, M. N., & Kim, K. E. (2010, April–May). *Governing young children's learning through educational reforms related to "best practice" and cognitive/academic success.* Paper presented at the Annual Meeting of the American Educational Research Association, Denver, Co.

Bowman, B., Donovan, M., & Burns, M. (2001). *Eager to learn: Educating our preschoolers.* Washington, DC: National Academy Press.

Bradley, K., & Szegda, M. (2006).The dance of learning. In B. Spodek & O. Saracho (Eds.), *Handbook of research on the education of young children* (pp. 243–250). Mahwah, NJ: Lawrence Erlbaum Associates.

Brown, E., Benedett, B., & Armistead, M. E. (2010). Arts enrichment and school readiness for children at risk. *Early Childhood Research Quarterly, 25*(1), 112–124.

Gadsden, V. L. (2008). The arts and education: Knowledge generation, pedagogy, and the discourse of learning. *Review of Research in Education, 32*(1), 29–61.

Goncu, A., & Gaskins, S. (Eds.). (2007). *Play and development: Evolutionary, sociocultural, and functional perspectives.* Mahwah, NJ: Lawrence Erlbaum Associates.

Hamre, B. K., & Pianta, R. C. (2005). Can instructional and emotional support in the first-grade classroom make a difference for children at risk of school failure? *Child Development, 76*(5), 949–967.

Hamre, B. K., & Pianta, R. C. (2007). Learning opportunities in pre-school and early elementary classrooms. In R. Pianta, M. Cox, &

K. Snow (Eds.), *School readiness and the transition to kindergarten in the era of accountability* (pp. 49–84). Baltimore, MD: Brookes.

Hirsh-Pasek, K., Golinkoff, R., Berk, L., & Singer, D. (2009). *A mandate for playful learning in preschool: Presenting the evidence.* New York, NY: Oxford University Press.

Pellegrini, A. (2005). *Recess: Its role in education and development.* Mahwah, NJ: Erlbaum.

Pellegrini, A., & Bohn, C. (2005). The role of recess in children's cognitive performance and school adjustment. *Educational Researcher, 34*(1), 13–19.

Pellegrini, A., & Holmes, R. M. (2006). The role of recess in primary school. In D. Singer, R. Golinkoff, & K. Hirsh-Pasek (Eds.), *Play = learning: How play motivates and enhances children's cognitive and socio-emotional growth* (pp. 36–57). New York, NY: Oxford University Press.

Stipek, D. J. (2004). Teaching practices in kindergarten and first grade: Different strokes for different folks. *Early Childhood Research Quarterly, 19*(4), 548–568.

Stipek, D. J. (2006). No Child Left Behind comes to preschool. *The Elementary School Journal, 106*(5), 455–465.

Welch, G. F. (2006). The musical development and education of young children. In B. Spodek & O. Saracho (Eds.), *Handbook of research on the education of young children* (pp. 251–267). Mahwah, NJ: Lawrence Erlbaum Associates.

Zigler, E. F., & Bishop-Josef, S. J. (2006). The cognitive child versus the whole child: Lessons from 40 years of Head Start. In D. G. Singer, R. M. Golinkoff, & K. Hirsh-Pasek (Eds.), *Play = learning: How play motivates and enhances children's cognitive and social–emotional growth* (pp. 15–35). New York: Oxford University Press.

Contributors

Foreword

Bernard C. Watson is a distinguished citizen of Philadelphia, having received (a) an Endowed Chair in Urban Education named in his honor at Temple University in 2005, and (b) The 2001 Philadelphia Award, presented to a citizen of the region who has done the most to "advance the best and largest interest" of the community. A former public school teacher and administrator for the Philadelphia School District, he established a graduate program in urban education at Temple University and became its first African American vice president, improving student services and enhancing diversity as vice president for academic administration. His reputation in the academic world earned him appointments on educational advisory councils by three U.S. presidents. An alumnus of the University of Illinois, and of the University of Chicago where he received his doctorate, Dr. Watson left Temple to become the president of the William Penn Foundation from which he retired in 1993 after 12.5 years. Since 1993, Dr. Watson has served as Chairman of the Board of Directors for the Pennsylvania Convention Center Authority, and since 1999, as President of the Barnes Foundation and its Board of Trustees.

Clayton Lecturers

Barbara Bowman is Co-Founder and Professor of the Erikson Institute for Advanced Study in Child Development, and the Irving B. Harris Professor of Child Development. Currently, she continues her affiliation with Erikson in Chicago, IL, and she is also working with the Chicago Public School District as Chief Officer, Office of Early Childhood Education. Dr. Bowman is a nationally recognized authority on early education and is one of three faculty who founded Erikson Institute in 1966. She has had experience teaching at both preschool and primary levels as well as in colleges and universities; her specialty areas are early education, cultural diversity, and education of at-risk children. Dr. Bowman has served on numerous professional boards, including the Family Resource Coalition and the National Association for the Education of Young Children, of which she was President (1980–1982). She chaired the Committee on Early Childhood Pedagogy for the National Research Council. Dr. Bowman is the recipient of honorary doctorates of humane letters (D.H.L.) and of Education (D.Ed.), having initially received a B.A. from Sarah Lawrence College and an M.A. in Education from the University of Chicago.

James P. Comer is the Maurice Falk Professor of Child Psychiatry at the Yale University School of Medicine's Child Study Center. A Yale medical faculty member since 1968, he centered his career on promoting a focus on child development as a strategy for school improvement. Dr. Comer is best known, nationally and internationally, for founding the Comer School Development Program. The Program promotes the collaboration of parents, educators, and community members to improve social, emotional, and academic outcomes for children. Dr. Comer is a member of the Institute of Medicine and the American Association for the Advancement of Science (AAAS). He has been awarded 47 honorary degrees and has been recognized by many organizations. For example, in 1996, he won both the prestigious Heinz Award in the Human Condition for his profound influence on disadvantaged children and the Health trac Foundation Prize (renamed the James F. and Sarah T. Fries Foundation). In 2004, he received the John P. McGovern Behavioral Science Award from the Smithsonian. In 2006 he received the John Hope Franklin Award, given to those who have demonstrated the highest commitment to access and excellence in American education, and in 2007 he received the University of Louisville Grawemeyer Award for Education. Dr. Comer received an A.B. degree in 1956 from Indiana University, an M.D. in 1960 from Howard University College of Medicine, and an M.P.H. in 1964 from the University of Michigan School of Public Health. Between 1964–1967, he trained in psychiatry at the Yale University School of Medicine and its Child Study Center.

Linda Darling-Hammond is currently Charles E. Ducommun Professor of Education at Stanford University. Her research, teaching, and policy work focus on issues of school restructuring, teacher education, and educational equity. Dr. Darling-Hammond is past president of the American Educational Research Association, a two-year term member of the National Board for Professional Teaching Standards, and a Member of the National Academy of Education. Dr. Darling-Hammond received her B.A. magna cum laude from Yale University in 1973, and her doctorate in urban education, with highest distinction, from Temple University in 1978. She received the

Phi Delta Kappa George E. Walk Award for the most outstanding dissertation in the field of education in 1978, the American Educational Research Association's Research Review Award in 1985, the American Federation of Teachers' Quest Award for Outstanding Scholarship in 1987, the Association of Teacher Educators' Leadership in Teacher Education Award in 1990, Educational Equity Concepts' Woman of Valor Award in 1995, the Association of Teacher Educators' Distinguished Educator Award in 1997, and the Council for Chief State School Officers' Distinguished Leadership Award in 1998. She has received honorary degrees from several universities, but she began her career as a public school teacher and was co-founder of a preschool and day care center.

Edgar G. Epps is Professor of Education Emeritus at the University of Chicago. He retired on June 30, 1998 after 28 years as the Marshall Field IV Professor of Urban Education in the University's Department of Education. Presently, he is Professor of Education at the University of Wisconsin, Milwaukee. Professor Epps has served as a consultant to the U.S. Department of Education and other federal agencies. In 1994, he served as an expert witness in the *Knight v. Alabama* higher education desegregation case, and in 1996, he was a member of the American Sociological Association's expert panel on Social Science Perspectives on Affirmative Action. Professor Epps received the Du Bois, Johnson, Frazier Award of the American Sociological Association (1996). On October 10, 1998, he was honored at a University of Chicago symposium, the papers of which were subsequently published as a book celebrating his life and work upon retirement from Chicago, and entitled, *African American education: Race, community, inequality, and achievement – A tribute to Edgar G. Epps.* Professor Epps received a B.A. from Talladega College, an M.A. from Atlanta University, and the Ph.D. from Washington State University.

Susan Fuhrman is the 10th President of Teachers College, Columbia University, and President of the National Academy of Education. Prior to this, she served for 11 years as Dean of the University of Pennsylvania's Graduate School of Education, where she was also the George and Diane Weiss Professor of Education, at the time of her Clayton lecture. She was at Rutgers' Eagleton Institute of Politics and a professor of education policy before joining the University of Pennsylvania. In addition to her deanship and teaching, she has been chair and director of the management committee of the Consortium for Policy Research in Education (CPRE) since 1985. Dr. Fuhrman is a former vice president of the American Educational Research Association, a member of the National Coalition on Asia and International Studies in the Schools, and she serves on the board of The Fund for New Jersey. She has a B.A. and M.A. in History from Northwestern University and a Ph.D. in Political Economy from Columbia University.

Louis M. Gomez is presently the MacArthur Chair in Digital Media and Learning at the Graduate School of Education and Information Studies at UCLA. At the time of his Clayton lecture, he was Aon Professor of Learning Sciences and Professor of Computer Science at Northwestern University. Professor Gomez's primary interest is in working with school communities to create social arrangements and curriculum that support school reform. Professor Gomez is dedicated to collaborative research and development with urban schools that will bring the current state-of-the-art in computing and networking technologies into pervasive use in urban schools in order to transform instruction and support community formation. Prior to joining the faculty at Northwestern Professor Gomez was director of Human-Computer Systems Research at Bellcore (Bell Communications Research) in Morristown, NJ. At Bellcore, he pursued an active research programs investigating techniques that improve human use of information retrieval systems and techniques that aid in the acquisition of complex computer-based skills. Professor Gomez received a B.A. in Psychology from the State University of New York at Stony Brook and a Ph.D. in Cognitive Psychology from the University of California at Berkeley.

James M. Jones received his doctorate from Yale University in 1970, where he specialized in social psychology. He is Professor of Psychology at the University of Delaware. A student of race and race relations for over 30 years, his research and scholarship also address the African cultural basis for African American psychological status and the implications of the adaptations and coping mechanisms of persons of African descent for the general processes of adapting to culturally stressful, challenging, and oppressive circumstances. He developed a psycho-cultural model known as TRIOS. The acronym represents the five psycho-cultural variables of Time, Rhythm, Improvisation, Orality, and Spirituality, posited to follow from African cultural origins and to characterize personality, including interpersonal and intergroup dynamics. For over 20 years Professor Jones served as Director of the Minority Fellowship Program of the American Psychological Association. He has been President of the Society for the Psychological Study of Social Issues (SPSSI), an organization of scientists committed to applying psychological knowledge to education of the public and identifying means of addressing social issues through interventions or public policy advocacy. In 2004, he led a delegation of SPSSI members and other colleagues in the psychological sciences to South Africa under the sponsorship of the People to People Ambassador Program.

Pamela Trotman Reid is President of Saint Joseph College in Hartford, CT. She was appointed Provost and Executive Vice President at Roosevelt University in July 2004 when she delivered the Clayton lecture. She has held professorial and administrative ranks at the University of Michigan where she served as head of the Women's Studies Program, was Professor of Education and Psychology, and Research Scientist at the Institute for Research on Women and Gender. She was Professor of Developmental Psychology and served as Associate Provost and Dean for Academic Affairs, then as Interim Provost at the City University of New York's Graduate Center. Over her 30-year career she focused her research interests on gender and ethnic issues, such as racial socialization particularly in girls and women. She has served on boards and committees of the American Psychological Association (APA) and other professional organizations. A Fellow of APA, Dr. Reid is the recipient of national awards, among them: the Distinguished Leadership Award given by the APA Committee on Women in Psychology; and the Distinguished Contribution to Research Award from the Society for the Psychological Study of Ethnic Issues. Named among the 100 Distinguished Women in Psychology in 1992, she holds a B.S. from Howard, an M.A. from Temple, and a Ph.D. from the University of Pennsylvania.

Lawrence Schweinhart is an early childhood program researcher and speaker for policy makers, educators, and advocates throughout the U.S. and in other countries. He has conducted research at the High/Scope Educational Research Foundation in Ypsilanti, MI, since 1975, and chaired its educational research division beginning in 1989. In 2003, the High/Scope Board of Directors appointed him President of the High/Scope Foundation. Dr. Schweinhart is the lead researcher on the High/Scope Perry Preschool Study—the landmark study establishing the extraordinary human and financial potential of high-quality early childhood programs by following the original preschool participants to midlife, ages 33 to 40—and the High/Scope Preschool Curriculum Comparison Study—which provides persuasive evidence that child-initiated learning activities are central to high-quality early childhood programs. Dr. Schweinhart has authored numerous articles and essays on research topics that impact children's educational issues as well as technical reports and program evaluations. He also has addressed a range of audiences that include early childhood educators, researchers, advocates, and policymakers. Dr. Schweinhart earned a B.A. in philosophy from St. Mary's Seminary and University in Baltimore in 1969. He received his Ph.D. in Education from Indiana University in 1975. He has taught fourth and seventh grades as well as graduate and undergraduate college courses.

Diana T. Slaughter-Defoe was the Inaugural Constance E. Clayton Professor in Urban Education at the University of Pennsylvania at the time of her Clayton lecture and became Clayton Professor Emerita, July 2011. Her research interests include culture, primary education, and home-school relations facilitating in-school academic achievement. Before joining Penn in 1998, Dr. Slaughter-Defoe taught for 20 years at Northwestern University's School of Education and Social Policy. Prior to joining Northwestern, she had served on the faculties of the Department of Psychiatry at Howard University in Washington, DC, the Child Study Center at Yale University, and the Committee on Human Development and Department of Education at the University of Chicago. At Northwestern, she was a member of the Institute for Policy Research Studies and the Department of African American Studies. In 1994, the American Psychological Association cited Dr. Slaughter-Defoe for Distinguished Contributions to Research in Public Policy. Dr. Slaughter-Defoe has been an elected member of the Governing Council of the Society for Research in Child Development. In June 2007, the University of Chicago awarded her its Lifetime Professional Achievement Citation. She received a B.A. from the Committee on Human Development, University of Chicago, in 1962; an M.A. from the Committee in 1964; and the Ph.D. from the Committee with emphasis on Developmental and Clinical Psychology in 1968; and in 1969 her dissertation received a distinguished research award from Pi Lambda Theta. She and Dr. Constance Clayton are members of Delta Sigma Theta Sorority, Inc.

Other Contributors

Davido Dupree was a Research Associate in UPENN-GSE's Center for Health Achievement Neighborhood Growth and Ethnic Studies at the time of the Clayton lecture. He is currently a Lecturer in the UPENN Graduate School of Education and a Research and Evaluation Consultant for research and evaluation projects designed to promote the healthy psychological, social, and cognitive development of youth of color.

Marybeth Gasman was an Assistant Professor of Higher Education in the Graduate School of Education at the University of Pennsylvania in 2003. She is currently Professor of Higher Education. Dr. Gasman received a Ph.D. in higher education from Indiana University in 2000. She is a historian of higher education. Her work explores issues pertaining to philanthropy and historically Black colleges, Black leadership, contemporary fund-raising issues at Black colleges, and African-American giving. In 2006, Dr. Gasman was awarded the Association for the Study of Higher Education's Promising Scholar/Early Career Award for her scholarship.

Tondra L. Loder-Jackson is currently an Associate Professor in the Educational Foundations program in the School of Education, housed within the College of Arts and Sciences at The University of Alabama at Birmingham (UAB). She is also the Associate Director of the UAB Center for Urban Education. Her research and teaching interests include life course perspectives on African American education, urban education, multigenerational life stories, and the influence of social movements on education. Following receipt of her PhD from Northwestern University, she was a

Clayton Postdoctoral Fellow in Urban Education at the University of Pennsylvania.

Audrey Mbeje is from Durban, in Kwa-Zulu Natal, South Africa. She is Director of the African Language Program at the African Studies Center, where she supervises African language instruction. In addition to overseeing the African Language Program at the University of Pennsylvania, Dr. Mbeje teaches courses in Zulu, her native language, and African Language and Culture. She has a Ph.D. in Applied Linguistics from Ball State University, and has taught Zulu at various institutions in the U.S. including the University of California-Berkeley, University of Wisconsin-Madison, and Yale.

Laura Murray is a doctoral student in Applied Psychology and Human Development at the University of Pennsylvania's Graduate School of Education. Prior to returning to school in 2009, she worked for ten years as a documentary producer, director, and editor on social issue films and television. Laura holds a B.A. in Film and Drama from Vassar College, an M.A. in Communication from Stanford University, and an M.S.Ed. in Human Development from the University of Pennsylvania.

Alton Strange, received his B.A. degree from Morehouse College in Atlanta, GA and his doctorate degree in Education from the University of Pennsylvania. He was Special Projects Assistant in the Office of Transition and Alternative Education, the School District of Philadelphia (SDP), at the time of the Clayton lecture. Currently, Dr. Strange is Special Projects Assistant II to the Deputy Chief Office of Specialized Instructional Services in SDP.

ROCHELLE BROCK &
RICHARD GREGGORY JOHNSON III,
Executive Editors

Black Studies and Critical Thinking is an interdisciplinary series which examines the intellectual traditions of and cultural contributions made by people of African descent throughout the world. Whether it is in literature, art, music, science, or academics, these contributions are vast and far-reaching. As we work to stretch the boundaries of knowledge and understanding of issues critical to the Black experience, this series offers a unique opportunity to study the social, economic, and political forces that have shaped the historic experience of Black America, and that continue to determine our future. Black Studies and Critical Thinking is positioned at the forefront of research on the Black experience, and is the source for dynamic, innovative, and creative exploration of the most vital issues facing African Americans. The series invites contributions from all disciplines but is specially suited for cultural studies, anthropology, history, sociology, literature, art, and music.

Subjects of interest include (but are not limited to):

- EDUCATION
- SOCIOLOGY
- HISTORY
- MEDIA/COMMUNICATION
- RELIGION/THEOLOGY
- WOMEN'S STUDIES

- POLICY STUDIES
- ADVERTISING
- AFRICAN AMERICAN STUDIES
- POLITICAL SCIENCE
- LGBT STUDIES

For additional information about this series or for the submission of manuscripts, please contact Dr. Brock (Indiana University Northwest) at brock2@iun.edu or Dr. Johnson (University of San Francisco) at rgjohnsoniii@usfca.edu.

To order other books in this series, please contact our Customer Service Department:

(800) 770-LANG (within the U.S.)
(212) 647-7706 (outside the U.S.)
(212) 647-7707 FAX

Or browse online by series at www.peterlang.com.